The Art of
Value Investing

Founded in 1807, John Wiley & Sons is the oldest independent publishing company in the United States. With offices in North America, Europe, Australia and Asia, Wiley is globally committed to developing and marketing print and electronic products and services for our customers' professional and personal knowledge and understanding.

The Wiley Finance series contains books written specifically for finance and investment professionals as well as sophisticated individual investors and their financial advisors. Book topics range from portfolio management to e-commerce, risk management, financial engineering, valuation and financial instrument analysis, as well as much more.

For a list of available titles, visit our Web site at www.WileyFinance.com.

The Art of Value Investing

*How the World's Best
Investors Beat the Market*

JOHN HEINS
WHITNEY TILSON

WILEY

Library of Congress Cataloging-in-Publication Data:

ISBN 978-0-470-47977-3 (Hardcover)
ISBN 978-1-118-22029-0 (ePDF)
ISBN 978-1-118-25863-7 (Mobi)
ISBN 978-1-118-23396-2 (ePub)

Printed in the United States of America

10 9 8 7 6 5 4 3 2 1

Contents

Introduction

When we launched the newsletter *Value Investor Insight* in early 2005, our motivation was not to tout the "10 Best Stocks to Buy Now" or peddle a proprietary system that would "Triple Your Money in Six Months!" Primarily through two in-depth interviews with highly successful money managers, our goals for each issue have been to deliver not only timely investment ideas, but also timeless wisdom about the craft of investing. To that end, our *Value Investor Insight* interviews explore the full spectrum of stock investing: from the definition of an underlying philosophy, to the identification of potential ideas, the research and analytical process, the discipline around buying and selling, all aspects of portfolio management and, maybe the most important, keeping emotion and common behavioral biases from ruining the best efforts of all of the above.

As befits the title of our newsletter, we're unrestrained proponents of the core value-investing philosophy first espoused by Benjamin Graham and then embellished and popularized by Warren Buffett. Value investing means different things to different people (more on that later), but value investors' core belief is that equity markets regularly offer—for a variety of different but predictable reasons—opportunities to buy stakes in companies at significant discounts to conservative estimates of what those businesses are actually worth. If you can consistently get the value of the underlying businesses right, pay deep discounts to those values in buying the companies' stocks, and maintain your conviction and discipline while conventional wisdom regularly goes against you, you can beat the market.

While the core precepts of value investing strike us as eminently sound, age and experience have also made it equally clear that, like fingerprints, no two value-investing strategies are exactly alike. So many elements make up a given strategy and its execution that when combined with inevitable differences in judgment, it's perfectly normal for equally talented and accomplished investors to assess the landscape of investment opportunities or a specific idea and come to diametrically opposed conclusions. That's what makes investing—and making judgments about investors—so difficult . . . and endlessly fascinating.

As encouraging as it may be that there are a multitude of paths to investment success, that in no way argues for trying to pursue several at the same time. The best investors, in our experience, can articulate in a clear and focused way what they're looking for, why they're looking for it and where they're trying to find it. They have a well-defined and consistently applied process for research and analysis. They follow specific disciplines for buying, for selling, for diversification, and for managing risk. They are well-versed in the behavioral traps investors can fall into and take concrete steps to avoid them. Obvious as that all should be, we're constantly surprised by the number of professional money managers who can't credibly argue why and how they expect to outperform.

Our goal with *The Art of Value Investing* is to offer a comprehensive set of answers to the questions every equity money manager should have thought through clearly before holding himself or herself out as a worthy steward of other people's money. Because there is not just one credible answer to each of these questions, we've provided a full range of potential answers and the justifications for each. What market inefficiencies will I try to exploit? How will I generate ideas? What will be my geographic focus? What analytical edge will I hope to have? What valuation methodologies will I use? What time horizon will I typically employ? How many stocks will I own? How specifically will I decide to buy or sell? Will I hedge, and how? How will I keep my emotions from getting the best of me?

We've delegated the task of providing answers to such questions to the experts: the market-beating money managers who have graced the pages of *Value Investor Insight*. Hedge-fund superstars such as Julian Robertson, Seth Klarman, Lee Cooperman, David Einhorn, Bill Ackman and Joel Greenblatt. Mutual fund luminaries including Marty Whitman, Mason Hawkins, Jean-Marie Eveillard, Bill Nygren and Bruce Berkowitz. Lower profile but no less accomplished money managers such as Maverick Capital's Lee Ainslie, Highfields Capital's Jon Jacobson, Ralph Whitworth of Relational Investors, and Jeffrey Ubben of ValueAct Capital. We hope to provide useful context and organization to the discussion, but we leave it to these superior investors and dozens more like them to describe how they practice their craft and why. We can't imagine more credible sources of information and insight.

We should emphasize that our goal is not to present a single answer to any strategic question an investor faces. Any investor's given performance is a function of thousands of individual decisions about the strategy he or she employs and how it's executed over time. One investor may invest only in large-cap stocks, while another may never touch them. One may consider spending time with management to be the most important component of research, while another may find it a complete waste of time. One may specialize in energy stocks, while another avoids them like the plague. What we will do is present the conclusions that a set of uniquely qualified investors have reached on a wide variety of subjects, as well as their explanations for why they've chosen the strategy and methods they have. While their conclusions will frequently differ, we hope the diversity of opinion helps inform the decisions you ultimately will have to make as an investor.

Who should read *The Art of Value Investing*? Our aspiration is for it to be as vital a resource for the just-starting-out investor as for the sophisticated professional one. The former are provided a comprehensive guidebook for defining a sound investment strategy from A to Z; the latter are provided challenges to all aspects of their existing practice and provocations to potential improvements.

We also want the book to be a must-read for any investor—institutional or individual—charged with choosing the best managers for the money they are allocating to equities. Choosing the right managers for you consists of knowing all the right questions to ask as well as the answers worthy of your respect and attention—both of which we aim to deliver.

Our organizing principle for the content roughly matches the chronological progression one would follow in defining and executing an investment strategy. In Chapter 1 we explore the core principles investors rely on to guide their strategies. While those principles for all the investors we hear from fall under the value-investing umbrella, that umbrella covers a diverse spectrum of thought and opinion. In the section "Field of Play," the best investors in the business describe how they define their circle of competence, the types of situations and inefficiencies on which they look to capitalize, and how they generate ideas. In the section "Building the Case," we examine how top investors go about their research, where they focus their analytical efforts, how they value companies, and the disciplines they follow in deciding what to buy and when.

While most of the literature on stock investing stops at getting to the buy decision, the final two sections of *The Art of Value Investing* address equally important contributors to investment success. The section titled "Active Management" describes best practices in all aspects of portfolio management, including position sizing, diversification, responding to changing circumstances, and the decision to sell. In the section "Of Sound Mind," we hear how superior managers learn from mistakes, what motivates them, and how they face the many threats to rational thinking that investing serves up.

All of the quotes used have appeared in the pages of *Value Investor Insight*, with the vast majority coming from first-person interviews we have conducted over the past eight years. In a small number of cases—most prominently the timeless wisdom from The Baupost Group's Seth Klarman and Oaktree Capital Management's Howard Marks—certain quotes have come from investor communications that were either publicly available or for which we were granted permission to use. In all cases, we offer our sincere thanks to everyone we've interviewed, whose generosity in sharing their experiences and insights is truly an inspiration.

The quest for knowledge is a never-ending process for investors and is what helps separate the best from the rest of the pack. To contribute in even a modest way to that learning process is truly our honor.

John Heins
Whitney Tilson

CHAPTER 1

"All Sensible Investing Is Value Investing"

A walk down any supermarket aisle makes it clear we live in a world of increasing product specialization. To break into a new market or grab more of an existing one, companies launch a dizzying array of new products in ever-more-specific categories. Want your soda with more caffeine or less? You've got it. More sugar? Less sugar? Six ounces, 10 ounces, 20 ounces? Whatever you like.

This trend has not been lost on marketers of investment vehicles. Specialized mutual funds and exchange-traded funds exist for almost every imaginable combination of manager style, geographic reach, industry sector, and company market capitalization size. If you're looking for a mid-cap growth fund focused on the commodity sector in so-called BRIC countries (Brazil, Russia, India and China), you're likely to find it.

We understand the marketing reality of specialization, but we argue that the most important factor in judging an investor's prospective gains or losses is his or her underlying philosophy. As you might guess from the fact that we co-founded a newsletter called *Value Investor Insight*, we agree 100 percent with Berkshire Hathaway's Vice Chairman Charlie Munger, who says simply that "all sensible investing is value investing."

But what exactly does it mean to be a value investor? At its most basic level it means seeking out stocks that you believe are worth considerably more than you have to pay for them. But all investors try to do that. Value investing to us is both a mindset as well as a rigorous discipline, the fundamental characteristics of which we've distilled down to a baker's dozen.

Value investors typically:

- Focus on intrinsic value—what a company is really worth—buying when convinced there is a substantial margin of safety between the company's share price and its intrinsic value and selling when the margin of safety is gone. This means not trying to guess where the herd will send the stock price next.

- Have a clearly defined sense of where they'll prospect for ideas, based on their competence and the perceived opportunity set rather than artificial style-box limitations.
- Pride themselves on conducting in-depth, proprietary, and fundamental research and analysis rather than relying on tips or paying attention to vacuous, minute-to-minute, cable-news-style analysis.
- Spend far more time analyzing and understanding micro factors, such as a company's competitive advantages and its growth prospects, instead of trying to make macro calls on things like interest rates, oil prices, and the economy.
- Understand and profit from the concept that business cycles and company performance often revert to the mean, rather than assuming that the immediate past best informs the indefinite future.
- Act only when able to draw conclusions at variance to conventional wisdom, resulting in buying stocks that are out-of-favor rather than popular.
- Conduct their analysis and invest with a multiyear time horizon rather than focusing on the month or quarter ahead.
- Consider truly great investment ideas to be rare, often resulting in portfolios with fewer, but larger, positions than is the norm.
- Understand that beating the market requires assembling a portfolio that looks quite different from the market, not one that hides behind the safety of closet indexing.
- Focus on avoiding permanent losses rather than minimizing the risk of stock-price volatility.
- Focus on absolute returns, not on relative performance versus a benchmark.
- Consider stock investing to be a marathon, with winners and losers among its practitioners best identified over periods of several years, not months.
- Admit their mistakes and actively seek to learn from them, rather than taking credit only for successes and attributing failures to bad luck.

WHAT IT MEANS TO BE A VALUE INVESTOR

Elaborating in detail on all aspects of the bare-bones list above is essentially what this book is about. We begin by turning to the uniquely successful investors we've profiled over the years as co-editors of *Value Investor Insight* to examine what they consider to be the key components of a value-investing philosophy, from general fundamental principles to the overarching mindset needed to make it work.

* * *

Our entire process is rooted in Ben Graham's simple philosophical framework for investing. He believed there were two values for every stock, the first being the current market price, and the second what the share would be worth if the entire company were acquired by a knowledgeable buyer or if the assets were liquidated, the liabilities paid off and the proceeds paid to stockholders. He called that the intrinsic value and argued that the time to buy was when there was a large spread between the current price and that value, and the time to sell was when that spread was narrow.

Over time we've developed different ways of applying that —by valuing income streams rather than just assets, by calculating private market values, by investing internationally—but the essence of what we do has remained consistent. Our work every day is essentially directed at valuing what businesses are worth.

—Will Browne, Tweedy, Browne Co.

At the heart of being a value investor is having a contrarian bent. Beyond that, though, there are many different flavors of value investing. Tweedy Browne is a great deep-value investment firm. Chuck Royce at Royce Funds is a wonderful GARP [Growth At a Reasonable Price] practitioner—he's focused on value but definitely doesn't like to own bad companies. Mason Hawkins at Southeastern Asset Management and Marty Whitman of Third Avenue are oriented toward stocks trading at significant discounts to net asset value. Bill Miller is probably best described as an all-out contrarian. The fact that all these people have been successful proves that there's no single way to do it. What the market offers up as opportunity is constantly changing, so being able to deploy a variety of strategies as the situation warrants allows us great flexibility to go almost anywhere and never get shut out of the market. That's important because our investors don't ask us to move in and out of cash depending on how overvalued or undervalued we think the market is. And frankly, having an eclectic view makes investing a lot more interesting.

—Preston Athey, T. Rowe Price

We've found that to earn repeatable, excellent returns over time with reasonable risk exposure requires being able to assign something approximating a fair value to a business, making conservative estimates. Then it's a question of looking at the price. If price is significantly below that fair value, you're likely to have a good outcome by investing in it. If the price is significantly above that fair value, you can make good money by shorting it.

—*Zeke Ashton, Centaur Capital*

There's nothing particularly earth-shattering about what we try to do. We believe the market often misprices stocks due to neglect, emotion, misinterpretation or myopia, so our value-add comes from bottom-up stock selection. We're trying to buy at low prices relative to our current estimate of intrinsic value and we want to believe that intrinsic value will grow.

—*Steve Morrow, NewSouth Capital*

When I got much more interested in individual securities analysis in the early 1990s I read as widely as I could and a light bulb just switched on when I read everything Marty Whitman wrote. I was thinking it was critical to understand the ins and outs of how the stock market really worked, but his basic message was to ignore the market, which was just the bazaar through which you had to make trades. He was all about valuing what a company was worth—independent of what the market was saying it was worth at the time—and buying when the market was giving you a big discount and selling when it was paying you a premium.

As obvious as that sounds, it was very liberating to come across such a straightforward approach. Using whatever analytical tools I want, whether it's valuing net assets, calculating private-market values or discounting future cash flows, I can arrive at a clear estimate of what a company is actually worth. From there, the actual buying and selling decisions aren't that hard.

—*Jim Roumell, Roumell Asset Management*

I've heard it said many times that value investing is not as much about doing smart things as it is about *not* doing dumb things. Avoiding mistakes, resisting market fads, and focusing on allocating capital into ideas that are highly likely to produce satisfactory returns and that offer a margin of safety against permanent capital loss – these are the dominant themes of the value investing approach. Contrary to how it sounds, these elements don't make value investing easier than other approaches. In fact, cultivating the discipline to avoid unproductive decisions, refining the craft of valuing businesses and assessing risk, and developing the emotional and mental equilibrium required to think independently in a field in which there is tremendous pressure to conform requires constant diligence and effort.

—*Zeke Ashton, Centaur Capital*

Long-term-oriented value investors have greater scope to produce superior risk-adjusted returns when the seas are rocky. The valid response when there's chop is to focus on the end destination—what value investors call intrinsic value—and not worry about whether the next wave is going to push the boat up or down. If you don't invest with a very clear notion of underlying value, how do you do it? Nothing else makes sense.

Your ability to maintain focus on the long term comes from experience. You go through a couple cycles where everybody else is screaming at you not to try to catch a falling knife, and then when you do so and make some money, it does wonders for you . . . and for your ability to do it next time.

—*Howard Marks, Oaktree Capital*

We make no heroic assumptions in our analysis, hoping, instead, that by compounding multiple conservative assumptions, we will create such a substantial margin of safety that a lot can go wrong without impairing our capital much or even at all. We never invest just to invest and don't bet blindly on mean reversion or on historical relationships holding up. Our settings are permanently turned to "risk off."

—*Seth Klarman, The Baupost Group*

In traditional-value ideas we're looking for a large discount to our estimate of value based on a company's normal earnings power, where normal means that general business activity is not too hot and not too cold. These tend to be more average-quality businesses, which can get very cheap in the down part of a cycle or when dealing with a self-inflicted problem.

The priority in these ideas is on margin of safety, which we look at in two primary ways. The first is by making sure the potential downside is a small fraction of the upside. That means we avoid stocks that are cheap on an equity-value basis primarily because there's a mountain of debt. The second important way to have a margin of safety is to have more than one way to win, through earnings growth, multiple expansion or free options in the business.

—Lee Atzil, Pennant Capital

Whenever Ben Graham was asked what he thought would happen to the economy or to company X's or Y's profits, he always used to deadpan, "The future is uncertain." That's precisely why there's a need for a margin of safety in investing, which is more relevant today than ever.

—Jean-Marie Eveillard, First Eagle Funds

People should be highly skeptical of anyone's, including their own, ability to predict the future, and instead pursue strategies that can survive whatever may occur. [Nassim] Taleb advises us to be "anti-fragile" – i.e., to embrace those elements that benefit from volatility, variability, stress and disorder. This is exactly what we strive to do.

—Seth Klarman, The Baupost Group

The person with the highest probability of outperforming over time is the one who knows how to value companies and buys at a significant discount from that. I've heard for 45 years why all these other things have become more important. You know what? It's all crap.

—Robert Olstein, Olstein Capital Management

Much of what we do is focused on the concept of mean reversion. For a wide variety of inputs, such as P/E ratios, profit margins, sales growth and dividend yields, we assume everything will end up in seven years at normal. There's obviously judgment involved in defining what's normal, but we're pretty faithful historians who are also trying to use our brains and trying desperately not to lose money. For a long time we used 10-year forecasts, but have concluded through research that seven years is closer to the average time it takes for a financial series to mean revert.

—Jeremy Grantham, GMO

Price is perhaps the single most important criterion in sound investment decision-making. Every security or asset is a "buy" at one price, a "hold" at a higher price, and a "sell" at some still higher price. Yet most investors in all asset classes love simplicity, rosy outlooks, and the prospect of smooth sailing. They prefer what is performing well to what has recently lagged, often regardless of price. They prefer full buildings and trophy properties to fixer-uppers that need to be filled, even though empty or unloved buildings may be the far more compelling, and even safer, investments. Because investors are not usually penalized for adhering to conventional practices, doing so is the less professionally risky strategy, even though it virtually guarantees against superior performance.

—Seth Klarman, The Baupost Group

If I had to identify a single key to consistently successful investing, I'd say it's "cheapness." Buying at low prices relative to intrinsic value (rigorously and conservatively derived) holds the key to earning dependably high returns, limiting risk and minimizing losses. It's not the only thing that matters—obviously—but it's something for which there is no substitute. Without doing the above, "investing" moves closer to "speculating," a much less dependable activity.

—Howard Marks, Oaktree Capital

When you look back as far as 80 years for which we have data, rather than moving about without rhyme or reason, the stock market methodically rewards certain investment strategies while punishing others. There's no question the value-based strategies that work over long periods of time don't work all the time, but history shows that after what turn out to be relatively brief periods when other things seem to be all that matter, the market reasserts its preference for value, often with ferocity. My basic premise is that given all that, investors can do much better than the market if they consistently use time-tested strategies that are based on sensible, rational, value-based methods for selecting stocks.

—James O'Shaughnessy, O'Shaughnessy Asset Management

Warren Buffett has made the point many times that being contrarian really isn't the full answer—it's having conviction in your own opinion and filtering out the noise. If the market happens to be right, being a contrarian for the sake of being a contrarian isn't a very good strategy. You have to have the discipline to stick to the situations where you have an edge and sit out the rest of them.

—Jon Jacobson, Highfields Capital

There isn't really a strong value-investing culture in Europe—at least that operates the way we do. Most of the big institutions here define value in terms of high dividend yields and low P/E multiples on reported earnings. That's why so many of them did poorly in 2008, because they owned too many banks and cyclical companies. The majority of European hedge funds are traders who care little about valuation but are investing based on short-term news or momentum. Some are very good at it, but that's not at all what we do. We tell our investors that while they're betting on our skill in identifying corporate assets to invest in, in the end, they own high-quality assets. That's very different than investing in a trading hedge fund, where you're investing in the trading skill of the portfolio manager. If I have a bad day, that's not going to hurt the future prospects of the companies I own. If a trader has a bad day, it can be a disaster.

—Richard Vogel, Alatus Capital

In a rising market, everyone makes money and a value philosophy is unnecessary. But because there is no certain way to predict what the market will do, one must follow a value philosophy at all times. By controlling risk and limiting loss through extensive fundamental analysis, strict discipline, and endless patience, value investors can expect good results with limited downside. You may not get rich quick, but you will keep what you have, and if the future of value investing resembles its past, you are likely to get rich slowly. As investment strategies go, this is the most that any reasonable investor can hope for.

—Seth Klarman, The Baupost Group

Do those things as an analyst that you know you can do well, and only those things. If you can beat the market by charts, by astrology, or by some rare and valuable gift of your own, then that's the row you should hoe. If you're good at picking the stocks most likely to succeed in the next twelve months, base your work on the endeavor. If you can foretell the next important development in the economy, or in the technology, or in consumers' preferences, and gauge its consequences for various equity values, then concentrate on that particular activity. But in each case you must prove to yourself by honest, no-bluffing self-examination, and by continuous testing of performance, that you have what it takes to produce worthwhile results.

If you believe—as I have always believed—that the value approach is inherently sound, workable, and profitable, then devote yourself to that principle. Stick to it, and don't be led astray by Wall Street's fashions, its illusions, and its constant chase after the fast dollar. Let me emphasize that it does not take a genius or even a superior talent to be successful as a value analyst. What it needs is, first, reasonable good intelligence; second, sound principles of operation; third, and most important, firmness of character.

—Benjamin Graham, Common Sense Investing

Consultants in the investment world work so hard to pigeonhole investors that I think even the word "value" is misconstrued to just mean low multiples of book value or earnings. Even Ben Graham early on talked about how growth is of great value, it's just riskier and more difficult to quantify. I'm always amazed that someone would say they weren't a value investor—I wouldn't admit it even if I wasn't. It just seems silly to think about investing any other way.

—Thomas Gayner, Markel Corp.

DOES QUALITY MATTER?

No less an authority than Warren Buffett has described his evolution as a value investor from being more interested early on in "cigar-butt" types of companies—distinguished by little more than how inexpensive their stocks were relative to their tangible assets—to an emphasis on less-cheap, but higher-quality businesses with a sustainable ability to compound shareholder value over long periods of time. The relative importance one places on business quality remains a central element of just about any value-investing approach.

* * *

I started out in 1974 with a Ben Graham value strategy, which suited my personality. For eight years the market did nothing, but it was a great time for stock pickers and value investing, so things went very well. Around 1982 it hit me that there were a lot of lousy stocks in my portfolio and I started wondering why. While it sounds like an obvious conclusion now, the common denominator of the losers was that they were in lousy businesses. I realized I should be more of a business analyst than a stock analyst, meaning that to create value as an investor I had to better understand how companies themselves created value. I moved more away from classical stock metrics of P/E and book value to business metrics of return on capital and cash flows.

—Andrew Pilara, RS Investments

Value to me often derives from competitively strong companies in structurally attractive industries supported by secular growth. In financial terms it's easy to describe a high-quality business. They generate high returns on unlevered capital and high returns on equity on an after-tax basis. They produce free cash flow or have attractive enough reinvestment opportunities to invest cash flow at high returns.

Great businesses are worth more, so I would rather own that type of company at a reasonable price than a mediocre company at a really cheap price. But I've also learned the hard way never to disregard valuation—you can easily overpay for even the best business.

—Morris Mark, Mark Asset Management

As a value investor, I was initially almost exclusively focused on companies with good balance sheets selling at low valuation multiples. There's nothing inherently wrong with that, but I've learned from experience that when cheapness blinds you to not-so-hot businesses or poor management, it's a recipe for disaster. We still only buy bargains, but we pay a lot more attention to things like whether the company's returns on capital are as good as they should be and at how adept and disciplined management is at allocating cash flow. When returns are inadequate or capital is allocated recklessly, equity value is usually destroyed.

—David Herro, Harris Associates

Our view is simply that superior long-term investment performance can be achieved when financially strong, competitively entrenched, well-managed companies are bought at prices significantly below their business value and sold when they approach that corporate worth. The quantitative piece of that is that we only want to buy when we can pay less than 60 percent of a conservative appraisal of a company's value, based on the present value of future free cash flows, current liquidation value and/or comparable sales.

—Mason Hawkins, Southeastern Asset Management

I began as a traditional value investor in the Ben Graham mold, looking for net-nets [companies trading for less than their current assets minus liabilities], discounts to book value and all of that. I would say, though, that I have graduated over time to be more focused on very good companies selling at fair prices.

—Prem Watsa, Fairfax Financial

I have come to the conclusion, as others have, that in general you find better investments in businesses with good economics, secular tailwinds, and sustainable competitive advantages than you do in trying to get one last puff out of proverbial cigar butts. When everything's out of favor and you can buy businesses with bright futures without having to pay for that future, that's a wonderful thing.

—David Winters, Wintergreen Fund

I've learned that to meet my return goals I can't have big losers. So regardless of how cheap something is or how much potential upside there is, that means avoiding companies that can wipe out—with too much debt, unproven business models, secularly challenged end markets or no durable competitive advantages.

—Zeke Ashton, Centaur Capital

What I'm looking for are steady cash flows, reinvested on owners' behalf by honest and able management. Steady cash flows come from businesses that, for one reason or another, enjoy the perception of indispensability for their products. This perception of indispensability often comes from a brand, but can also be from real barriers to competition. If you have the only quarry in town, it's hard for competitors to ship into your market because transportation costs are so high.

—*Thomas Russo, Gardner Russo & Gardner*

For the past 30 years we've sort of floated in style between Ben Graham and Warren Buffett. Graham's approach is static, quantitative, and focused on the balance sheet. There's no attempt to look into the future and judge the more qualitative aspects of the business.

Buffett's major idea was to also look more qualitatively for those few businesses with apparently sustainable competitive advantages, where the odds were fairly high that the business would be as successful ten years from now as it is today. In those situations, one makes money not so much from the elimination of the discount to intrinsic value, but more from the growth in that intrinsic value.

When I started out in 1979, both in the U.S. and Europe, there were many Ben Graham-type stocks to uncover after the dismal stock performance of the 1970s. As we grew and markets changed, we've moved more to the Buffett approach, but not without trepidation. If one is wrong in judging a company to have a sustainable competitive advantage, the investment results can be disastrous. With the Graham approach, the very large discount to static value minimizes that risk. Overall, I'd like to believe we've learned well from both Graham and Buffett and that we own securities that would attract each of them.

—*Jean-Marie Eveillard, First Eagle Funds*

We have moved more from a pure Benjamin Graham style of value investing to one closer to Phil Fisher and Warren Buffett, in the sense that we're putting even more weight on the quality of the business. I don't know, maybe when you're younger you just care about getting things that are cheap and making money fast. But as you become old you see that buying companies with high and sustainable returns on capital at reasonable prices tends to work a little bit better.

—*Francisco Garcia Parames, Bestinver Asset Management*

What we've tried to do is marry the Graham-and-Dodd type emphasis on margin of safety with the more modern version of value investing that focuses on a company's sustainable ability to generate returns on invested capital (ROIC) that exceed its cost of capital. For ROIC we use earnings before interest and taxes, divided by the sum of net working capital and property, plant and equipment, less cash. That measure consistently exceeding the cost of capital means the net asset value is likely to grow and the business can be worth considerably more than the net value of those assets.

—Ari Levy, Lakeview Investment Group

Speaking broadly, probably 10 percent of the businesses out there are lousy, such as selling pure commodities where the marginal cost of production drives the pricing and companies find it very hard to earn even the cost of capital over time. I may own such a company from time to time, but it's rare.

At the other end of the spectrum are another maybe 10 percent of businesses which are of excellent quality. A perfect example would be money management firms, which in aggregate earn obscene returns on equity. We love to own these types of companies, but the opportunities to buy them cheaply are relatively few and far between.

So that leaves us most occupied with the other 80 percent, in which there's a changing roster of winners and losers. Those changes in fortunes are typically tied to cycles and how individual companies are managed, which are the types of things we believe we can analyze and judge. In a lot of our companies, just getting back to average operating performance can result in excellent investment results.

—Preston Athey, T. Rowe Price

We would love to own great businesses as much as the next guy, but the problem is finding them at the right price. We're perfectly happy looking for the average company, where we think there's something going on which the market hasn't recognized that can make it better than average. You're rewarded as much for that as for a good company becoming very good.

We do make every effort to understand what edge the company has in facing competitive threats or maintaining pricing power. When that edge isn't clear, you have to be very careful about the valuation you assign to the earnings and cash flow stream. But business quality, in and of itself, isn't paramount to our decision to buy.

—Vincent Sellecchia, Delafield Fund

We aren't obsessed with perfection and quality. I've made some very nice investments in companies that were going from terrible to bad or bad to fair. We're just looking for the biggest mismatch between value and price—where those occur on the quality scale can change over time.

—Carlo Cannell, Cannell Capital

Everything doesn't have to be the next Microsoft—we may invest in a company because the market thinks it's going to fail, and we don't.

—Lee Ainslie, Maverick Capital

When I talk about the companies I invest in, you'll be able to rattle off hundreds of bad things about them—but that's why they're cheap! The most common comment I get is "Don't you read the paper?" Because if you read the paper, there's no way you'd buy these stocks.

They're priced where they are for good reason, but I invest when I believe the conditions that are causing them to be priced that way are probably not permanent. By nature, you can't be short-term oriented with this investment philosophy. If you're going to worry about short-term volatility, you're just not going to be able to buy the cheapest stocks. With the cheapest stocks, the outlooks are uncertain.

In my whole career I have yet to find the great business with a wonderful management team, high margins, a dominant market position and all the conditions everybody wants, at a low price. The stocks of such companies don't sell at a low price. If I find one, I'll cheer, but it hasn't happened yet.

—Richard Pzena, Pzena Investment Management

People often say they emphasize the quality of management or the competitive moat of a company, but the problem with some of those generalizations is that companies with those attributes are very often not attractively priced. Procter & Gamble may today be considered one of best-managed companies in the world, with some of the best brand franchises and with very low-risk equity, but if the stock is not attractive at the current price, none of the rest matters.

—Ric Dillon, Diamond Hill Investments

I'm generally not obsessed with quality. Good assets bought at the wrong price can be terrible investments, just as lousy ones bought very cheaply can generate excellent results.

That anything is attractive at a price might seem intuitively obvious, but many investors consistently ignore it. People feel better in our business when prices are going up, so you consistently see buyers come in after markets have been good, while people tend to move to the sidelines and watch when markets are bad. People are, in general, momentum investors, which is completely at odds with being a value investor and which can create opportunities for those who are disciplined and patient.

—Jon Jacobson, Highfields Capital

THE VALUE OF GROWTH

A corollary issue to business quality is the emphasis value investors place on a company's ability to grow. Distinctions tend to be made in how heavily weighted growth is in the assessment of value and in the conservatism with which future estimates are made, but avowed value investors typically resist being labeled as unconcerned with growth in assessing a company's intrinsic value.

* * *

Positioning value versus growth sets up a false comparison. They are not opposite ends of the spectrum—value investing and momentum investing are at opposite ends. All else equal, after a stock price falls with no change in its estimated value, a value investor will find it more attractive. A momentum investor reacts in the opposite way; a price decline makes the stock less attractive, and vice versa.

A value investor needs to be able to assess the value of many business characteristics, such as balance sheet strength, cash-generating ability, franchise durability, and so on. Growth is also one of those factors. The ability to grow organically is almost always a positive. It would be a negative only if that growth required so much investment that it had a negative present value. That almost never happens. Ten to 15 years ago, investors were paying a very high price for growth. Many stocks traded at barely double-digit P/Es, but large-cap companies that had above-average expected growth were trading at 50 times earnings and higher. At that spread, we believed growth was way too expensive, and it was an easy choice to avoid it. More recently, valuations have compressed, meaning the price of growth has sharply fallen. When we can get more growth without having to pay for it, the choice again becomes very easy.

I see value investing as applying a consistent discipline to a changing marketplace. As the price investors pay for growth becomes excessive, applying our price discipline moves us away from growth. As the price for growth declines, our discipline moves us toward higher-growth businesses.

—Bill Nygren, Harris Associates

I don't get overly concerned with how my portfolios are categorized. Our mutual fund was originally called a value fund, then it was a "core" fund, and now it shows up sometimes as a growth fund. Through all that, we haven't changed anything we do since day one—the notion that growth is a creator of value is an important part of how we invest.

—Chuck Akre, Akre Capital Management

People often make it sound complicated, but investing is really all about estimating what something is worth and then buying it at an attractive price. Even though we have a classical value approach— analyzing stocks as an ownership stake in a business, calculating intrinsic values, requiring a margin of safety—we don't call ourselves value investors in any of our marketing or other communications. Borrowing from Warren Buffett, as we so often do, we see growth and value as all part of the same equation—to separate them strikes us as kind of dumb. There should be fairly broad agreement that what constitutes value are a company's discounted future cash flows—the growth in those cash flows is obviously central to figuring that out.

—Ric Dillon, Diamond Hill Investments

We believe the most important contributor to the long-term investment performance of the companies we own is earnings growth, not a change in valuation. Because growth is driven by earning high returns on capital and successfully reinvesting cash flow, we tend to be very long-term investors—our average holding period runs about seven years—in order for this virtuous process to bear fruit. Because of that orientation, we put primary emphasis on market structure, the sustainability of the business's competitive advantage, and management's track record in creating shareholder value over time.

If you step back and think about the basics of what we're doing, we're interested in companies that are better than their competitors and which have shown the ability to take the cash they earn and do something smart with it. There's nothing earth-shattering about that, but to the extent you can apply it, understand the business dynamics and not pay foolish prices for things, there's no reason you shouldn't get the attractive long-term returns we believe we and our predecessors have produced.

—Eric Ende, First Pacific Advisors

When I started in the business and for a long time, my concept of value was absolute value in terms of a price-earnings ratio. But I would say my concept of value has changed to a more relative sense of valuation, based on the expected growth rate applied against the price of the stock. Something trading at 30× earnings that is growing at 25 percent per year—where I have confidence it will grow at that rate for some time—can be much cheaper than something at 7× earnings growing at 3 percent. Some people call that GARP (Growth-at-a-Reasonable-Price) investing, I'd call it value. I think that's just semantics.

We've always had excellent analysts, and a good analyst is more adept at making judgments on growth. That's their job—based on the business and the company's position in it, how fast is the company going to grow? It's pretty hard to lose if you're right on the growth rates when the growth rates are high. In that 30× P/E company growing 25 percent per year, you'll be bailed out pretty quickly because in about $2^1/_2$ years the earnings will double and the multiple on that will go to only 15×.

—Julian Robertson, Tiger Management

I'm a value investor, which says I want to buy 50-cent dollars, but given my firm's predilection for serving the needs of taxable investors, I also want that dollar to tax-efficiently compound in value over long periods of time. That means the businesses I find attractive must have great capacity to reinvest, which is not all that common.

—Thomas Russo, Gardner Russo & Gardner

In such a value-focused world, we need to be all the more contrarian in our views. It also requires additional research focus on unique, future-potential situations that might traditionally have been called growth ideas. This is just a practical response. As defined in classical Graham and Dodd terms, a bargain-basement stock has a market capitalization lower than its net working capital—current assets minus current liabilities. The approximate number of companies selling at a discount to net working capital today is zero.

—Murray Stahl, Horizon Asset Management

In my experience, it's been more important to be involved with a powerful trend with accelerating potential returns than to get too hung up on valuation. That's not at all to say valuation doesn't matter, but there have been many times when I've been right about the trend but didn't buy a leader because it was 20 percent too expensive and that turned out to be a mistake.

—John Burbank, Passport Capital

To me, investing success is 50 percent analytical ability and 50 percent understanding and playing off the market's psychology. We are serious students of macroeconomic influences and trends, and are most interested when industry sectors that should benefit from major demographic, technological, or economic shifts are out of favor.

—Ralph Shive, Wasatch Advisors

If you're looking, as we are, for extraordinary returns—from companies whose stocks can go up 10× rather than 2×—it's far more likely to happen because the company's earnings turn out to be so much better than anyone expected than because you found a temporary 50-cent dollar.

—John Burbank, Passport Capital

I'm looking for opportunities in which I have a differentiated view on forward earnings, preferably revenue-driven. You generally make money in three ways on the long side: your estimates are higher than the Street's and the consensus moves to your numbers, the earnings grow, or the earnings multiple expands. By and large, the multiple is likely to expand the most in situations where revenue is accelerating.

—Jed Nussdorf, Soapstone Capital

I tend to look at multiples in absolute terms and am quite comfortable with 12 to 13× multiples of net income when I believe there's an opportunity for faster growth in earnings—for clearly defined reasons—than the market expects.

I do think it's dangerous to lock yourself into rules. So many people miss out on great opportunities because a stock only gets within a quarter point of their price target. I try to avoid being overly rigid.

—Thomas Russo, Gardner Russo & Gardner

While price obviously matters, if we're right on the big picture, I don't need a screaming bargain to do well—compounding value can cover up a lot of sins.

—Thomas Gayner, Markel Corp.

We have learned from experience that the credible expectation of intrinsic-value growth is a helpful guard against value traps. We'd rather own a full-priced business with potential 15 percent per year intrinsic value growth than something at a 30 percent discount that has no growth. The math works in your favor. Ideally, of course, we're shooting for both the growth and the discount.

—Steve Morrow, NewSouth Capital

I've read that the average holding period on the New York Stock Exchange is nine months, which I don't even consider investing. Over such a short period of time you're just betting on the overall direction of the market or on the next quarterly earnings. I typically don't even make quarterly projections, but get excited when I see excellent growth potential over time for which I'm paying next to nothing because the market is ignoring it.

—Aaron Edelheit, Sabre Value Management

Many value investors are primarily focused on price and valuation, which we obviously think are important, but we also believe that when constructing a portfolio you should have companies with promise beyond just going from undervalued to fairly valued.

Basic-value stocks make up about 40 percent of the portfolio [and] consistent earners, blue-chip companies that tend to have long records of steady organic revenue and profit growth but every once in a while become out of favor, also make up around 40 percent of the portfolio. The last category we try to own are emerging franchises, which are typically younger companies with excellent growth prospects. Because they often have a narrow product lineup, they fall out of favor when one or a few important products suffer from inevitable hiccups in growth. I often say the only small company we want to buy is one that can become a big company—that's what we're looking for in emerging franchises.

—William Fries, Thornburg Investment Management

We tend to like equity ideas that have almost bond-like qualities, where cash is being generated in a fairly predictable way and being used to pay down debt or return capital to shareholders through dividends or stock buybacks. Companies in growth mode, reinvesting all of their cash, are more like zero-coupon bonds and are more difficult for us to get our hands around. It's not that we never invest in growth ideas, but it's not our focus.

—Mitchell Julis, Canyon Capital

We expect to generate the vast majority of our returns not from the growth in the value of the business, but from the unwinding of the value discount. We're more than happy to see growth potential and we recognize how valuable it can be, but higher-growth businesses typically expose us to more valuation risk than we're comfortable with.

—David Samra, Artisan Partners

THE VALUE MINDSET

While the success of any investment strategy bears heavily on the intelligence and technical skill of its practitioners, value investors also believe their competitive advantage rests upon the unique and multifaceted value mindset they possess. It's an attitude as much as a strategy, born more than bred, and indispensible to their ability to outperform over time.

* * *

Starting with the first recorded and reliable history that we can find—a history of the Peloponnesian war by a Greek author named Thucydides—and following through a broad array of key historical global crises, you see recurring aspects of human nature that have gotten people into trouble: hubris, dogma, and haste. The keys to our investing approach are the symmetrical opposite of that: humility, flexibility, and patience.

On the humility side, one of the things that Jean-Marie Eveillard firmly ingrained in the culture here is that the future is uncertain. That results in investing with not only a price margin of safety, but in companies with conservative balance sheets and prudent and proven management teams. If you acknowledge your crystal ball is at best foggy, you follow the advice of Ben Graham and invest to avoid the landmines.

In terms of flexibility, we've been willing to be out of the biggest sectors of the market, whether it was Japan in the late 1980s, technology in the late 1990s or financials the late 2000s. That wasn't necessarily because of any particular gift of foresight, but reflected a recognition that each of those areas embodied very widely accepted and high expectations. It's painful and not socially acceptable to be out of the most revered sectors of the market, but those types of acts of omission have been a key contributor to the strong performance.

The third thing in terms of temperament we think we value more than most other investors is patience. We have a five-year average holding period. Particularly in a volatile market like today's, people are trying to zig and zag ahead of every market turn that they're hoping they can forecast with scientific precision. We like to plant seeds and then watch the trees grow, and our portfolio is often kind of a portrait of inactivity. That's kept us from making sharp and sometimes emotional moves that we eventually come to regret.

—Matthew McLennan, First Eagle Funds

The key to the success of value investing is that it is basically contrarian investing. How can you buy something at a value price if it's desired by the world? Investors go out of their way to look for companies with certain cash flow characteristics, returns on assets that are stable and that have objectively verifiable tangible assets that could be liquidated at some point. If that's going to be the focus for literally thousands of funds . . . how could you possibly have outstanding results by just doing the same thing?

—Murray Stahl, Horizon Asset Management

It's important to play to your strengths. As an investor, I'm not a home-run hitter and can't think of a lot of securities on which I've made 10 times my money. But I also can't think of a lot of securities, post-1970, on which I've lost a meaningful amount of capital. Success in investing is not really much more complicated than that.

—Spencer Davidson, General American Investors

It's hard for most people to grasp that a great company is not always a great stock, and that a great stock is not always a great company. Value works because you're consistently paying less to get more. Over time that works a lot better than paying more to get less.

—James O'Shaughnessy, O'Shaughnessy Asset Management

Going against the grain is clearly not for everyone—and it doesn't tend to help you in your social life—but to make the really large money in investing, you have to have the guts to make the bets that everyone else is afraid to make.

—Carlo Cannell, Cannell Capital

Our worst mistakes have been far more likely a result of our being a follower rather than a leader. We've been much less successful buying into stories that are out there already than ones that we're anticipating in advance.

—Sam Isaly, OrbiMed Advisors

It's important to remember as a contrarian investor that the consensus is often right. My colleague François Sicart likes to say, "Just because everyone says it's raining outside is no reason not to take an umbrella." But because we believe the consensus is priced into any given investment, going along with that is a very hard place from which to make money.

—Robert Kleinschmidt, Tocqueville Asset Management

Value investors tend to have a different default question in looking at a potential opportunity. Most investment managers ask "Can I own this?"—to which the answer is generally yes. Value investors put a different burden of proof on every idea by asking, "Why should I own this?" That degree of skepticism is a valuable trait.

—James Montier, Société Générale

We do tend to be a little dour at times and we definitely take a skeptical view of the facts. Warren Buffett once said, "You pay a very high price for a cheery consensus." Value investors simply don't believe in cheery consensus. That's not a criticism—I'd consider it a badge of honor.

—Daniel Bubis, Tetrem Capital

Most investors take comfort from calm, steadily rising markets; roiling markets can drive investor panic. But these conventional reactions are inverted. When all feels calm and prices surge, the markets may feel safe; but, in fact, they are dangerous because few investors are focusing on risk. When one feels in the pit of one's stomach the fear that accompanies plunging market prices, risk-taking becomes considerably less risky, because risk is often priced into an asset's lower market valuation. Investment success requires standing apart from the frenzy—the short-term, relative performance game played by most investors.

—Seth Klarman, The Baupost Group

What you should do is take a dim view of what's been appreciating and be interested in what hasn't been good to you. You certainly want to understand why any asset class has been going down, but you should celebrate the fact that it has been getting cheaper. To say price going down is a good reason to look the other way is like saying you'd never go shopping when stores are running sales.

—Howard Marks, Oaktree Capital

We're classic value investors in the sense that when share prices are low, we think risk is low as well. Most people can understand that in theory but don't believe it in practice and even act as if it's heresy. It's actually when prices are rising and stocks are converging with our share-price targets that we find risk far more uncomfortable.

—Sarah Ketterer, Causeway Capital

Someone asked me the other day whether watching what was going on [in troubled markets] felt lousy, and of course it does. But you can only buy quality cheap when people are afraid. We earn our keep much more in difficult markets than when everybody's serene and happy.

—David Herro, Harris Associates

I'm perfectly fine if Mr. Market wants to go down another 15 to 20 percent—we'll just buy more stocks. It's not during up years that great investment track records are made!

—Charles de Vaulx, International Value Advisers

The market is extremely noisy, but you just can't let that distract you from your discipline and your framework. We've said this since we started out: The market is really just a pendulum that forever swings between unsustainable optimism, which makes stocks too expensive, and unjustified pessimism, which makes them too cheap. All we're trying to do is keep a level head, sell to the optimists, and buy from the pessimists.

—Jonathan Shapiro, Kovitz Investment Group

Warren Buffett is right when he says you should invest as if the market is going to be closed for the next five years. The fundamental principles of value investing, if they make sense to you, can allow you to survive and prosper when everyone else is rudderless. We have a proven map with which to navigate. It sounds kind of crazy, but in times of turmoil in the market, I've felt a sort of serenity in knowing that if I've checked and rechecked my work, one plus one still equals two regardless of where a stock trades right after I buy it.

—Seth Klarman, The Baupost Group

When you have a model you believe in, that you've used for a long time and which is more empirical than intuitive, sticking with it takes the emotion away when markets are good or bad. That's been a central element of our success. It's the emotional dimension that drives people to make lousy, irrational decisions.

—Will Browne, Tweedy, Browne Co.

I like to say that changing investment styles to the latest fad produces the same results as changing lanes during rush-hour traffic jams: You increase the risk of an accident with little chance of achieving better results. The psychological pain of sticking to your guns, though, is tough. I was up 35 percent in 1999 but had people telling me I didn't have enough technology in my fund and they were taking money out. This is not nuclear physics, but [it's] hard to stick to your guns when the crowd's running over you. We don't believe value investing is ever out of style—it just doesn't work all of the time.

—Robert Olstein, Olstein Capital Management

The real secret to investing is that there is no secret to investing. Every important aspect of value investing has been made available to the public many times over, beginning with the first edition of *Security Analysis*. That so many people fail to follow this timeless and almost foolproof approach enables those who adopt it to remain successful. The foibles of human nature that result in the mass pursuit of instant wealth and effortless gain seem certain to be with us forever. So long as people succumb to this aspect of their natures, value investing will remain, as it has been for 75 years, a sound and low-risk approach to successful long-term investing.

—Seth Klarman, The Baupost Group

It is occasionally possible for a tortoise, content to assimilate proven insights of his best predecessors, to outrun hares which seek originality or don't wish to be left out of some crowd folly which ignores the best work of the past. This happens as the tortoise stumbles on some particularly effective way to apply the best previous work, or simply avoids standard calamities. We try more to profit by always remembering the obvious than from grasping the esoteric. It is remarkable how much long-term advantage people like us have gotten by trying to be consistently not stupid, instead of trying to be very intelligent.

—Charlie Munger, Poor Charlie's Almanack

In a world in which most investors appear interested in figuring out how to make money every second and chase the idea *du jour*, there's also something validating about the message that it's okay to do nothing and wait for opportunities to present themselves or to pay off. That's lonely and contrary a lot of the time, but reminding yourself that that's what it takes is quite helpful.

—Seth Klarman, The Baupost Group

One investor who has greatly influenced me from a conceptual standpoint is Howard Marks, the Chairman of Oaktree Capital. He's not an equity investor, but he describes this notion of running a core strategy, focused on beating the market through the accumulation of small but high-probability advantages over a long period of time. The alternative, which can also be a legitimate strategy, is to swing for the fences with the goal of hitting enough home runs to drive outstanding performance. The high-probability approach is consistent with my personality.

—Zeke Ashton, Centaur Capital

I feel strongly that attempting to achieve a superior long-term record by stringing together a run of top-decile years is unlikely to succeed. Rather, striving to do a little better than average every year, and through discipline to have highly superior relative results in bad times, is: (1) less likely to produce extreme volatility; (2) less likely to produce huge losses which can't be recouped, and (3) most importantly, more likely to work.

—Howard Marks, Oaktree Capital

One of the temptations of a professional investor is that one is often drawn towards difficult analytical problems in search of a big pay-off. If anything, this temptation has been amplified in recent years by the acclaim and financial rewards that have accrued to those who end up on the right side of a big, dramatic bet – the more complex, the better. The problem is that such success is hard to maintain, hard to predict, and generally creates further pressure to find similarly difficult, large-scale mispricing opportunities to exploit in the future. Such opportunities may not be available most of the time, which may explain why many of those investors who get things dramatically right one year find themselves getting it dramatically wrong the next. At the end of the day, being consistently smarter than the rest of the market is probably next to impossible to do.

—Zeke Ashton, Centaur Capital

I don't think being a value investor is something you can learn. You can learn how to be better at it and the analytical support for it, but you can't sit there and say, "I'm going to make an intellectual decision that I'm going to become a value investor." My personal belief is that you're either born as a bargain-hunter type or you're born as a bright-eyed optimist. You have to be skeptical and pessimistic, and you have to really enjoy the bargain-hunting process, and it has to be part of your whole life. I find that the people who are the best at this are the type of people who are absolutely thrilled to find a pair of shoes for $20 that they could have paid $150 for at a department store.

—Richard Pzena, Pzena Investment Management

Some of the best early advice I got was to forget all I'd learned in business school about efficient markets and instead read Ben Graham. You either take to it or you don't, and I knew right away that this was how I wanted to do it.

—Prem Watsa, Fairfax Financial

We consistently articulate two goals—to achieve positive returns and to outperform the market. If you aren't going to make money owning our mutual fund, then there's no point in buying it. And if you aren't going to make more money than you would have in an index fund, we're not worth our fees.

At the end of 2010 I looked at the previous decade for the Oak-mark Fund, to see in how many quarters we could tell our investors that we both made money and that we made meaningfully more—which I defined as 100 basis points—than the S&P 500. Of the 40 quarters, only eight qualified as winners. That's like hitting .200 in baseball, just one out away from a ticket to the minor leagues.

For those 10 years, however, the fund returned 74 percent, versus 15 percent in total return for the S&P 500. So even though we were most often frustrated because we lost money or didn't make as much as somebody else, over that period we beat 96 percent of competing funds and did more than 400 basis points better per year than the market. That to me is kind of the essence of value investing. We often don't keep up with strong markets, but make up for it by losing less during market declines. Expectations for companies we own are typically quite low, which means they don't usually fall as much as the market does when times get tough.

It is a limited set of people who have the personality and discipline to successfully invest this way. I guess that's why we can continue to put food on the table.

—Bill Nygren, Harris Associates

Value investing strategies have worked for years and everyone's known about them. They continue to work because it's hard for people to do, for two main reasons. First, the companies that show up on the screens can be scary and not doing so well, so people find them difficult to buy. Second, there can be one-, two- or three-year periods when a strategy like this doesn't work. Most people aren't capable of sticking it out through that.

—Joel Greenblatt, Gotham Capital

If you are a value investor, you're a long-term investor. If you are a long-term investor, you're not trying to keep up with a benchmark on a short-term basis. To do that, you accept in advance that every now and then you will lag behind, which is another way of saying you will suffer. That's very hard to accept in advance because, the truth is, human nature shrinks from pain. That's why not so many people invest this way. But if you believe as strongly as I do that value investing not only makes sense, but that it works, there's really no credible alternative.

—Jean-Marie Eveillard, First Eagle Funds

Field of Play

CHAPTER 2

Circle of Competence

In a 1989 *Fortune* article profiling 10 young money managers—under the title "Are These the New Warren Buffetts?"—Marshall Weinberg, of the brokerage firm Gruntal & Co., recalls a dinner in Manhattan he had with Buffett himself: "He had an exceptional ham-and-cheese sandwich. A few days later, we were going out again and he said, 'Let's go back to that restaurant.' I said, 'But we were just there,' and he said, 'Precisely. Why take a risk with another place? We know exactly what we're going to get.' And that is what Warren looks for in stocks too. He only invests in companies where the odds are great that they will not disappoint."

This anecdote says a great deal about a core tenet of successful investing: combining an understanding of what Buffett calls your "circle of competence" with the discipline to remain within its boundaries. There's certainly no one right circle of competence to have, nor should it remain static over time. But when successful investors talk about ideas that have gone awry, one key reason often cited has been venturing into an industry, company, or market situation with which they don't have experience or don't yet have a full command. Enough can go wrong even when you're in the center of your circle of competence, why increase the chance of mishap by operating outside of it?

Regardless of how broad or narrow their field of play, the best equity investors are able to articulate clearly where they expect to find investing opportunity and why. This circle-of-competence definition includes the characteristics of companies of interest, with respect to such things as their size, where they operate geographically, their business models, and the industry or industries in which they compete. It also includes the situations that the investor has found can lead to potential share mispricing, such as where a company is in its evolution, where an industry is in its cycle, and when a company or industry is likely to be neglected or misunderstood. All of this informs where the investor will—and won't—look for ideas, and the tactics he or she uses to generate them.

In an interview in 2009 we asked Julian Robertson, the founder of Tiger Management and one of the most successful hedge fund managers of all time, what advice he might have for students interested in pursuing an investing career. He spoke about them getting experience working with the best investors possible, and about learning to focus:

> *A baseball player never really gets paid, no matter how many homeruns he hits or what his batting average is, unless he gets to the big leagues. Then he's guaranteed to make a lot of money. But in the fund business you can find a minor league where you can hit for a better average, because that's what you're paid on.*
>
> *I remember one of our guys taking us into Korea in the early 1990s, and the market was so inefficient that it was a gold mine if you knew what you were doing. One of our Tiger funds today focuses on gold—a league that is inhabited by some of the crazier investors out there—and it just has a phenomenal record. They know more about gold than anyone else in the world and they just kill all the rest.*
>
> *My point is that to be successful in this business, you don't have to be better than everybody everywhere, just better than everybody in the league in which you play. It's maybe today more difficult to find those inefficient areas, but it's not impossible.*

This section assembles the myriad answers the best investors give when asked to explain where they look for opportunity and to justify why they've chosen the focus they have. Again, it's important to keep in mind that there is no narrow set of right answers here. What matters is that some level of clear focus exists and that the rationale behind it is sound. From there, it's all about execution.

THE RIGHT SIZE

One of the most basic distinctions investors make in defining their field of play concerns company size. How big a company is can say a lot about its complexity, the sustainability of its business model, how actively followed it is, the volatility of its stock price, and why it might be mispriced. Practical concerns can obviously come into play: A manager with $5 billion in assets will find it much more difficult to invest in microcap stocks—where he or she might have to own 100 percent of the company in order to take a position size that is material to his portfolio—than will someone managing $50 million. But managers typically can identify their sweet spot in terms of market cap, or, alternatively, should be able to explain why they're agnostic on the point.

*　　*　　*

Our strategy from the beginning has been to focus on areas where we believe we can have some advantage, where there is a greater prevalence of irrationality and higher likelihood of mispriced assets. For us, that's not going to be investing in Microsoft or in some quantitative strategy against a room full of Goldman Sachs' PhD's with Cray supercomputers. We have to be guerrilla investors, lying in the weeds and picking off opportunities among the obscure and mundane.

That usually means small, ignored companies that no one else is talking about. We'll invest in companies with up to $1 billion or so in market cap, but have been most successful in ideas that start out in the $50 million to $300 million range. Fewer people are looking at them and the industries the companies are in can be quite stable. Given that, if you find a company doing well, it's more likely it can sustain that advantage over time. We can also take a significant-enough stake in any company that, if necessary, we can have an impact on how it's run.

—James Vanasek, VN Capital

My basic premise is that the efficient markets hypothesis breaks down when there is inconsistent, imperfect dissemination of information. Therefore it makes sense to direct our attention towards the 14,000 or so publicly traded companies in the U.S. for which there is little or no investment sponsorship by Wall Street, meaning three or fewer sell-side analysts who publish research. Money is made in the dark, not the light.

You'd be amazed how little competition we have in this neglected universe. It is just not in the best interest of the vast majority of the investing ecosphere to spend 10 minutes on the companies we spend our lives looking at.

I consider myself better off buying an index fund or an ETF rather than trying to figure out how to own Johnson & Johnson or Coca-Cola or Exxon, very high-quality companies with dozens of analysts fine-tuning their estimates by the penny every week. I love Coca-Cola and find its financial characteristics to be outstanding, but how can I have an edge in buying and selling its stock? How can something like that ever be a fat pitch?

I would point out that most ignored companies are not investable, either because they're not really public or are just complete garbage. But within that flea market is where you find the greatest bargains, so we troll through it to find the small percentage of companies that are ignored for improper reasons.

—Carlo Cannell, Cannell Capital

I accept the proposition that public markets are most of the time efficient in pricing large-cap companies, but I've never believed there was sufficient trading volume or research coverage of very small companies to make their prices similarly efficient. So it ought to at least be theoretically possible for an investor in microcaps to have an informational advantage. We focus on companies with an average market cap of $400 million, which either don't have Wall Street coverage or the value-added of that coverage is, shall I say, modest. It can turn your stomach, but we also see it as an opportunity that frequent imbalances of supply and demand in the stocks we follow are capable of producing enormous price swings.

We found Roger Ibbotson's recent study of the impact of investors' preference for liquidity to be quite consistent with our experience. He's done seminal research on the superior performance over time of small-caps over large-caps and of value investing over growth investing, but in this case he found going back over 40 years that investors overpay so much for the perceived safety and lower frictional costs of liquid stocks that the opportunities to earn gains in the less-liquid stocks they neglect are significant. One could certainly argue that the extreme increase in market volatility that started in 2008 has exacerbated this inefficiency.

—David Nierenberg, D3 Family Funds

The potential value added by the research into a microcap company is substantially greater. I have a lot less competition. I'm also much more able to speak directly with the CFO or CEO, who may not be as polished in the ways of Wall Street and might be more open and forthcoming about their business. All of that makes it easier to uncover new and previously unknown facts, which can be an important edge.

—Paul Sonkin, Hummingbird Value Fund

We focus on smaller-cap companies that are largely ignored by Wall Street and face some sort of distress, of their own making or due to an industry cycle. These companies are more likely to be inefficiently priced and if you have conviction and a long-term view they can produce not 20 to 30 percent returns, but multiples of that.

—*Robert Robotti, Robotti & Co.*

Our process is meant to identify where short-term fears have created inefficiencies in pricing, and as you go down in market cap, the market reactions get more extreme. Because so many people are looking at large caps, when a stock gets even a little undervalued the market tends to take advantage of that. If you're investing on bad news, it's best to look where the overreaction on the downside is the biggest, and that's more often in small caps.

—*Canon Coleman, Invesco*

I'm also not going to spend any time trying to figure out what a conglomerate like General Electric is worth. Too many moving parts, and there are so many other people who have to own it that it's very unlikely it will be dramatically mispriced anyway.

—*Zeke Ashton, Centaur Capital*

In the same year I started my firm, 2000, I read David Swensen's *Pioneering Portfolio Management*. He talked a lot about how institutions using a multi-manager approach ought to find managers who concentrate capital in their best ideas and who look off the beaten path to produce above-average results. That dovetailed perfectly with what we thought made sense anyway: The market gets less efficient as you go down the market-cap spectrum, so running a concentrated portfolio of around 12 stocks in the least-efficient segments would offer the best opportunity to produce above-average returns. We started out primarily in microcaps, which we define as $300 million in market value or less, and have since started a small-cap strategy as well, investing in companies with up to $2 billion in market cap.

—*Brian Bares, Bares Capital*

We believe we can generate alpha in smaller companies in part because the market overemphasizes the income statement and underemphasizes the balance sheet in valuing them. We try by focusing first on the balance sheet to take out some of the risk that comes with relying so heavily on inherently unpredictable future prospects.

—*Bruce Zessar, Advisory Research, Inc.*

Maybe the biggest reason small companies outperform is just their entrepreneurial nature. We're almost always more comfortable investing behind management with significant ownership in the business than in big companies where that's rarely the case.

—*William Nasgovitz, Heartland Advisors*

We stick primarily to smaller companies because if we can't speak with senior management on a regular basis, we aren't interested. Otherwise we're just playing with numbers. We've always focused on small caps, but what makes them even more interesting today is that sell-side Wall Street research has never been worse. Everyone has cut back on research staff, which means more and more companies are ignored or getting very superficial work done on them. I was reading an analyst report over the weekend where the price target on the company had gone from $6 to $16, but as far as I could tell nothing at all had changed. The worse the research, the better the chance we find something that's being overlooked.

—*Candace Weir, Paradigm Capital*

Multiples tend to contract further when small companies mess up than when large ones do, so there's more room on the upside when a small company grows out of a turnaround. I'd also argue that it's generally quicker and easier for a small company to be turned around, which improves your chances of investment success.

—*Kevin O'Boyle, Presidio Fund*

In my second year at Columbia I took Bruce Greenwald's value investing class, and on the first day he showed us a table from Eugene Fama and Kenneth French's famous *Journal of Finance* paper called "The Cross-Section of Expected Stock Returns." The table showed how low-price-to-book stocks and small caps tended over long periods of time to outperform the market as a whole. The whole idea made so much sense to me that I decided that was the basic direction I wanted to go.

—*Paul Sonkin, Hummingbird Value Fund*

I'm never going to run $1 billion while sticking with these teeny-weeny companies. That suits me, because I much prefer managing a portfolio to managing the staff I'd need with a lot more assets. Most important, though, is that I just love the thrill of the hunt involved with these types of companies. Why give that up?

—*Paul Sonkin, Hummingbird Value Fund*

Small-cap investing can be more labor intensive due to the sheer number of companies, but at the same time you can more quickly know just about everything you need to know about a company to make an investment judgment. I can't say that in looking at a company like AIG, for example.

—*Philip Tasho, TAMRO Capital*

We're looking for the prospect of an accelerating rate of positive change. That means we're naturally drawn to management changes, turnarounds, or, more generally, to situations in which changes in the macroeconomic, competitive or regulatory landscape require a company to remake what it does or how it does it.

That strategy is particularly tailored to small caps. Simpler business models are easier to analyze and cross-check, while at the same time change happens faster in small companies, making for more investable inflection points. One or two people can also make a big difference, quickly.

—*Mariko Gordon, Daruma Capital Management*

The traditional reason for looking at a small-cap stock, which is less liquid, less known, and therefore theoretically riskier, is because it can grow faster. What happens as a result is that people crowd into the same 200 names that are rock-star growers, leaving aside a large number of smaller companies that may still have excellent prospects but fall between the cracks. We have always been about finding those types of companies and learned through experience early on that (1) you want to invest in companies with great balance sheets; (2) you want to take a long-term view; (3) the price you pay matters a lot; and (4) you have to be diversified. To be good at it you have to focus on it, so we believe our edge is in bringing a formidable amount of knowledge and experience to a part of the stock market that is not always well understood or effectively followed.

—*Whitney George, Royce & Associates*

For quality-of-business reasons, we now focus on companies with between roughly $1 billion and $8 billion in market cap. The $500 million company is unlikely to have as global a footprint and as diversified a customer base as we want, and the business generally is less mature and more volatile. We've invested successfully in smaller companies over the years, but it can be more hair-raising than I'm comfortable with at our current asset size.

We avoid the biggest companies because we want to eliminate the "what you don't know" risk. With bigger companies there can be many different business units with distinctly different trajectories, making it harder to identify the core engine that truly drives the bottom line. There's also just a greater possibility that you miss something important, like environmental liabilities, or underfunded multi-employer pension plans, or work rules in a region that limit your ability to sell businesses.

—*Jeffrey Ubben, ValueAct Capital*

I do believe mid caps to some extent offer the best of both worlds. They're usually not as well followed as large caps and by the rule of large numbers can have longer growth runways. At the same time, they're broader-based and therefore less volatile than small caps, with better liquidity. I also think it's been an advantage that the investing world seems more focused on small-cap or large-cap exposure, leaving mid-caps relatively neglected.

—*Tom Perkins, Perkins Investment Management*

Our sweet spot tends to be in small and mid-size companies that often aren't particularly well followed by Wall Street. It would be illogical for us to know or uncover something about Procter & Gamble or Texas Instruments before 100 smart analysts did. I'd add that as brokerage firms have gone out of business or cut back on the number of companies they follow, it's not as if we need to focus on tiny or new companies to find those that are relatively ignored. You can find plenty of established, decent-sized companies that just don't get the attention from Wall Street that they once did.

—Dennis Delafield, Delafield Fund

We try to be cap-agnostic, but we do want businesses that are easier to understand, and smaller to mid-size companies are generally easier to understand. They have fewer divisions and we can usually get more of our questions answered. Our median market cap in the fund is around $5 billion.

—Steven Romick, First Pacific Advisors

We generally want to own only those things that can be bought out. That number keeps getting bigger, but it does tend to keep us out of the very biggest names.

—Christopher Browne, Tweedy, Browne Co.

Our sweet spot tends to be in companies with market caps from $1 billion to $5 billion. Illiquidity in smaller-cap companies is fine for a portion of your book, but it's nice to have the ability to change your mind and more easily sell if things don't develop as you hoped. The largest companies can certainly be mispriced, but our ability to create an analytical edge given the number of people looking at them is more limited.

—Brian Feltzin, Sheffield Asset Management

The high-quality characteristics we look for in companies to own at the right price tend more often to be in large-caps than small-caps. We agree with all the arguments that small-caps may benefit from persistent market imperfections that can lead to them being mispriced—which is one reason we like them—but the fact is that large-caps meeting our criteria get mispriced from time to time as well. Maybe the inefficiency has a different trigger, but whatever the reason, we're glad it exists.

—C.T. Fitzpatrick, Vulcan Value Partners

It is hard for us to have an edge in analyzing Microsoft's or Intel's business, but we do believe it's possible through understanding macro trends and market psychology—and through the use of a clear valuation discipline—to buy even the most widely followed companies when they're out of favor and sell them when they're too highly regarded. If Intel's historical valuation range is between 12 and 25 times earnings, with discipline and patience there should be opportunities to buy at the low end of that range and to sell at the high end, making good money along the way.

—Ralph Shive, Wasatch Advisors

We gravitate toward larger, diversified companies where the inefficient pricing comes from an excessive focus on short-term issues that we expect to mean-revert. If we're wrong, in a big company our downside risk is limited because there are other parts of the business that can hold up value or even increase overall value if we bought cheaply enough. In my experience, if we're wrong with a smaller company focused on one product or one geography, there's too much risk it's going to zero.

—Daniel Bubis, Tetrem Capital

I build an earnings model from scratch for every material position in the fund, which is the best way to understand the key drivers of the business and its profitability. I'm looking for opportunities in which I have a differentiated view on forward earnings, preferably revenue-driven. By focusing on better-followed mid-cap and large-cap stocks, I can have a much better understanding of what constitutes consensus, and specifically how and where my view varies from it. In smaller companies that attract little attention, it's harder to know the expectations embedded in the share price.

—Jed Nussdorf, Soapstone Capital

It's much easier to find large-cap stocks that are out-of-favor—they're on the front page of *The Wall Street Journal* and the folks at CNBC are all over them. But in addition to looking for what others don't like, we also look for what is relatively neglected, which are almost always smaller to mid-cap names. In these cases our anticonsensus view is that the quality of the business and its prospects are just being missed by the market.

—Robert Kleinschmidt, Tocqueville Asset Management

We want to maintain the discipline that we will invest in a company, regardless of size, if it meets our criteria. Part of that is because we learn from all the companies we own. Part of that is because it keeps us fresh and engaged and not stuck in the rut of looking at the same 100 companies everyone else is. We also take the position that a penny more in return for our shareholders than we would have had otherwise is a penny worth having. If smaller-cap companies can give us that, we'll buy them.

—Clyde McGregor, Harris Associates

[The SEC's] Regulation FD, for better or worse, is used by many bigger companies to restrict access to senior management and limit communication to the canned presentation. We learn a lot from sitting down with management at smaller companies and really talking about their businesses, competitors, and opportunities.

—Edward Studzinski, Harris Associates

The information-inefficiency tale commonly told about the small-cap universe is over-hyped. In a diversified institutional portfolio, with 50-plus names, you're deluding yourself if you think you can have some unique inside scoop on more than a handful of the names you own. That's all the more true in recent years, with all the concentrated hedge funds out there selling themselves as small-cap experts.

—James Kieffer, Artisan Partners

INDUSTRY PREFERENCE

Central to any accomplished investor's definition of his or her circle of competence is a description of the industries—or more generally, the types of businesses—on which he or she focuses. Hard-earned experience would appear to be the most impactful teacher here—the emphasis is usually more on where they will not invest, rather than on where they will.

* * *

Stepping outside your areas of competence is often a seductive siren song, but I've learned from experience not to listen anymore. Without the confidence that comes from experience and the ability to recognize patterns, the risk is higher that you'll overpay or sell too soon in a panic. If you're a value investor, it's pretty easy to explain to yourself or your investors why a deep-value idea hasn't worked out yet. But if you bought JDS Uniphase at $100, which was down from $200 but on the way to $2, that's tougher to explain.

—Shawn Kravetz, Esplanade Capital

The more specialized the knowledge necessary to understand a business, the less likely we'll invest in it. Who's going to be the better biotech investor, the person who ran drug trials for Merck for 25 years or us? We do little in pharmaceuticals, healthcare, and computer technology.

—James Vanasek, VN Capital

We've struggled to underwrite moats based on intellectual capital, say in a company like Qualcomm, where its earnings power is enormous if all its patents hold up. That's another reason we're not active in things like pharmaceutical or biotech companies.

—James Crichton, Scout Capital

In general, the best thing for us is to find companies that have really stumbled, but where you can look at their past and understand why they are going to earn something much better in the future. That's opposed to looking at a company like Amazon.com, for example, which might be a great business, but where understanding exactly what the model is going to be in the future isn't easy. It's a lot easier to look at the prospects for a rail-car manufacturer, whose business has been the same for decades.

—Steven Romick, First Pacific Advisors

We don't typically bet on scientific innovation, so we rarely find things we'll consider in healthcare. We avoid many areas in technology because of the speed of the product cycles and the magnitude of change from cycle to cycle.

—Adam Weiss, Scout Capital

Successful technologies change something, creating an efficiency or demand that wasn't there before. But the very fact that the change happens means that somebody else can come along and change it again. If because of the threat of technological obsolescence I'm uncertain about a company's cash flows several years out, I'll put a big discount on those cash flows and conclude they're not worth much. Because Wall Street tends to put a large value on the future cash flows of technology companies, we rarely find one that we consider very attractive.

—Ed Wachenheim, Greenhaven Associates

Back in the late 1990s we invested in a few too many "concept" stocks—earlier-stage companies with developing technologies where the stories were compelling and indicated that there would be considerable future value. The problem is that without a real underpinning of asset value or earnings, these types of companies can run into big trouble when the thesis doesn't pan out as quickly as expected or new competition disrupts the story.

—Randall Abramson, Trapeze Asset Management

We're drawn to companies with long product lifecycles, in which the product or service will be more or less the same five years from now. If that's not the case, we don't believe we can with adequate confidence make reliable long-term earnings forecasts.

—Murray Stahl, Horizon Asset Management

We'd like to believe any business is analyzable, but when you have product cycles of only twelve months, as an investor you're very reliant on the company hitting that window exactly right. If they don't and somebody else does, you can buy low all you want, but you find out pretty quickly that you were buying a future income stream that was a mirage.

We haven't sworn off technology entirely, but we've essentially sworn off investing in short-product-cycle technology. We look for technology companies where the business cycles are glacial in comparison.

—Larry Robbins, Glenview Capital

We're typically not attracted to most technology businesses because of cut-throat competition, potential technology obsolescence, short product cycles, and the excessive use of stock options. The return on time is also a problem—you spend so many hours analyzing new products and technology trends that 50 percent of your time gets spent on 5 to 10 percent of your portfolio.

At the same time, technology is an important driver of economic growth and grows at above-GDP rates, so we want to have exposure to it. We like to attack difficult industries through the side door, so to speak. With Arrow Electronics, for example, we can own a leading distributor of technology products—including semiconductors, software and electronic components—that supplies mostly small and medium-sized companies. That allows it to benefit from the growth in high tech without the typical risks associated with tech stocks.

—Pat English, Fiduciary Management, Inc.

I first got interested in technology stocks after watching things like Micron Technology go from $20 to $40 to $20 to $40 to $20 to $40. The cyclicality in many of these businesses can be more regular than is often believed, so it's possible to buy on the down leg of a cycle because there will inevitably be an up leg. We've had considerable success, in particular, in buying technology companies that also have great balance sheets. Companies like this have the flexibility to invest in new initiatives, buy new technology and invest in R&D. Even if they aren't profitable today, you have the potential for a goldmine if the business turns around.

—John Buckingham, Al Frank Asset Management

From the beginning we have occasionally come across products or technologies that we thought were too compelling to ignore by sticking rigidly to our playbook. These ideas are higher risk and so they won't make up a big part of the portfolio, but we make room for them when the potential is as high as we think it is.

—Charles Mackall, Avenir Corp.

Circle of competence essentially comes down to whether we understand the business. There are several sub-questions under that: Do we know the right people in the industry? How well do we understand the products and the customer decision-making process? Are there unanalyzable things that could have a big impact? No matter how well you understand the steel industry, for example, there's tremendous volatility and variability in the business that may not be susceptible to prediction, which makes it difficult for us to underwrite the business with adequate confidence.

—James Crichton, Scout Capital

We tend to find more special situations in industries with higher cyclicality, which most often aren't the most glamorous sectors of the economy. How companies both prepare for and respond to industry capacity utilization rates going from 100 percent to 30 percent and earnings falling off a cliff has a dramatic impact on their future prospects. If the down cycle makes entry points attractive, that can create excellent opportunities.

—Vincent Sellecchia, Delafield Fund

We find that at times companies—or even industries—can trade at big discounts to their inherent growth rates because of the perception that the earnings are highly cyclical.

—Jon Jacobson, Highfields Capital

We're far more interested in cyclical companies that are well capitalized, that don't lose money at the bottom of the cycle, and whose peaks and troughs are both higher over time. We'd be less apt to buy into something like a capital-intensive pulp and paper manufacturer, which bleeds money at the trough and, when they do generate some cash flow, needs to spend much of it on new or upgraded plant and equipment.

—Charles de Lardemelle, International Value Advisers

Cyclical industries don't scare us if we understand the long-term supply and demand dynamics of the industry and believe that the company we're interested in is on the right side of that. We think, for instance, that insurance is a lousy business. There's way too much capital, too little differentiation and way too many managements doing the same dumb things. That's all contributed to there being a generally soft pricing market for six or seven years. That said, we're happy to own insurance companies that don't think like everyone else and zig when the others zag.

—*Steve Morrow, NewSouth Capital*

We don't have a problem with cyclicality. Wall Street still looks for certainty in areas that are uncertain. We feel good about lumpiness. We just try to be cash counters—if you can buy something at 5× free cash with limited chance of permanent impairment, even if it earns only half of what we thought, that's okay.

—*Bruce Berkowitz, Fairholme Capital*

The downside of an industry cycle is a consistent reason why things get cheap. We'll put a reasonable multiple on the normalized earnings power of the business over three to four years—knowing it can take five or six—and, given the types of things we look at, often come up with intrinsic values that are three to five times where the stock is trading today. Which is not to say the wait can't sometimes be painful.

—*Robert Robotti, Robotti & Co.*

Cyclicals by their nature repeatedly experience boom and bust periods that create opportunities for investors like us who pay careful attention to supply/demand economics and believe in mean-reversion.

If you look at the average equity holding period over the last 15 to 20 years, it's clear that there are a lot of people out there just renting stocks. The primary inefficiency we're trying to exploit is that investors don't like it when things aren't going well and a company is under-earning its potential or what's normal, so our focus on the long side is to identify overreactions in the stock when that happens. Companies can get put in the penalty box if they stumble. It doesn't happen all the time, but reliably enough that we're rarely at a loss for ideas by focusing on cyclical but temporary issues in a company's business.

—*Brian Feltzin, Sheffield Asset Management*

High-quality businesses tend to be characterized by things like strong brand names, customer loyalty, pricing control, some cost advantage and growing long-term markets. Low-quality businesses, which don't have much control over their futures, exhibit the opposite characteristics. We generally consider cyclical, commodity businesses to fit this more negative profile and so are less invested there.

—Bill Nygren, Harris Associates

There can certainly be a cyclical component [to what we find interesting], but the more salient observation is that there is variability over time in how the market looks at the company or industry. Perceptions don't vary much for things like electric utilities or even a stable blue-chip business like Coca-Cola. In those cases it's difficult for us to find the valuation dispersion and reflexive selling at nonsensical prices that we look for.

—Brian Barish, Cambiar Investors

We're unlikely to invest in a pure cyclical like a steel company, where the returns are governed primarily by macro forces.

—Boykin Curry, Eagle Capital

In areas like basic materials and other commodity businesses, there usually just isn't enough of a moat, which makes it hard for us to get interested on a fundamental basis.

—Adam Weiss, Scout Capital

I'm very leery of any business that is so cyclical that it burns cash at or near the bottom. I've concluded there are enough alternatives out there that I don't need to accept that kind of risk.

—Chris Mittleman, Mittleman Brothers, LLC

One of the lessons I took from Warren Buffett years ago was to define the areas you're comfortable with and stick to them. I generally stay focused on food, beverage and tobacco companies. Branded consumer businesses are those for which I have a natural affinity and that I think I understand. While I would have a hard time on the weekend observing what DRAM chip is in the cellphone of the person walking next to me, I pay a lot of attention to—and think I learn a lot from—what people are wearing, or eating, or smoking or drinking. Of course these are also all businesses that lend themselves to the types of global growth opportunities I most value.

I'm always tempted to look in other areas, but I come back to asking whether my ability to gather information and develop insights about a business are substantive enough to justify a position I want to own for a very long time. That happens very rarely.

—*Thomas Russo, Gardner Russo & Gardner*

There is something inevitable to me about positional goods. Once you've provided for your basic needs, you start to march up the consumption curve and it is often the more traditional brands that attract the consumer as he reaches a new position in life. The more you prosper, the more narrow the universe of items through which you can express your prosperity.

—*Thomas Russo, Gardner Russo & Gardner*

We prefer companies without heavy reinvestment needs. The average company has to pour more than half its earnings every year back into the business to maintain itself. If you don't have to do that—like most consumer products companies, for example—you have more to invest in new businesses, to give back to shareholders, or to keep on hand for a rainy day. That's a huge advantage that we don't think people are correctly evaluating.

—*Stephen Yacktman, Yacktman Asset Management*

I like to invest in consumer brands in areas like chocolate, whiskey, beer and wine. These are products that have been around for thousands of years, that people like, and I don't think that's going to change. Changes in technology or the trend toward outsourcing don't diminish the fact that people like to have a drink at the end of the day, or that they enjoy chocolate.

—*Thomas Gayner, Markel Corp.*

I've always had an affinity for companies that actually make things. We favor companies with transparent businesses that we can understand fairly quickly and those that have large and recurring maintenance, repair, and overhaul revenues from an installed base, such as elevator companies or aerospace-parts firms.

—*Alexander Roepers, Atlantic Investment Management*

We're focused on four sectors that have exhibited unvarying demand regardless of economic activity and that have key fundamental strengths that help explain why they've been around for hundreds of years. The inherent demand of people to smoke, drink and gamble and of nations to arm themselves is clearly strong and long-lasting.

—*Charles Norton, The Vice Fund*

I'm biased more towards industrial and capital-goods businesses, which I find more rational than those that are tied primarily to consumer demand. I'm not much of a consumer myself, so I don't have a great feel for what makes a lasting consumer business. Why do people like Coach bags? How do you predict the extent to which they'll like them tomorrow? I just don't know. When Motorola was doing so well with the Razr phones, I didn't recognize what a fad that was and got hurt in the stock as a result.

—*Ralph Shive, Wasatch Advisors*

I have often made the mistake of investing in businesses that needed and used more capital to operate than I thought they would. That's one reason I tend to avoid heavy industrial companies. Some very smart people own General Motors now—I hope they make money and it's probably good for the country if GM survives, but I can't figure out how to make that work as an investment. We just don't own those types of companies.

—*Thomas Gayner, Markel Corp.*

One thing about being an investor for 20 years is that experience leads you to write off big chunks of the market. I don't do retail because you have to recreate the demand every day. I don't do financial services because it's a spread business with no real free cash in it—you have to grow equity to grow assets to make more spread. I don't do much in industrials because the capital demands are high and, long term, the cost structure—particularly with labor and energy prices—is challenging in a global economy. I don't do commodities—we like price-makers that set prices based on value added, as opposed to price takers.

If you buy a high-quality business, you only have to be right once—buying at the right price. The sale is fairly easy to execute. In cyclical or commodity areas, you have to be right twice, on the buy and the sell. If you miss the exit, it might be awhile before it comes back around.

—Jeffrey Ubben, ValueAct Capital

It's easier to describe what we don't do: oil and gas, commodities, utilities and biotech. We fundamentally believe that energy and commodities have been value-destroying businesses over time. At the same time, their value tends to be driven by the price of a commodity that we have no ability to predict. With utilities, they don't tend to be businesses that can create excess value. They might be nice surrogates for bonds, but not much more. In biotech, we just have no illusions that we know how to analyze the business. Outside of these few areas, just about anything else is fair game.

—Ricky Sandler, Eminence Capital

As long as it's a good-quality business selling at an attractive price, I don't care much about what the company makes or sells. One thing we are very conscious of is the degree of leverage in a business. That can be financial leverage, which is reflected on the balance sheet. It can be operational leverage, where you look at how much of the cost base is fixed or variable. It can also be the degree of leverage to a particular industry or geography. In general, I'm uncomfortable with companies that are vulnerable to more than one of those kinds of leverage going against them at the same time. A cyclical business that has a lot of fixed costs, for example, should not have a lot of financial leverage or be too levered to one geography or industry. If things go the wrong way, management has its hands tied in trying to get out of trouble. This is a big reason we rarely find opportunity in more commodity-type businesses.

—David Herro, Harris Associates

We avoid industries in which information arbitrage is extremely important to stock prices. I don't think we'd buy a single-product biotechnology firm, for example. The same holds true in a crisis situation like Bear Stearns [in 2008]. I had no idea whether it was a zero or if it was going to be fine. In cases like that, our time-horizon advantage is dwarfed by our competitors' short-term information advantage.

—Boykin Curry, Eagle Capital

We believe in reversion to the mean, so it can make a lot of sense to invest in a distressed sector when you find good businesses whose public shares trade inexpensively relative to their earnings in a more normal environment. But that strategy [in 2008] helped lead many excellent investors to put capital to work too early in financials. Our basic feeling is that margins and returns on capital generated by financial institutions in the decade through 2006 were unrealistically high. "Normal" profitability and valuation multiples are not going to be what they were during that time, given more regulatory oversight, less leverage (and thus capital to lend), higher funding costs, stricter underwriting standards, less demand and less esoteric and excessively profitable products.

—Steven Romick, First Pacific Advisors

One way of dealing with information being more available is to stop playing the game and seek out securities or asset classes where there's less information or competition.

—Seth Klarman, The Baupost Group

We tend to be less invested in areas in which there's less differentiation between the winners and the losers and in which results are more macro-driven than company-specific. We typically do not have significant investments in utilities or REITs, for example.

—Lee Ainslie, Maverick Capital

We don't like businesses that are completely reliant on human capital that can walk out the door. We have no rule against it, but you generally won't find us investing in things like investment banks or consulting firms.

—Don Noone, VN Capital

Because five or six unique holdings make up 60 to 70 percent of each of my portfolios, I exclude companies with idiosyncratic risk profiles that I consider unacceptable in such a concentrated portfolio. That means I exclude high-tech and biotech companies with technological-obsolescence risk, tobacco or pharmaceutical companies with big product-liability risks, utilities and other regulated companies where the government can change the rules of the game, and companies that lack sufficient transparency, like banks, broker-ages and insurance companies.

—Alexander Roepers, Atlantic Investment Management

We have not done well in fashion-related businesses, which I'd extend to retail, where our record is almost unblemished by success. We tend to be susceptible to value traps in these businesses. One example was our investment years ago in Bombay Company, a home-furnishings specialty retailer. We were attracted by an enthusiasm for the CEO, combined with the apparent financial anomaly of a company trading at only 30 percent of its $700 million in revenues. We would still be awaiting the turnaround had we not decided to sell out at a modest loss and move on.

—David Nierenberg, D3 Family Funds

We've never been that fond of the hotel business because the tenants move out every night. That makes the business susceptible to economic swings in a way that office buildings with long-term leases to credit-worthy tenants aren't. We prefer to see more predictable streams of cash flow than lodging companies typically have.

—Michael Winer, Third Avenue Management

Some areas lend themselves better to our types of analysis than others. It's very hard for us to figure out what brands are worth, for example. It's also hard for us to figure out what future scientific developments are worth. We tend to stay away from those kinds of things. But at the right price, we'll consider anything.

—David Einhorn, Greenlight Capital

Most people say they want to stay within their circle of competence, and that's smart. But there's no reason to say "Here's my circle of competence and, guess what, it's never getting any bigger because I'm not going to learn anything new." We're trying to understand new things if we can.

—Bill Miller, Legg Mason Funds

There's a real premium in this business on innovation. That doesn't mean chasing the latest fad, but it does mean recognizing new opportunities and taking advantage of them even if they don't fit exactly into your historical playbook.

—Jeffrey Tannenbaum, Fir Tree Partners

I have a problem with the concept of circle of competence as defined by many value investors, who won't invest in energy, won't invest in commodities, won't invest outside the U.S. This business requires constant learning, even sometimes abandoning precepts about industries and geographies that no longer apply. If you're not willing or able to do that, I think the environment ahead means you're in for a very tough time.

—John Burbank, Passport Capital

WHERE IN THE WORLD?

When we first started interviewing highly accomplished investors for *Value Investor Insight* in early 2005, a U.S.-centric focus was more the norm than the exception. For any number of legitimate reasons—language barriers, accounting-principle differences, limited research capacity—value-investing orthodoxy still argued for geographic focus rather than expansiveness. While this stance remains prevalent, in clear ascendance is the argument that as industries and companies have become ever more global in scope, so must the investors who follow them. Regardless of the position taken, all investors today must think carefully about their geographic field of play and how they expect to cover it.

*   *   *

It has become increasingly clear to me that the best opportunities in coming years are going to be outside the U.S. That wasn't the case when I started out, when buying a stock in Canada seemed awfully unusual to people.

Over the past five years we've more than doubled our international exposure, to the point where 65 to 70 percent of our portfolio on a look-through basis is invested outside the U.S. Companies able to tap into growing affluence and people's innate desire to improve what they eat, what they wear and how they live will have decided advantages over those focused on mature economies like the U.S. and Europe, where deleveraging will take a long time to work out.

—David Winters, Wintergreen Fund

From day one we've had a significant portion of our assets invested outside the U.S.—it's currently about 30 percent of our gross exposure. This is probably too broad a generalization, but in our view non-U.S. markets tend to be less efficient than the U.S. market. If you look at our core opportunity set, which we define as the 3,000 or so stocks that trade more than $10 million a day, on average we took advantage [in 2005] of about 12 percent of the available opportunities in the U.S., 6 percent in Europe and 3 percent in Asia. In an ideal world, I'd like to be more selective in the U.S. and take advantage of more opportunities outside the U.S.

—Lee Ainslie, Maverick Capital

I'd argue that literally every investor today has to be a global investor to understand what's going on—certainly in markets like energy and commodities, but also to take advantage of where we think the best opportunities are going to be.

—John Burbank, Passport Capital

We believe it's prudent for long-term investors to have a significant and growing portion of their portfolios allocated to equities in foreign countries that are growing faster than the U.S. and whose currencies will likely appreciate against ours.

—David Nierenberg, D3 Family Funds

In general, you still see less long-term commitment to owning equities by investors outside the U.S. When markets run into trouble, you'll see more wholesale selling of equities by big non-U.S. institutional holders. There may be some historical precedent to that, but we hope it continues.

—Will Browne, Tweedy, Browne Co.

We probably held 35 to 40 percent in non-U.S. stocks five years ago and that number today is closer to 70 percent. Most of that is a result of company-by-company assessment, but I will admit to casting an eye toward history and wondering if today's U.S.-centric investor isn't like the similarly positioned British investor in the early 1900s who would have left a lot of money unearned as a result of his nation losing economic relevance due to progress elsewhere while he or she stayed invested only domestically.

—*Thomas Russo, Gardner Russo & Gardner*

There's increasingly a distinction without a difference. Nestlé is Swiss, Diageo is British, Johnson & Johnson is American and Philip Morris International is headquartered down the street from us but no longer has any business in the U.S. We own all of them and in most of the ways that matter to investors, the analysis and valuation of their businesses is very similar.

Businesses are dynamic entities, moving capital and assets to maximize opportunity. They increasingly operate on a worldwide basis, so we have to as well. We've found that knowledge of businesses and companies is quite transferable and have often applied our experience in one market to another. For example, we've had success over the past several years in buying Coca-Cola bottlers at different times and in different markets.

—*Will Browne, Tweedy, Browne Co.*

Another reason it's important to be more international in your outlook: If you're not paying attention to what competitors in emerging markets can do, you're likely taking on risk with U.S.-company investments that you shouldn't.

—*Robert Williamson, Williamson McAree Investment Partners*

For our type of investing, which involves buying big stakes in companies and investing for the long term, we need transparency and a firmly established rule of law. If we can't believe the financial statements or we see too much risk of the rules being changed after the game starts, the whole exercise is pointless. As a result, we won't invest in Russia. We've also never owned a mainland Chinese company, because most of them are controlled by the state and there's too much potential conflict between shareholder and state interests.

—*David Herro, Harris Associates*

The foundation of our process is the ability to arrive at a reasonable estimate of intrinsic value, which is often undermined in emerging markets by a variety of reporting, governance, legal and regulatory obstacles. In South Korea, for example, consolidated financial statements aren't always available. In Russia, the government hasn't kicked the habit of controlling companies that are supposed to be owned and controlled by shareholders. Even in countries where government is less intrusive, regulation can be inconsistently and unfairly applied, adding uncertainty to business models that makes forecasting very difficult.

At a low enough valuation, of course, the incremental uncertainty can be worth taking on. But valuations have only rarely gotten low enough in emerging markets relative to the developed world for us to step over the border. It's not for lack of effort—we're always looking—but so far we've found plenty of opportunity elsewhere to keep us busy.

—Dan O'Keefe, Artisan Partners

For better or worse, the Anglo-Saxon business model puts the interests of shareholders first. We are less comfortable in markets where loyalties are more divided.

—Jeffrey Schwarz, Metropolitan Capital

There are still language barriers, particularly in Japan, but that's gotten better over the years as English has become firmly entrenched as the international language of business. Culturally, in some parts of the world we're up against a kind of social-democracy attitude, that says shareholders are equal constituents with employees and customers and suppliers and banks. I don't ascribe to that at all, so in some cases we have some convincing to do. Most often, if that attitude is too prevalent we just won't be very active.

—David Herro, Harris Associates

We like to operate under the illusion that if we see something that is out-and-out unacceptable being done, that there's a clear rulebook and well-defined avenue to complain about it. It's not clear that's yet the case in China.

—Will Browne, Tweedy, Browne Co.

In general, there aren't many countries in which we wouldn't invest. But if a country is too economically or politically troubled or the rule of law doesn't really prevail, we pass. The main country in which we won't invest today is Russia. There's still too much risk for foreign (or even local) investors that you'll think you own an asset and then Mr. Putin decides you don't.

—*Jean-Marie Eveillard, First Eagle Funds*

We do very little direct investing in Eastern Europe, where the level of disclosure and the quality of corporate governance is still poor. Many leading companies are controlled by government-related entities or majority shareholders who couldn't care less about the interests of minority shareholders. We also aren't very active in the U.K. London has its own well-established and well-capitalized investment community, so we find value there is arbitraged out quicker than it is in continental Europe.

—*Richard Vogel, Alatus Capital*

For the types of companies I generally invest in—sophisticated global companies like Diageo, Nestlé, Pernod Ricard—the information is generally accessible and complete, so I don't require a greater margin of safety or lower multiples because they're international. Also, partly because the field hasn't been as crowded, I've had as good, if not better, access to senior management at non-U.S. companies.

—*Thomas Russo, Gardner Russo & Gardner*

We're not afraid of political risks, which we generally think are exaggerated. We invested in Thailand after the coup. We're investing in Turkey in the face of political uncertainty. It's not a big component of what we do, but there are always small pockets of mispriced risk and political uncertainty can create very nice bargains.

—*Oliver Kratz, Deutsche Asset Management*

Over the next 10 years it's far more likely that the huge amount of capital owned by the rest of the world will grow by investing somewhere other than the U.S., whether it's in infrastructure in China or the Middle East, or to develop consumer markets in places like India.

—*John Burbank, Passport Capital*

We haven't been traditional emerging-markets investors because we do not chase growth or glamour, but we like nothing better than to invest in emerging markets on a contrarian basis. Strong economic growth is never steady, so you can find nice opportunities to invest after booms have gone temporarily bust.

—Charles de Vaulx, International Value Advisers

One of the keys to Warren Buffett's early success was investing in high return on capital consumer businesses that were relatively immature when he bought them and that grew enormously along with the U.S., the largest economy in the world. He owned companies like Gillette, Wells Fargo, and Washington Post Co. over a period in which consumer products, financial, and media companies grew from being a relatively small part of the S&P 500 to a very large part of it. That's a natural evolution in any large, developing economy and we expect that dynamic to create considerable value in places like India for a long time.

—John Burbank, Passport Capital

We keep heading more toward direct international investing, but worry that we're going to be the patsy. We looked at South Korea, but kept asking ourselves what edge we really had there. How do we understand the culture, the management?

The U.S. is going through the same decline faced by all past great civilizations. It's in the nature of things. It takes a very long time and happens in 10,000 different ways. All smart companies and investors need to respond to that. We actually look at our energy bets as more of a global play on the fact that 3 billion new capitalists in Asia are going to have a significant impact on future energy demand.

The good thing about investing is that you don't have to do everything to be successful. There are plenty of different ways to make money.

—Bruce Berkowitz, Fairholme Capital

Because we put such a strong emphasis on companies based in close proximity to us—two-thirds of our portfolio companies are in the upper Midwest, with 50 percent very nearby in Minneapolis/

St. Paul—we commit ourselves to knowing all the public companies in that limited universe very well.

Our initial research is very qualitative, focused on getting to know management and letting them explain what their markets are, how they're addressing them, where they're investing and how they make those investment decisions. From that, we also want to learn from various other constituencies, from suppliers to customers to current and former employees. All of that is considerably easier when you're close to where these people are.

—*William Frels, Mairs & Power, Inc.*

My feeling is that it's beyond my skill set to try to buy local companies outside the U.S. Some people will make a lot of money doing that, but not me. What I am doing is buying companies like GE and Citigroup and Diageo, who already have tremendous expertise and operations outside the U.S. to take advantage of international growth and development opportunities.

—*Thomas Gayner, Markel Corp.*

I once heard someone say that every time you double the distance from where you are to where you are investing, you should divide the quality of your assessment in half.

—*Francisco Garcia Parames, Bestinver Asset Management*

I did have the good fortune in the 1980s and into the 1990s to have our style of value investing not be widely practiced, particularly in continental Europe. Value stocks were largely neglected and it was possible, if one was willing to be patient, to often buy them for a song. That's no longer true—many of the more secular inefficiencies are gone.

But the fundamentals of value investing—which to my mind are based on common sense—still work, and work equally well across borders. We look at stocks exactly the same way, whether in Hong Kong or Japan or Paris. People always ask, "But don't you want to invest like the locals, understanding the local idiosyncrasies?" and my answer is simply no. We never buy stocks based on what we think other investors are going to do.

—*Jean-Marie Eveillard, First Eagle Funds*

People tend to lump international investing into this general bucket of opportunity, which to us is kind of silly. We expect a closing of the relative GDP-per-capita gap between the developed world and many emerging markets, but as that happens we believe you're still going to have stocks be cheap or expensive based on cyclical ups and downs and on valuations that overshoot and under- shoot. Unless you're smart about picking your spots, you're not going to be successful no matter where you invest.

—*David Samra, Artisan Partners*

CHAPTER 3

Deficient Market Hypothesis

An all-too-common error that novice investors make is to assume a consistent connection between the success of a business and the success of an investment in that business. There's no question that successful companies can also be outstanding investments, but that's not necessarily the case. Winning investments arise when the current market price of a company's stock underestimates what you believe its current value is—and you turn out to be right. The market today has to be missing something, say the level and/or timing of future cash flows or the value of hidden assets. These are the inefficiencies that the most strident Efficient Market Hypothesis proponents argue don't exist, but which smart investors count on for their success. Long-time *Daily Racing Form* Publisher Steven Crist captured this verity well in describing how to think about betting on horses: "The issue is not which horse in the race is the most likely winner," he says, "but which horse or horses are offering odds that exceed their actual chances of victory. There is no such thing as 'liking' a horse to win a race, only an attractive discrepancy between his chances and his price."

Look at almost any company's market value over a multiyear period if you want assess the efficiency of the market. Even the largest, most stable and most liquid company will often exhibit a surprising variability in market price from high to low—a variability that almost certainly goes beyond the underlying change in the company's actual value. This spells opportunity for astute investors.

In articulating any investment strategy, then, managers should be able to describe the typical inefficiencies on which they are looking to capitalize and the types of situations in which they expect to find them. For any given idea, they should be able to explain how their view on a company's prospects differs from what is built into the current share price. Quite simply, if an investor doesn't know why something might be mispriced, the chance of it actually being mispriced significantly decreases.

THE HUMAN ELEMENT

The Baupost Group's Seth Klarman has proven not only to be one of the best investors of his generation, but also one of the most articulate in explaining the underlying value-investing principles on which his strategy is based. In one of the many annual letters that he allowed us to excerpt in *Value Investor Insight*, he captured nicely a common impetus for market inefficiency, the human element involved in the setting of prices:

> *Imagine that every adult in America became a securities analyst, full-time for many, part-time for the rest. Every citizen would scour the news for fast-breaking corporate developments. Some would run spreadsheets and crunch numbers. Others would analyze competitive factors for various businesses, assess managerial competence, and strive to identify the next new thing. Now, for sure, the financial markets would have become efficient, right? Actually, no. The reason that capital markets are, have always been, and will always be inefficient is not because of a shortage of timely information, the lack of analytical tools, or inadequate capital. The Internet will not make the market efficient, even though it makes far more information available, faster than ever before, right at everyone's fingertips. Markets are inefficient because of human nature—innate, deep-rooted, permanent. People don't consciously choose to invest with emotion—they simply can't help it.*

All human beings are susceptible to the emotions and biases that can cause stock prices to be inefficiently priced. The best investors would appear better able to keep theirs in check, and to recognize when the emotions and biases of others are creating investment opportunity.

* * *

At the center of all market pricing are human beings. I joke that the Four Horsemen of the investment apocalypse are fear, greed, hope, and ignorance, only one of which is not an emotion. Fear, greed and hope have wiped out more money than any market downturn ever could. Because of all the foibles of human nature that are well documented by behavioral research—and now by neurological research—people are always going to overshoot and undershoot when pricing securities. A review of financial markets all the way back to the South Sea Company nearly 300 years ago proves this out. As long as human nature doesn't fundamentally change, we can continue to arbitrage the pricing inefficiencies it creates.

—James O'Shaughnessy, O'Shaughnessy Asset Management

The mood swings of the securities markets resemble the movement of a pendulum. Although the midpoint of its arc best describes the location of the pendulum "on average," it actually spends very little of its time there. Instead, it is almost always swinging toward or away from the extremes of the arc. In fact, it is the movement toward an extreme itself that supplies the energy for the swing back.

Investment markets follow a pendulum-like swing between euphoria and depression, between celebrating positive developments and obsessing over negatives, and thus between overpriced and underpriced.

There are a few things of which we can be sure, and this is one: Extreme market behavior will reverse. Those who believe the pendulum will move in one direction forever—or reside at an extreme forever—eventually will lose huge sums. Those who understand the pendulum's behavior can benefit enormously.

—Howard Marks, Oaktree Capital

I'd argue the market isn't terribly efficient any of the time. Underpinning the efficient markets hypothesis is the notion that markets tend toward an equilibrium price and that there's a normal distribution around that efficient price. It's a nice theory, but I don't see evidence for it in the real world. Quite the opposite, valuations tend to orbit some sort of appropriate valuation, but spend no more time in the middle of the range as they do at the various ends—it's not a normal distribution at all.

We focus on taking advantage of reflexive selling that we don't believe is well considered. It may be due to some recent bad news at a company or from the perceived impact of a more macro trend or event. We become increasingly interested in a stock as misinformation and disinterest on the part of sellers serves to compress its valuation.

Brian Barish, Cambiar Investors

I had an inkling that 2009 would be a good year when *Institutional Investor* magazine published an article in late 2008 titled "The Death of Value Investing." In my experience, "Death of . . . " articles usually mark a turning point, irrespective of the subject. In this instance, I was struck not only by the article's potential as a contrary indicator, but also by the utter preposterousness of its assertion. For value investing to die, either humanity would have to die too, or people would have to become entirely and consistently rational. The very reason price and value diverge in predictable and exploitable ways is because people are emotional beings. That's why the distinguishing attribute among successful investors is temperament rather than brainpower, experience, or classroom training. They have the ability to be rational when others are not.

—*Bryan Jacoboski, Abingdon Capital*

I was originally trained as an economist and it took me two different degrees in economics to work out that it really wasn't what it purported to be. It claims to be a science of behavior, but actually all of the behavior was assumed. I became disenchanted with that and the longer I worked in the markets the more I became convinced that the paradigm of rational economic beings was deeply, deeply flawed—it just didn't match up with the reality I was observing.

—*James Montier, Société Générale*

Human beings are subject to wild swings in their levels of fear, risk tolerance, and greed. That won't change. I base my whole approach on buying when others are fearful and selling when others are greedy. The reason Shakespeare is so relevant still today is that his plays were all about human nature, and human nature never changes.

Mark Sellers, Sellers Capital

I've been around long enough to see irrationality in all flavors, so less and less surprises me. I no longer think I must be missing something, and realize the madness of investor crowds can do some nutty things.

Ricky Sandler, Eminence Capital

It's always important to ask whether you have any competitive advantage in analyzing a particular company. Can we know the business better because no one else seems to be paying attention? Is the market's view being distorted by some behavioral or structural bias that we don't have?

—Brian Bares, Bares Capital

A[n] argument is made that there are just too many question marks about the near future; wouldn't it be better to wait until things clear up a bit? You know the prose: "Maintain buying reserves until current uncertainties are resolved," etc. Before reaching for that crutch, face up to two unpleasant facts: The future is never clear [and] you pay a very high price for a cheery consensus. Uncertainty actually is the friend of the buyer of long-term values.

—Warren Buffett (quote from Forbes)

Comfort in investing comes at a high cost. Selling stocks in 2007 would have felt uncomfortable, but in retrospect we all should have done more of that. Buying or even holding stocks in early 2009 was equally uncomfortable, but investors should have done that as well. We get comfort from the consensus, but making the same investment choices as a large number of other intelligent people almost mathematically insures you'll do the wrong thing at the wrong time because security prices reflect that consensus.

—Staley Cates, Southeastern Asset Management

Wall Street sometimes gets confused between risk and uncertainty, and you can profit handsomely from that confusion. The low-risk, high-uncertainty [situation] gives us our most sought after coin-toss odds. Heads, I win; tails, I don't lose much!

—Mohnish Pabrai, Pabrai Funds

There are probably five main behavioral impediments that keep our industry from spotting and avoiding bubbles. First is basic overoptimism. Nobody gets married expecting to get divorced, a mindset that bedevils most of what we do. In our industry that translates into this sort of innate bullish bias.

Second, people suffer from an illusion of control, that even if things do go wrong, they'll be able to sort them out. A lot of the modern risk-management techniques created a totally false illusion of safety. The idea that by quantifying risk using a tool like VaR [Value at Risk] that you can therefore control it is one of the slightly more ridiculous things to have come along in years.

Third, there's a self-serving bias in our industry. Generally people make more money when markets go up than when they go down, so it's not often that people stand in the way. You can imagine a risk manager several years ago arguing against buying a pot of collateralized debt obligations—he would have been fired for obstructing a sterling opportunity.

The next impediment would be myopia, a natural short-sightedness reminiscent of St. Augustine's plea, "Lord make me chaste, but not yet." This is probably the most cynical of the biases because you often know what you're doing is wrong, but rationalize that you'll promise to be good after getting one more good bonus out of it.

Finally, there's change blindness or inattentional blindness. We just don't see what we're not looking for. We're governed by our recent experiences and don't actually ponder the bigger picture very often. Just because something hasn't happened in the past 12 months, or five years, doesn't mean it can't.

James Montier, Société Générale

Humans have a strong desire to be part of a group. That desire makes us susceptible to fads, fashions and idea contagions.

Michael Mauboussin, Legg Mason Funds

People tend to suffer greater pain from losing a given amount of money than they experience pleasure from gaining the same amount, so the typical investor is a pain avoider who shuns stocks when there's any hint of trouble. That tendency results in a consistent over-reaction to bad news that we believe creates investment opportunity.

Daniel Bubis, Tetrem Capital

When we find ourselves in trouble, when we find ourselves on the cusp of falling, our survival instinct—and our fear—can evoke lurching, reactive behavior absolutely contrary to survival. The very moment when we need to take calm, deliberate action, we run the risk of doing the exact opposite and bringing about the very out-comes we fear.

—*Jim Collins in How the Mighty Fall*

There's a great chapter [in Dan Ariely's *Predictably Irrational*] about the ways in which we tend to misjudge price and use it as an indica-tor of something or other. That links back to my whole thesis that the most common error we as investors make is overpaying for the hope of growth. Dan did an experiment involving wine, in which he told people, "Here's a $10 bottle of wine and here's a $90 bottle of wine. Please rate them and tell me which tastes better." Not surpris-ingly, nearly everyone thought the $90 wine tasted much better than the $10 wine. The only snag was that the $90 wine and the $10 wine were actually the same $10 wine. When they were tasted blind, with-out the signaling of the price, people came to exactly the right conclu-sion about which was the better wine. That to me was a tremendous example of the bias against value that people tend to have.

—*James Montier, Société Générale*

It is very hard to avoid recency bias, when what just happened in-ordinately informs your expectation of what will happen next. One of the best things I've read on that is *The Icarus Syndrome*, by Peter Beinart. It's not about investing, but describes American hubris in foreign policy, in many cases resulting from doing what seemed to work in the previous 10 years even if the setting was materially dif-ferent or conditions had changed. One big problem is that all the people who succeed in the recent past become the ones in charge go-ing forward, and they think they have it all figured out based on what they did before. It's all quite natural, but can result in some really bad decisions if you don't constantly challenge your core beliefs.

—*Jed Nussdorf, Soapstone Capital*

One of the unfortunate lessons of speculative bubbles is that they always go on longer than we expect. It's what has caught me out more than anything over the years—I'm always too early. I usually see the bubble and talk about how I wouldn't touch this or that with a barge pole, but then watch painfully as it goes on for two or three more years. For professional investors, that can be a job killer. You can see how in a world in which people are benchmark-measured and totally obsessed with relative performance, career concern can be a driving force in all this. People are afraid of getting it "wrong" for two or three years, so they just go along and the problem festers.

—James Montier, Société Générale

Humans have a tendency toward overconfidence, which may be reinforced by the stories that are prevalent at any given time and by the fact that we tend to act on a biased information set to make decisions. The list of facts we retain in our consciousness very likely excludes other facts we either aren't observing or choose to ignore. That's a big reason people become overconfident, which plays a big role in bubbles forming.

—Robert Shiller, Yale University

In general, I believe markets are basically efficient and that the academics are right when they say markets are even more efficient as market-caps go up. The inefficiencies that haven't gone away, though, have to do with crowd mentality, when specific news or market events cause the crowd to rush in one direction. If you have the ability to think independently and to be patient, you can find opportunities when that happens.

—John Rogers, Ariel Investments

Investors overreact to the latest news, which has always been the case, but I think it's especially true today with the Internet. Information spreads so quickly that decisions get made without particularly deep knowledge about the companies involved. People also overemphasize dramatic events, often without checking the facts. It's the classic, "Are more people killed each year by sharks or by being trampled by pigs?" type of situation—the dramatic event can get more play than it deserves. These types of overreactions are what we're trying to take advantage of.

—John Dorfman, Thunderstorm Capital

What the media should be criticized for is the cheerleader aspect to its coverage. Champagne corks would pop with every new 1,000 points on the Dow, as if that was the natural state of things and that imagining that it could go down—or even rooting for it to go down—was un-American. It's gotten better when you start to see people like Warren Buffett show up more on channels like CNBC, but I still find financial news as entertainment, with someone like Jim Cramer, sort of sad. Coverage of the market is always about making money, when in fact sometimes you should be worried about preserving your money. Since you don't get advance warning about what kind of environment is coming next, you should always be concerned about preserving your money. The person just watching cable TV might never know that.

—Seth Klarman, The Baupost Group

There is still a large and loud industry out there which on a daily basis tries to advise anyone listening exactly what they should do today—often *right now*—to be a better investor. For all but the smallest percentage of people involved in the market, that's bad for you and is not the way to build wealth over time.

—Chuck Akre, Akre Capital Management

March 2009 was a generational bottom, in my opinion, and it scared people to death. The market has doubled since then, but hedge fund net exposures are about where they were at the bottom, institutional assets allocated to equities are barely above where they were at the bottom, and the public investor in equity mutual funds hasn't come back. There is a skepticism and even disdain for equities.

They'll all be back. It may take a long time, but stocks will get overvalued again and people will be buying on tips they hear at a cocktail party without spending a minute thinking about them. People are people and will get greedy again.

In the meantime, the negativity should be great for us. It gives us time to identify attractive businesses and buy them at discounts.

—Steve Morrow, NewSouth Capital

I was always so impressed by John Templeton's enthusiasm, the fresh approach he seemed always to take and, of course, how independent a thinker he was. In 1939, right after Hitler marched into Poland, Templeton bought 100 shares of every stock on the Big Board selling for less than $1. Within a few years he had quadrupled his money. He always said the time to buy was at the point of maximum pessimism and pain—something we've all had experience with lately.

—John Dorfman, Thunderstorm Capital

IT'S A MATTER OF TIME

Top value investors almost universally consider their longer-term investment horizons to be a competitive advantage. With investment decisions
increasingly driven by short-term market, industry or company concerns,
the reasoning goes, individual share prices are more likely to misrepresent
the future potential, when industry dynamics are more normal, company
misfires are corrected or strong performance is more apt to be recognized.

*   *   *

Most investment institutions define success as having a good result in
each and every discrete time period, so it's quite logical that people in
those institutions look to buy stocks that will do well from the current moment in time until, say, the end of the year. As a result, favorable occurrences such as positive earnings reports or value-realization
events that are highly probable, but not likely to occur within the
discrete time period, are discounted at a fairly remarkable rate.

If you traveled through time and brought back the *Wall Street
Journal* from four years from now and could specifically identify
the highest-returning security between now and then—into which
you should put all your money—people wouldn't do it. The uncertainty of not knowing the pattern of return, even given the certainty
of the outcome, would keep people from buying it. Our opportunity is to take advantage of those kinds of inefficiencies.

—Murray Stahl, Horizon Asset Management

Time arbitrage just means exploiting the fact that most investors—
institutional, individual, mutual funds, or hedge funds—tend to
have very short-term time horizons, have rapid turnover, or are
trying to exploit very short-term anomalies in the market. So the
market looks extremely efficient in the short run. In an environment
with massive short-term data overload and with people concerned
about minute-to-minute performance, the inefficiencies are likely to
be looking out beyond, say, 12 months.

—Bill Miller, Legg Mason Funds

The most important change in the business over the past
40 years is probably investors' time horizons. Today the majority of

investors—Ben Graham would call them speculators—are focused so closely on this week, this month and this quarter. Did this company meet the estimates or did that one meet its guidance? Stocks are bought and sold on penny deviations from those estimates, which is mind-boggling. Crazy as it is, we can't complain—it just creates more opportunities for investors with longer time horizons.

—William Nasgovitz, Heartland Advisors

It's still true that the biggest players in the public markets—particularly mutual funds and hedge funds—are not good at taking short-term pain for long-term gain. The money's very quick to move if performance falls off over short periods of time. We don't worry about headline risk—once we believe in an asset, we're buying more on any dips because we're focused on the end game three or four years out.

—Jeffrey Ubben, ValueAct Capital

Music to my ears is when something is considered dead money and people say, "It looks okay, but I'll come back to it later when this or that issue resolves itself." That to me shouts, "Look here."

—Jeffrey Schwarz, Metropolitan Capital

One the last great arbitrages left is to be long-term-oriented when there is a large class of shareholders who have no tolerance for short-term setbacks. So it's interesting when stocks get beaten-up because a company misses earnings or the market reacts to a short-term business development. It's crazy to me when someone says something is cheap but doesn't buy it because they think it won't go anywhere for the next 6 to 12 months. We have a pretty high tolerance for taking that pain if we see glory longer term. I actually think doing that is one of the few ways left to make an incremental return versus the market.

—Mario Cibelli, Marathon Partners

When I was starting out in the business, I was pitching a stock as a buy to an account in Boston. It was a conglomerate trading at 4x earnings. My pitch was that it was really cheap and was going to go up a lot over the next couple of years. When I finished, the chief investment officer said, "That's a really compelling case, but we can't own that. You didn't tell me why it's going to outperform the market in the next nine months." I said I didn't know if it was going to do that or not, but that there was a very high probability that it would do well over the next three to five years. He said, "How long have you been in this business? There's a lot of performance pressure in this business, and performing three to five years down the road doesn't cut it. You won't be in business then. Clients expect you perform right now." So I said "Let me ask you, how's your performance?" He said, "It's terrible, that's why we're under a lot of performance pressure." I said "If you bought stocks like this three years ago, your performance would be good right now and you'd be buying stocks like this to help your performance over the next three years." That's our approach. We buy today with an eye on performance several years out. I can think of only twice when what we did in the year that we did it helped that year.

—Bill Miller, Legg Mason Funds

Investors come up with all kinds of reasons to own or not own stocks, and in times of stress the reasons can become nonsensical because people get driven by this cascade of negative information. We see analyst reports all the time that say they don't like a stock short-term or they don't see a catalyst in the next six months, but that it's attractive long-term. Implicit in that is the notion that, "I'm going to know exactly the right time to step in and I'll let you know a few days before it's obvious to the rest of the market." Based on our experience and everything we've seen about people's ability to time the market, we don't understand how to make money on that basis.

—Will Browne, Tweedy, Browne Co.

With the frayed nerves of investors after the 2008 crisis and with the continued rise of hedge funds, ETFs, and computerized trading, time frames have truncated. Our investment horizon is three years, give or take, which allows us to invest with no obvious catalyst other than mean reversion and a return to normalcy. That works when nobody is patient anymore.

—Sarah Ketterer, Causeway Capital

The average holding period on the New York Stock Exchange is nine months or less, which I don't even consider investing. Over such a short period of time you're just betting on the overall direction of the market or on the next quarterly earnings.

—Aaron Edelheit, Sabre Value Management

Many investors don't start with the question of whether General Electric or Procter & Gamble is undervalued, they start by trying to match the weighting in the benchmark. In 2001 when we were short GE, people thought we were crazy: How could you short the greatest company in the world with the best CEO in the world? I had no argument with that, but we were focused only on what it was worth and where it was trading and concluded there was no chance it was worth $55 per share, which we said publicly at the time.

The reason it traded there was because I'd estimate that 95 percent of the dollars invested in the U.S. stock market were either indexed or closet indexed—people had to own it to keep up with the benchmark. If they thought it was overvalued, their response would be to maybe buy only a 3 percent position rather than the 4 percent weighting in the benchmark. That's the type of irrational behavior that can create inefficiency.

—Ric Dillon, Diamond Hill Investments

I would assert the biggest reason quality companies sell at discounts to intrinsic value is time horizon. Without short-term visibility, most investors don't have the conviction or courage to hold a stock that's facing some sort of challenge, either internally or externally generated. It seems kind of ridiculous, but what most people in the market miss is that intrinsic value is the sum of *all* future cash flows discounted back to the present. It's not just the next six months' earnings or the next year's earnings. To truly invest for the long term, you have to be able to withstand underperformance in the short term, and the fact of the matter is that most people can't.

—David Herro, Harris Associates

Classic opportunities for us get back to time horizon. A company reports a bad quarter, which disappoints Wall Street with its 90-day focus, but that might be for explainable temporary reasons or even because the company is making very positive long-term investments in the business. Many times that investment increases the likely value of the company five years from now, but disappoints people who want the stock up tomorrow.

—*Mason Hawkins, Southeastern Asset Management*

The human brain is incapable of conceptualizing something vastly different from what's happening today. But the big-money ideas are those where the changes are far beyond what you can conceive today. The closer you can get to conceiving those types of changes and the higher the probability they might happen, the more likely you are to find big winners.

—*Lisa Rapuano, Matador Capital Management*

While we may not always be able to estimate it with great confidence, every stock has an intrinsic value that is independent of its current market price and tends to be far less volatile than that market price. That's because market prices partly reflect investor emotions, while intrinsic values reflect business fundamentals. Given that over sufficiently long periods of time market prices tend to revert to intrinsic values, we're simply looking to go long when the price is at a discount to a value we believe we can estimate, and to go short when it's at a premium to that value.

What that typically means on the long side is that we're assuming things remain more or less normal or get back to normal when the implicit assumption reflected in the stock price is that things are going to fall off or never recover.

—*Chris Welch, Diamond Hill Investments*

We have no problem buying things that take a long time to play out. Call me lazy, but I don't want to worry about last week's same-store sales or next week's oil price.

—*Jeffrey Schwarz, Metropolitan Capital*

We're trying to capitalize on the incremental mindset of Wall Street. IBM beats earnings by 10 cents in a quarter and everyone cranks up their models and scurries around and takes their full-year estimate up by a total of 10 cents. We're trying to find companies where if Wall Street's EPS consensus is $1, $1.10 and $1.20 over the next three years, we're looking for something more like $1, $1.30 and

$1.80. Where we're seeing a material difference in the trajectory of the company's growth because of an expanding market opportunity, operating leverage or capital-redeployment opportunities that the Street is ignoring. In cases like that you don't have to be precisely right—approximately right can still make you a lot of money.

—Steve Morrow, NewSouth Capital

Our thesis often is based on the passage of time. What makes a negative story negative may just be that the next three to six months— the time space in which Wall Street analysts live—don't look so great. We try to look at companies as a private investor would. To that investor a company's near-term bad news is only instructive if it informs the long-term outlook. If it doesn't, why should we care?

—Robert Kleinschmidt, Tocqueville Asset Management

If you listen to earnings conference calls, most of the questions are about what happened this quarter or what next quarter looks like. That focus would indicate that near-term issues are generally extremely well understood, so there isn't that much value in our trying to figure that out.

But if you really understand how a company's business model works, how its industry is structured, the underlying trends impacting the industry, and where management is taking the company, there's a bit more opportunity to add value. That doesn't mean we own every stock for a long time, but we analyze and value it with a multiyear horizon.

—Morris Mark, Mark Asset Management

Typical investor behavior is to want to own things coincidental to success, so there are plenty of investors out there who will bail at any sign of disappointment. By extending our time horizon out three to five years, we're trying to take advantage of bargains that result when negative news and twitchy investors drive stock prices down.

—Sarah Ketterer, Causeway Capital

Most of the time the short-term outlook stinks for the companies we end up buying, for company-specific or cyclical reasons.

The best opportunities tend to be when the company now facing a lousy short-term outlook was not long before considered a darling of growth investors, and when the problems are now perceived to be more permanent. If you think those problems aren't really permanent, you can make very attractive investments if you turn out to be right.

—Jean-Marie Eveillard, First Eagle Funds

We evaluate businesses over a full business cycle and probably our biggest advantage is an ability to buy things when most people can't because the short-term outlook is lousy or very hard to judge. It's a good deal easier to know what's likely to happen than to know precisely when it's going to happen.

—Whitney George, Royce & Associates

I have a ready answer when people ask me why I'm such a long-term investor, which is because I failed miserably as a short-term investor. I'm not against making money in the short term, I just don't know how to do it.

—Thomas Gayner, Markel Corp.

CHAPTER 4

Fertile Ground

Great ideas are the lifeblood of successful investing. Joel Greenblatt, whose Gotham Capital was one of the most successful equity hedge funds ever and who remains active as a teacher, author, and managed-index-fund proprietor, distilled the essence of a great idea for us:

> *There's a clarity that comes with great ideas: You can explain why something's a great business, how and why it's cheap, why it's cheap for temporary reasons and how, on a normal basis, it should be trading at a much higher level. You're never sitting there on the 40th page of your spreadsheet, as Warren Buffett would say, agonizing over whether you should buy or not. If you find yourself there, it's either not yet clear enough in your head or it's not as striking an idea as it should be.*
>
> *I can describe why we own the stocks we do in a few sentences. The hard work, of course, comes in proving the assumptions that get you to that point. But if you've done the work correctly, the actual idea ends up being very simple. The most money we've made has been on ideas that, once you looked at it the way we did, were pretty obvious.*

The simplicity of the great idea, however, belies a more complex challenge every investor faces: How to focus attention on potential ideas that are more likely to be misunderstood by the market, and therefore mispriced. Methods vary widely for homing in on such ideas—and limiting the time devoted to running down blind alleys—but the best investors combine an avid curiosity with a keen ability to sift through the avalanche of available information to focus on the core elements of a company's situation that signal potential opportunity. They know and can describe well the situations they're looking for and the disciplines they use to find them.

IN SEARCH OF UNCERTAINTY

While value investors are typically considered a risk-averse lot, that's more a reflection of the price they're willing to pay for any given investment than the types of situations they most often pursue, which are often fraught with uncertainty. As companies constantly evolve and change in response to industry or company-specific challenges and opportunities, the lack of clarity around those changes—and the risks inherent in the potential outcomes—can cause share prices to diverge widely from underlying business values. The ability to recognize and capitalize upon that dynamic is a key element of what sets top investors apart.

*   *   *

There are two kinds of events that create volatility, which creates opportunity. The first revolve around individual companies, such as earnings misses, unexpected news, M&A activity, restructurings and legal issues—things that can make prices and valuations change relatively quickly. In general, prices change much faster than fundamentals of businesses change, so what we want to do is understand what made the price change and then figure out whether the facts have changed as much as the price. To the extent they haven't, that can be an opportunity.

The other major source of volatility is when a macro event or trend causes markets to move. These can be industry-specific, but also reflect interest rate moves, currency moves, political instability, and the overall economic outlook. The market reflects at any moment what investors think XYZ's business is worth, so if macroeconomic factors force people to buy and sell its securities but we believe those factors have nothing to do with the underlying fundamentals of the company—or less to do with the fundamentals than is being reflected in the share price—that can also be an opportunity.

—*Jon Jacobson, Highfields Capital*

Our reference to "misunderstanding" among our investment values refers to our having a variant perception versus consensus with respect to the earnings power or the free-cash-flow-generating potential of the business. Some misunderstandings come from Joel Greenblatt *You Can Be a Stock Market Genius*-types of events—such as spinoffs, emergence from bankruptcy, and recapitalizations—where the movement of debt, equity, or assets around on a balance sheet leads to analytical complexity or some form of irrational selling.

Variant perceptions can also arise from having a differential view about the ongoing business itself, such as new product launches, the impact of a change in management, or on how operating or financial leverage plays out over time.

The key in almost all these cases is that something is changing. If a business has been around for 20 years and public for the last 15, it's hard to argue that people are really missing something if there's nothing relatively big going on. That gets to the importance of knowing why there is information asymmetry. If you can zero in on that, you're better able to handicap how likely you really are to be seeing something other people aren't.

—James Crichton, Scout Capital

Change brings uncertainty, so many investors want to wait out that uncertainty until the situation is easier to analyze. We think that uncertainty is what creates opportunities.

—Peter Langerman, Mutual Series Funds

You can usually only pay an undemanding price when there's fear or uncertainty associated with a name. That can result from a variety of things: when companies are restructuring, acquiring or divesting; when a turnaround is necessary, either company-specific or in the industry; or when there's been a big operating disappointment of some kind. The common denominator is typically very low expectations.

—James Kieffer, Artisan Partners

The hedge-fund industry grew up by preying on the inefficiencies created by the mutual-fund mentality of only departing from a benchmark index weighting with reluctance. Events that transform companies can complicate things when you're focused on, say, having an 8 percent weighting in industrials. That's why these types of companies can often be mispriced. There's also change going on and the market can be remarkably slow in shifting its focus from how things have been to how they will be.

—Gary Claar, JANA Partners

Companies going through operating or financial restructuring can go into a bit of an information vacuum, which can provide a good entry point into a position. There's often uncertainty about the specific programs being instituted, management may be less apt to provide guidance and, because the change is ongoing, the results are by definition unclear.

—Jerry Senser, Institutional Capital LLC

We want to have a high conviction based on our research that we can achieve a 50 percent rate of return on long investments over a two-year period. That potential return can come from any number of sources: turnarounds, changing product cycles, shifts in competitive dynamics, a revamp of the capital structure, or even cyclical recovery. The key is whether we believe we have an edge in understanding the magnitude or timing of the improved performance.

—Ellen Adams, CastleRock Management

In our experience, it's revenue and earnings momentum that catapults a stock out of the swamp. We're looking for elements of positive change—fresh management blood, a changing market, a changing regulatory environment, a shift in competition—which suggest a future characterized by reliable and increasing earnings. We have to be predictors of growth to be able to buy at bargain prices.

—Carlo Cannell, Cannell Capital

You make a lot of money in stocks when they get revalued. We want situations in which the probabilities are favorable for margin recovery and a return to normal revenue levels coming out of a difficult period, which would result in multiple expansion.

—Alan Fournier, Pennant Capital

We named our firm Thunderstorm Capital because a thunderstorm is a frightening but temporary event that usually passes without lasting damage. In constructing our portfolios, we try to invest in good companies whose stocks are depressed by frightening but temporary bad news. The trick, of course, is to distinguish thunderstorms from Category-5 hurricanes.

—John Dorfman, Thunderstorm Capital

The market missing an opportunity often has more to do with the psychology around companies that run into trouble. "Everybody knows" the business is in trouble. "Everybody knows" the management is incompetent. If we take a more nuanced view, see some positives among the negatives and have some insight into management's capability of turning things around, that's what makes it a good idea.

—John Osterweis, Osterweis Capital Management

We specialize in the highly complex while mostly avoiding plain vanilla, which is typically more fully priced.

—Seth Klarman, The Baupost Group

Financial complexity is one reason companies get mispriced. People talk about investing only in easy-to-understand businesses, but we're not afraid of tackling complicated financial analysis. If we think we can get a handle on what's going on, the fact that others tend to shy away from these situations can provide an opportunity for us.

—Curtis Macnguyen, Ivory Capital

We're not reluctant to invest in pretty hairy situations. That by no means suggests complexity or controversy is always better, but it can often scare enough people away to create opportunity.

—Tucker Golden, Solas Capital

Companies in severe financial stress tend to be overlooked and under-loved, because they have a risk or fundamental profile that many equity investors are not comfortable with.

—Mitchell Julis, Canyon Capital

What a lot of people don't realize about distressed investing is that you can do this type of investing in a low-risk way. By analyzing the capital structure and the underlying asset values, you can figure out with some degree of confidence at what point you're fully covered. If you're buying at 50 cents on the dollar and are comfortable that you're covered at 80 cents or 100 cents on the dollar, that isn't such a risky proposition.

—Peter Langerman, Mutual Series Funds

A legitimate case can be made that low-beta stocks are consistently undervalued by the market. Portfolio managers tend to favor high-beta stocks as a way to beat the market. If a portfolio beta is 2.0, the portfolio should double the market returns, right? Of course it can go the other way as well, but with their bonuses dependent on beating the market, many managers are willing to take that risk.

—Bernard Horn, Polaris Capital

We don't like making assumptions about highly uncertain outcomes, such as how a new product will work or an industry transition will play out. If you look at most value traps—say newspapers or various industrials over time—they look extremely cheap if some significant problem goes away or isn't as bad as expected. I try not to deal in those big "ifs." Therefore many of the companies we own are quite boring, but they generate cash flows we believe we can value.

—Eric Cinnamond, Intrepid Capital

Avoid entirely what you can't totally get your mind around. It's just not worth it. There will be plenty of other things to invest in—keep the cash for them.

—Amit Wadhwaney, Third Avenue Management

SPECIAL SITUATIONS

Frequently the specific events that investors believe can create investment opportunity are prompted by the changing nature of the company's business. Maybe its core product line is maturing, its industry's growth has slowed, an ancillary business is booming, or it is investing heavily in new products or services. The emphasis is on change to which the company is responding. When smart investors' assessment of the ultimate impact those responses will have is at variance with conventional market wisdom, ideas can be born.

*   *   *

We are often looking for broken growth stories, when a once-great company is no longer considered to be great. The market tends to overreact in these cases, as growth and momentum investors move on to the next new thing and the shareholder base turns. Since I wasn't in the stock before, I'm not disappointed if something is no longer a high-flier. All I care about is the future potential relative to what I have to pay for it.

—Alan Schram, WellCap Partners

If you look at technology-driven growth industries over the past two centuries—steam engines, railroads, telephony, electric power, the Internet—people become too excited about growth and over-invest in it. When the bubbles burst, markets overcorrect on the downside, even though the fundamental growth drivers may still be as present as they were before. We love to find jewels buried amid the rubble after that kind of explosion occurs.

—David Nierenberg, D3 Family Funds

Most of the time we're picking up the pieces after a high-growth company hits the wall at 80 miles per hour, having made at least one too many investments to try to sustain an unsustainable growth rate. Public markets can actually conspire to screw companies up. When you're growing fast, you get this big P/E and pretty soon you have all the wrong investors with ridiculous expectations. You try to meet those ridiculous expectations and do things contrary to shareholder value.

—Jeffrey Ubben, ValueAct Capital

If you think about the lifecycle of a small company, it usually initially succeeds in a relatively small niche where it delivers unique value and becomes a market leader. The business inevitably starts to mature—producing strong cash flow with a lower growth rate—and the natural response from management is to take some of the cash generated and to invest it in new areas of potential growth. Hopefully these new growth initiatives are related to the core business and hopefully the company can have some competitive advantage. This pursuit of incremental growth is exactly what management should be doing.

One of two things will happen. Either the new initiatives work, everyone's happy, the stock has a high multiple and we never find it, or the new growth initiatives are not working, the market becomes disenchanted with the company because earnings and cash flow are depressed and that drives down the stock price. Those are the situations we find attractive.

—Jeffrey Smith, Starboard Value

We typically look for underperforming companies, against their peers and their own history, and then try to understand why that's happening. Sometimes the answer is something we can't do anything about. In other cases, though, the underperformance may come from the company having wasted money over the past three or four years on acquisitions and the market is concerned it's going to do it again and isn't assigning full credit to its future cash flows. That's probably an opportunity for us.

—Ralph Whitworth, Relational Investors

In many cases we're getting involved when a rapidly growing company is slowing down or maturing. There's a changing of the guard among the shareholder base and as that happens, there's often a disagreement over how quickly the growth is slowing and whether the slowdown is permanent. When you're right that the market is overreacting to the challenges faced, the investment result can be quite positive.

—Wally Weitz, Weitz Funds

An area we try to mine is busted IPOs. Buying at the IPO often means you're buying from smart sellers, but we'd much rather buy from dumb sellers—which is more likely to happen after an IPO company disappoints in some way and the people who bought in the initial offering bail.

—Steven Romick, First Pacific Advisors

We don't have any discernible edge determining whether IBM's earnings are going to beat the Street by a nickel, or whether the multiple should be 16, 18, or 20. We don't know where the price of oil is going or whether small-cap stocks are going to outperform large caps. These things are really unknowable and unpredictable. But there are a wide variety of situations in which there are dislocations—like mergers, spinoffs, short-term bad news, legal issues—where we think we understand why there might be a huge disconnect between supply and demand for a given security. Then if we can analyze what the true value of the business is and look across all the different securities on a company's balance sheet, we may be able to find something that's mispriced.

It's analogous to going to Las Vegas on Super Bowl weekend and betting on the game. By definition, the line on the Super Bowl is the most efficient on the board. Every piece of information is completely disseminated and the line is set by all the buyers and sellers coming together, of which there are thousands. The best bet on the board in Las Vegas is much more likely to be on a game between two college teams for which most people couldn't name the coach, any of the players, or even the team nicknames. But if you know one of the best players on a team is hurt, or that one team got in at 4 o'clock in the morning because there was a snowstorm—and the rest of the market doesn't know that—you have an edge making that bet.

—Jon Jacobson, Highfields Capital

One key situation we find of interest is when we believe unrepresentative accounting obscures the true value of the business. With DirecTV, for example, subscriber acquisition costs are expensed immediately rather than capitalized over time, which hides the true free cash flow. With Chesapeake Energy, the best deals they've done have been percentage interests they've sold in many key fields, but they haven't booked any of them so that doesn't show up in returns on equity, it doesn't show up in earnings, and it doesn't even really show up in book value as receivables. Bad accounting is often a common denominator in many of our biggest positions.

A second common situation is when the market seems to be making massively negative qualitative judgments that we believe, on deep analysis, are misplaced. With Chesapeake, everybody appears to hate natural gas forever and is angry at Aubrey McClendon [the co-founder and chairman, who was forced to liquidate nearly all his company shares in 2008 to meet margin calls], so the incredible assets they have sort of get lost in the discussion.

The last common thread would be when companies have an absolute jewel of a business that gets lost in the shuffle of a bigger conglomerate. Our success in Disney so far, and we believe in the future, is about ESPN, which nobody asks about on conference calls because they want to hear about movies or the animation business. With Olympus Corporation in Japan, it's about their medical-device business, not their cameras. Ruddick is about the Harris Teeter grocery business, not textiles. Worthington Industries is about gas containers, not the steel business.

—Staley Cates, Southeastern Asset Management

We've always put emphasis on finding hidden value and hidden assets. We like looking at multi-segment businesses where it's a bit more complicated to analyze all the parts and there's not an obvious answer to the question of what the entire company is worth. In this context, we pay a lot of attention to private-market values and trying to understand how underperforming segments should be valued.

—Peter Langerman, Mutual Series Funds

A common opportunity for us is when two businesses—which would trade on different valuation parameters if separate—operate under the same roof, resulting in the whole appearing mispriced.

—Timothy Mullen, VNBTrust

We like to invest in companies in which we think people are paying attention to the wrong thing, so if 80 percent of investor attention is focused on something that you think is less than 20 percent of the story, it's a good opportunity to take a look at the business.

—Bill Nygren, Harris Associates

One key source of opportunity is when companies are building new assets that will generate incremental revenues, prof- its and cash flows. Many times these are what we call "inside-out" growth stories, where a large legacy business is somehow perceived as challenged, but a newer one is thriving and taking on more prominence.

—Matthew Berler, Osterweis Capital Management

We often see value in holding companies, where there are several disparate businesses and a single earnings multiple doesn't capture the true value. Or in companies that own a significant asset that may not currently be earning anything but is quite valuable.

—Jon Jacobson, Highfields Capital

We find opportunity in looking at the different values ascribed to a company's different asset classes. If the debt markets would provide 100 percent financing of a company's total market value, that usually means the equity is undervalued. Whether Facebook is worth 15× sales or 10× sales is not something we'll take a position on. But if the debt market is telling us that a company's equity appears to be undervalued, that's something we're interested in."

—Steven Tananbaum, GoldenTree Asset Management

At PIMCO there are more than 70 different credit analysts covering just about every credit on the planet and producing research that very often has a valuable read across to the equity. That includes being on top of specific financing events that may be debt-negative, equity-positive, or vice versa. All of that is a very rich source of ideas and fundamental insight into companies.

—Charles Lahr, PIMCO

We find that geography makes a difference. The further a company is from New York, Boston, Chicago, L.A., and San Francisco, the less attention—and often less respect—they get. In the 1990s, we started finding a lot of companies in the upper Midwest that weren't well followed but had smart, entrepreneurial managers who were building great businesses. Minnesota is still probably our favorite state for stock ideas.

—Scott Hood, First Wilshire Securities

Special situations unfortunately aren't as plentiful as we'd like, but include things like companies going through large reorganizations or companies that are being spun off. As well-known as spinoffs are for being potentially mispriced, there appear to be enough structural reasons for inefficiency—having to do with limited information, forced selling, and management incentives—that they often still work. Over the past 30 years the average spun-off company has outperformed the market by 10 percent per year.

—Timothy Beyer, Sterling Capital Management

We take a close look any time a company is trying to create value through some type of spin-off or major restructuring, which can result in mispricings for the parent as well as the spinoff company. The documentation filed with the SEC when companies split up is quite complex and the pro-forma financials can be very fuzzy, dealing with tricky questions such as how debt and overhead are allocated, how assets are depreciated and how costs will evolve in the separate companies. Most people don't do the work of going through what can be hundreds of pages of financials, but we find it can often uncover interesting ideas.

—Edward McAree, Williamson McAree Investment Partners

Often spin-off opportunities are bond-like in nature, generating a lot of cash, with a great base of assets and excellent incentives in place for the right things to be done with the cash generated. But the numbers generally don't look so great at the beginning, because it's in management's interest to underpromise and overdeliver. Coupled with the fact that the shareholder base is usually in flux at the beginning—many holders of the parent-company stock don't want to or, because of their charters, can't own the spinoff—inefficiencies arise.

—Mitchell Julis, Canyon Capital

Many times companies find themselves in what the market considers predicaments because they have been farsighted and are spending on future opportunities. The good thing about that type of spending from a shareholder's standpoint is that if the company is right, you benefit, and if it turns out to be wrong, it stops spending the money and you also benefit.

—Murray Stahl, Horizon Asset Management

Most companies expand during good times and wind up over-leveraged and with too much capacity when the business goes south. We like to see the opposite, companies today investing on the cheap in additional capacity for when things turn up.

—James Vanasek, VN Capital

Obviously, just because a company makes a new, long-term investment doesn't mean it's the right one. As an investor, though, the existence of controversial initiatives like that creates a potential buying opportunity. It's up to you to decide whether to pursue it or not.

—Thomas Russo, Gardner Russo & Gardner

At the peak of the Internet bubble, I went to an investor presentation by [check manufacturer] Deluxe Corp. in which they described how the Internet was going to flatter, not tarnish, the check business. Then the CEO launched into a big discussion about how he was going to convert his core franchise to a new platform he called Internet gift sales, and that they were going to lose $50 million a year on it. I went away and didn't buy the stock, disgusted with that idea. What I learned from this, however, was that really dumb ideas like this one actually have a habit of meeting an early death. In fact, it turned out to be such a dumb idea that it died quite quickly, leaving the business to flourish under its core dynamics, unburdened by ill-considered strategic moves. That was a big lesson.

—Thomas Russo, Gardner Russo & Gardner

OPERATING TURNAROUNDS

The bad news that typically precipitates the need for an operating turnaround, as well as the ongoing uncertainty that revolves around management's turnaround effort, can wreak the kind of havoc on stock prices that value investors are keen to capitalize upon. That a company is in turnaround mode, of course, doesn't mean the turnaround will be successful. That makes the ability to distinguish eventual winners from losers in the turnaround game an essential—if decidedly nontrivial—skill in any contrarian investor's toolkit.

* * *

We're looking for the prospect of an accelerating rate of positive change. That means we're naturally drawn to management changes, turnarounds, or, more generally, to situations in which changes in the macroeconomic, competitive or regulatory landscape require a company to remake what it does or how it does it. Sometimes it's even more straightforward, where we see unrecognized assets that can generate significant value, or when a company blew something like an acquisition or a product rollout and we believe the fix will happen more quickly and with less pain than the market expects.

—*Mariko Gordon, Daruma Capital Management*

We search for companies in which change can alter the future for the better. That can mean a change in management. It can mean a change in management's attitude toward running the business, say by recognizing that 120 percent of the earnings come from 80 percent of the assets, so they should do something about that other 20 percent at some point. It can mean a new business opportunity that has yet to take off. It can mean a change in the dynamics of a company's cash flow and how it's to be used.

If we perform our analysis correctly, the value added we bring is an earlier and better understanding of the companies in our portfolio than other investors might have. If the companies then begin to improve, their earnings should increase and they're likely to earn a higher price/earnings multiple.

—*Dennis Delafield, Delafield Fund*

We're looking for businesses that are going through some kind of transition—in management, in the business mix, in the industry. Often a previous management team overextended and overleveraged the company and somebody new has been brought in to straighten it all out, by cutting costs, selling assets or paying down debt. A good business that happens to have a bad balance sheet is much easier to fix than the opposite.

—*James Rooney, Avenir Corp*

Just because a company is capable of throwing off lots of cash doesn't mean they're doing so at any given moment or that they're using the cash correctly. We're value investors first, so we're looking for depressed stock prices. Often what causes a depressed stock price is a misallocation of free cash flow, through ill-timed or ill-conceived acquisitions, pouring money into bad businesses, or any number of wrong capital-allocation decisions. But those tend to be fixable problems, which is a lot easier to do when the core business is intrinsically healthy.

—Andrew Jones, North Star Partners

Missing a product cycle, for example, is generally fixable. So are problems that result from a company out-growing its infrastructure—it's a high-class problem to have, but can result in some real earnings trouble. Botched acquisitions can also create interesting opportunities if we believe the delayed cost savings or strategic benefits will eventually show up and increase earnings.

—Kevin O'Boyle, Presidio Fund

Our experience shows there's a positive correlation between improvements in a company's return on invested capital and its stock performance. That makes sense, given that a company's earnings today are the result of project spending it made in the past. We obsess over ascribing value to today's capital projects, as well as on deconstructing businesses into their component parts so we can better value the existing asset base.

More than anything, we're looking for inflections in businesses where some sort of structural change will drive returns on invested capital to be materially higher. In all of our conversations with companies, their competitors, and their suppliers, we're trying to identify structural changes that we can get ahead of and believe will result in better returns on capital.

I'd say at least half the time it has to do with new leadership changing how things are done. For example, we love when management or a board changes compensation systems to move from a grow-grow-grow, earnings-per-share-driven culture to one focused on returns on invested capital.

—Joe Wolf, RS Investments

Three-year to five-year turnarounds almost always require a deep infusion of outside management talent, a change in culture, an overhaul of the cost structure and some fairly dramatic shifts in operational execution. We want to identify these potential turnarounds early, but it's often only after a year or so of careful study that we're ready to act. Depending on the situation, we want to see tangible evidence—say, an increase in gross margins, declining inventory levels or reduced operating expenses—that the turnaround is working.

If we believe the shares can double or triple if we're right—which isn't a stretch if earnings and valuations are starting from particularly depressed levels—we have no problem leaving the first bump in the stock price on the table. We're helped by the fact that once the market has given up on a company, it can be quite slow to embrace it again.

—Lloyd Khaner, Khaner Capital

Management changes can help a lot with timing. If a board of directors is serious about restructuring, they'll often hire someone from a best-in-class company to make it happen. Those people aren't cheap, which shows the board is serious, and the fact that the person is willing to come indicates they think they can add value. An executive from a first-class company taking over a laggard can mean an opportunity is ripe for the picking.

—Philip Tasho, TAMRO Capital

While management changes aren't always necessary, we often view management changes positively in turnaround situations. You're much more likely to get a frank, thorough appraisal of what has gone wrong and why, so you'll probably understand the situation better. My confidence also increases when a strong new manager has been attracted to a situation and is highly motivated to perform.

—Kevin O'Boyle, Presidio Fund

My best ideas, by far, have been in situations where a new CEO takes over an undermanaged franchise. If we only focused on one thing, that would be it. The market just does not pick up on the ramifications of change quickly enough.

The big question after identifying a CEO you have confidence in is getting the timing right. You can't wait for the CEO to come out with his restructuring plan in front of 250 analysts. The best thing is when you already know the person and the business and can act very quickly after the new CEO is named.

—Kenneth Feinberg, Davis Advisors

What will get me excited is when one of our analysts comes into me with a story like this: "Preston, I've been following this stock for two years but haven't found a good reason to write it up. It used to be kind of a high-flier, but the stock chart now looks like death warmed over. The shares were at $40, had a big drop and have been trading between $15 and $18 for months and nobody cares. The company is likely to have some big writeoffs this year to clean up the balance sheet. And, by the way, two months ago the board fired the CEO and the new guy is someone I know from a previous company where he did a great job. He's not even talking to the Street for six months as he gets a handle on things."

—Preston Athey, T. Rowe Price

Stock prices go up for two primary reasons. The first is investors' willingness to pay a higher multiple for a company's earnings or cash flows. That's what traditional value managers look for—undervalued securities that will be more richly rewarded in the future. We're trying to find that as well, but we're also looking for evidence of fundamental turnarounds and the additional stock-price upside that comes from higher earnings expectations.

—Ronald Mushock, Systematic Financial Management

The primary reason to invest in a turnaround is when you're able to invest in great management at value prices. The best people are attracted to a challenge, but the fact that it's a challenge keeps valuations in line early on. Wall Street tends not to believe something is turning until it's fairly obvious, which can give you time to do real work and build your position before the market starts paying attention.

Even in poor market environments, turnarounds can do well because they're usually coming off such low bases. As a result, we find that our results are less correlated to the overall stock market, especially in down markets.

—Lloyd Khaner, Khaner Capital

As a general point, we aren't seeking classic turnarounds. If we look back at mistakes we've made, particularly in smaller-cap companies, it's been when we needed some fundamental problem to be fixed for the investment to work out. We've developed a healthy respect for how hard it is to turn a business around.

—Timothy Hartch, Brown Brothers Harriman

Getting turnarounds right is very tough. It takes a tremendous amount of research effort, the turnarounds almost always take longer than you expect, and it's just easy to get it wrong. That doesn't scare us away, but we're very cognizant of the risks. We're unlikely to act until we see tangible signs of the turnaround happening or some clear positive sentiment from the industry or management.

—Scott Hood, First Wilshire Securities

The first basic thing I look for is that the business is currently profitable, which means generating good returns on capital without the excessive use of leverage. I was tempted in my youth by turnaround stories or betting on new product or service offers, where you could hit the ball out of the park if things got fixed or the new product took off. But I've had enough failures pursuing those types of ideas that I've for the most part lost the stomach for them. From a performance standpoint, I'm more focused on what something is than what it can be.

—Thomas Gayner, Markel Corp.

We don't do turnarounds. What attracts us to the whole concept of value investing is the idea of having a margin of safety, in terms of value over price. That margin of safety only exists if values are stable and it only improves if value increases. With turnarounds, you're making a bet—maybe a very intelligent one, but still a bet— that something broken can be fixed. Even in the best case, you may be looking at years when value declines or stagnates. Our experience is that we're better off investing in a good business that is constantly compounding value from the beginning of our ownership, without what to us is the unacceptable risk that the turnaround doesn't work. We just don't think we need to take that kind of risk to earn strong returns.

—C.T. Fitzpatrick, Vulcan Value Partners

Not to be flip, but all we count on in a number of our investments is just for things to return to normal. There's a lot less risk in wanting that to happen than looking for some huge transformation in a company's business.

—Christopher Grisanti, Grisanti Brown & Partners

CHAPTER 5

Generating Ideas

The active quest for ideas is a universal component of every investor's toolkit, but the methods chosen to do so are often all over the lot. Some investors use computer screens extensively, for example, while others don't use them at all. Some frequently pursue top-down ideas sparked by an industry trend or secular change, while others pursue only ideas that bubble up individually. Regardless of the methods employed, however, the idea-generation process typically reflects the same abiding curiosity and dogged pursuit of information seen in the research and analysis efforts that follow.

BEHIND THE SCREEN

The ever-increasing sophistication of financial and market databases and the technology available to use them make it easier and easier for investors to screen on all manner of attributes in the search for prospective investments. The extent to which top investors take advantage of that capability, however, is far from uniform, ranging from not at all to a near-total automation of the initial idea-generation process. Similarly diverse are the metrics on which they screen, not surprising given the diversity of company characteristics on which they focus.

*   *   *

I do a lot of screening, which can be a valuable check on emotion, if you like. I wouldn't necessarily suggest blind faith in them, but there is a degree of honestly about numbers that can be quite useful for disciplining yourself when looking at potential opportunities.

—*James Montier, Société Générale*

We often start with screens on all aspects of valuation. There are characteristics that have been proven over long periods to be associated with above-average rates of return: low P/Es, discounts to book value, low debt/equity ratios, stocks with recent significant price declines, companies with patterns of insider buying and—something we're paying a lot more attention to—stocks with high dividend yields.

—Will Browne, Tweedy, Browne Co.

Our heritage has been very much to focus on traditional value metrics of low P/E, price/book, and price/sales ratios. An initial screen for us might be looking for stocks trading at less than 2× book value, less than 1x sales and less than 15× forward earnings. That's still at the core of what we do, but we've evolved to also screen on a variety of other metrics. We have a Joel Greenblatt screen, for example, looking at stocks with a combination of high earnings yields and high returns on capital. We also look at a variety of balance sheet measures, including basic things like net cash versus market value. The art part of the process comes in deciding which companies that screen well deserve more fundamental analysis. The keys here are usually an initial assessment of the quality of the business and its growth potential. We want to buy cheap—particularly relative to where the stock has historically traded and where companies in its industry should trade—but usually only when there's real potential for growth.

—John Buckingham, Al Frank Asset Management

We start by screening for classic value. This could be a low price-to-net-assets ratio, a low premium or a discount to book value, a P/E ratio less than the return-on-equity ratio or, depending on the industry, a modest premium or a discount of the market value to revenues. We also have various screens that try to predict a build-up of cash. Companies that continually generate cash above and beyond their capital expenditure requirements are hopefully going to do good things with that cash and shareholders should benefit.

—Carlo Cannell, Cannell Capital

We screen for financial metrics that may show symptoms of the types of situations we look for. Say revenues have been flat for the past three years, but operating expenses have increased in each of those years. We also typically look for companies that are underperforming on any number of profitability or productivity measures, against peers and against their own history. Be cause they're under-earning, many of the companies that interest us look expensive based on current numbers, but are actually undervalued relative to the pro-forma earnings that can be generated if our plan is implemented.

—Peter Feld, Starboard Value

We have a computer model that ranks our value universe of the 1,000 largest domestic companies. It ranks all 1,000 companies from cheapest to most expensive, on the basis of current price to the normalized earnings we extrapolate from history five years into the future. From this computer screen, we do an initial review on the cheapest quintile of these stocks, looking more closely at the company financials and the industry dynamics. After this initial research, we reject about 75 percent of these companies. The other 25 percent we do detailed analysis on, including visiting the company and meeting management.

—Richard Pzena, Pzena Investment Management

Some of our most useful screens look to identify businesses that are either short on capital or have excess capital.

—James Crichton, Scout Capital

Our basic screening process weights three factors equally: return on tangible capital – which we define as operating cash earnings over working capital plus net property, plant and equipment – the multiple of EBIT to enterprise value, and free cash flow yield. We rank the universe we've defined on each factor individually from most attractive to least, and then combine the rankings and focus on the top 10%.

—Stephen Goddard, The London Company

We look at all the usual valuation screens to identify stocks that are cheap relative to book value, earnings and cash flow. I'm also interested in companies whose margins are significantly higher or lower than they've been historically.

—Jon Jacobson, Highfields Capital

Since we're trying first and foremost to limit our downside, our valuation screening is centered on where a stock is trading relative to its own history. We look at various measures, but we basically go back as far as we can and calculate for each calendar year the high multiple of cash flow, say, and the low multiple of cash flow at which the stock traded. (The cash flow number we use is for that entire calendar year.) From that, we determine the median high multiple over the entire history and the median low.

We'll then look at the upside to that high and the downside to that low from today's multiple on current-year estimated cash flow and calculate what we call a favorability ratio. We want to do further work only on companies where the favorability ratio is at least 3:1, meaning the upside to the median-high valuation level is at least 3x the downside to the low. In other words, for the multiple part of the return equation, we want the odds in our favor.

—Brian Krawez, Scharf Investments

Having an edge as an investor is a bit like having an edge as a radiologist or a mechanic or a pilot. The edge comes from being able see patterns and reliably diagnosing what they will mean. I'd like to think that the combination of inputs we use to correlate and predict is somewhat unique to us.

In identifying potential short sales, for example, seeing decreasing inventory turns for a company audited by a non-Big Six accounting firm is an interesting correlation. Or we might draw some conclusions over an increase in the gap between cash flow from operations and net income combined with increasing analyst coverage of a company.

—Carlo Cannell, Cannell Capital

The long-term rate of return on equities in this country is in the neighborhood of 10 percent, which correlates closely to the actual return on owners' capital for all those businesses over time. My premise then is that the return I'll earn on a stock—absent distributions and assuming a constant valuation—will approximate the company's ROE over a number of years. So we choose to swim in the pool of companies where the returns have been much better than average and where we believe over the next five to ten years that opportunity will remain largely intact. And because you're saying, "Akre, you fool, you know we don't have constant valuations," we also work hard to pay low valuations at the outset.

—Chuck Akre, Akre Capital Management

One of our best screens looks for companies that are earning higher and higher returns on invested capital, but are trading at a reasonable price based on free cash flow. These companies are becoming incrementally better businesses, but the market has not caught up with the fact that they're incrementally better.

—Zeke Ashton, Centaur Capital

Most of our initial research is on finding the true standouts in any given business. That's largely a numbers-driven exercise, focusing on returns on equity, margins, and growth in key sales and profitability metrics—all in comparison with the competition. We've identified more than 400 companies—primarily in the U.S., but not exclusively—that we could imagine owning and that we try to keep fairly close track of.

—Francois Rochon, Giverny Capital

We consider ourselves first and foremost value investors, but we don't start by looking for cheap stocks. We spend our time following outstanding businesses that we would want to own should they ever become cheap. They're rarely inexpensive when we start trying to understand them, but we follow them closely so that on the rare occasion they become discounted, we can act right away. Coming at it this way also means we're not wasting our time chasing statistically cheap companies that we will have no interest in owning. Time is precious in this business.

—C.T. Fitzpatrick, Vulcan Value Partners

With the market as volatile as it has been, we've been more diligent about maintaining watch lists to catch companies whose stocks trade off sharply for reasons that may be more overall-market related. We're not looking for short-term trades but, as we learned in late 2008 and early 2009, stocks of even the high-quality companies we want to own can get remarkably cheap quite fast. We want to be prepared for that.

—David Nierenberg, D3 Family Funds

One important change we've made is to develop a well-maintained list of companies we would want to own at the right price. Because of the suddenness of the [2008] crisis, there were so many securities on sale that we were a bit paralyzed in trying to analyze them all. We've made the investment to stay current about on-deck ideas so we can act more quickly when opportunities present themselves.

—Jason Wolf, Third Avenue Management

Our best ideas tend to come from what I call "old research, new events." That's typically the good company you've studied carefully and would love to own at the right price, that gets marked down after it trips or its industry goes out of favor.

—Ricky Sandler, Eminence Capital

Tapping into our own prior work has probably produced the largest number of ideas. The risk is that you let the prior experience—whether you bought into something or not—bias your view. We try to stay cognizant of that, but just find it can be very helpful to leverage the head start we have from work we've already done. We've tried to automate some of the process by setting up stock-price alerts on companies we've already analyzed, but it isn't an exact science as target prices can become obsolete fairly quickly.

—Tucker Golden, Solas Capital

I've concluded that if you find yourself going back to the well with the same idea a third time, you're not generating enough ideas and are likely to get killed. You're not as vigilant as you should be because you think you know it already. When I find myself doing that, I tell myself I'm just not working hard enough.

—Jeffrey Ubben, ValueAct Capital

One narrow screen I like targets insider buying—when a lot of insiders are buying, I don't care what the valuation is, that's always an interesting signal.

—Zeke Ashton, Centaur Capital

We often look at cases in which a company with significant insider ownership is aggressively buying back shares, but the insiders don't participate in the buy-back. That indicates that someone who may know more about the business wants to own more at a particular price.

—*Robert Robotti, Robotti & Co.*

We don't take all insider buying and selling at face value. Some people and some trades you pay a lot more attention to than others. When a founder CEO who has 100% of his net worth in a stock buys another $10 million worth on the open market, that's interesting. When a director buys nearly $100 million of a company's stock, that's interesting. When top management is exercising options that don't expire in 15 years, that makes us leery, especially when they're publicly talking about how great everything is at the company.

—*Stephen Goddard, The London Company*

[W]e basically spend our time trying to uncover the assorted investment misfits in the market's underbrush that are largely neglected by the investment community. One of the key metrics we assign to our companies is an analyst ratio, which is simply the number of analysts who follow a company. The lower the better—as of the end of last year, about 65 percent of the companies in our portfolio had virtually no analyst coverage.

—*Carlo Cannell, Cannell Capital*

We want to know the level of attention paid to the company by Wall Street, much preferring those that are under-followed and for which there are low expectations. The blessing of low expectations is that being right about things turning out better means the stock will probably do quite well, while being wrong usually means not much happens because the low expectations are built into the share price.

—*James Shircliff, River Road Asset Management*

We look for companies that don't have heavy institutional ownership and for which the sell-side is generally negative, but that we think are addressing their failings through management and strategy changes. Often we're just trying to do the work early before sell-side analysts jump on the story and the company finds its right shareholder base and valuation level.

—*Gary Claar, JANA Partners*

We do exactly one screen, which is to segment our potential opportunities by market cap. Starting with a rank-order valuation screen is more likely to lead you into less-than-optimal businesses, which we can't afford to be in with such a concentrated portfolio.

—Brian Bares, Bares Capital

One thing we don't do is a lot of computer screening for ideas. I've always considered screens to be too backward-looking. Many of our best investments would have screened very poorly—with negative cash flow, horrible returns on equity, declining sales and suspect management. We're trying to look beyond all that to the changes in management or changes in the business that can correct the problems. The key for us is to be able to make a credible case for the company looking very different in two to three years from how it looks today.

—John Osterweis, Osterweis Capital Management

We don't do traditional screens and are actually looking for situations in which the publicly available information that a computer can analyze is giving false signals. For example, we bought auto insurer Progressive in 1999 when their earnings looked bad because they were spending heavily on a direct-to-consumer strategy like Geico's. A computer would see that as a negative earnings trend resulting in a too-high multiple, but it doesn't know how to judge whether certain spending might generate big returns in the future.

—Boykin Curry, Eagle Capital

FOLLOW THE LEAD

The pursuit of good ideas is often a more top-down and iterative process than implied by the heavy use of computer screens. A trend, a theme, or even a throw-away line in an obscure industry journal inspires a line of inquiry that is always filled with blind alleys, but from time to time uncovers a mispriced gem.

*   *   *

It's very important to define where you're going to look for opportunities. Time is a precious resource and if you make it your
task not to miss anything, you set yourself up for failure. There
are too many opportunities out there and, by definition, you will
miss many of them. That's why we narrow where we want to look
first by the themes we consider most compelling. We're not necessarily seeing things others don't see, but we will likely have a very
different view on the magnitude of the trend or the speed at which
it happens.

—Oliver Kratz, Deutsche Asset Management

Our ideas typically have more to do with the trends in a particular
industry than whether XYZ stock looks very cheap. We want to
invest in good businesses with industry or company-specific tailwinds behind them, and which happen to be cheap. That's a different mindset from finding something that's cheap and constructing a
story about why the negative issues should go away.

—Brian Barish, Cambiar Investors

We take the traditional value investor's process and just flip it
around a little bit. If you're looking for something that's cheap,
you'll probably do a variety of screens—on price-to-sales, price-to-
earnings, price-to-book, whatever—to identify stocks that appear
to be inexpensive. Once you have that list, then you start to research if there are good reasons the stocks deserve to be cheap, or
if maybe there's an investment opportunity because they're cheap
without a good reason. We think that's the way most value investors approach it.

We never do screens like that. We start by identifying situations
in which there is a reason why something might be misunderstood,
where it's likely investors will not have correctly figured out what's
going on. Then we do the more traditional work to confirm whether, in fact, there's an attractive investment to make. That's as opposed to starting with something that's just cheap and then trying
to figure out why. We think our way is more efficient.

—David Einhorn, Greenlight Capital

I'd say most of the ideas that have made money for the portfolio have been the result of some form of reasoning by analogy.

One example of that is applying well-understood and successful U.S. investment ideas to markets outside the U.S.

—Guy Spier, Aquamarine Fund

As we extend our time horizons, we try to think about things not just unique to one security or situation but applicable across a bigger industry trend. Thematic umbrellas help us organize our thoughts about bigger opportunities. We then go systematically one company at a time, one security at a time, to try to identify where we can find the best investments.

—Larry Robbins, Glenview Capital

For me it's all qualitative and contextual. Once you begin to research an industry, you have to survey the entire landscape to understand it, from the competitors within the industry to the competitive threats from outside the industry. Ideas naturally flow out of that process.

—Thomas Russo, Gardner Russo & Gardner

Many opportunities I pursue have a thematic, top-down element, where an industry's structure or certain situational dynamics are a tailwind to the company's business. It may be the industry has consolidated or supply is otherwise tightening, resulting in pricing power for the key players. It may be a company with a structural cost advantage that will allow it to take market share and accelerate revenue growth over a long period of time. The point is that I focus on the fundamentals of the business first, not on how cheap the stock is or how much it's off its 52-week high. That helps me avoid value traps and/or businesses with structural challenges.

—Jed Nussdorf, Soapstone Capital

We believe our job is to look out two or three years, to identify who's winning and who's losing in each industry, and to recognize the discrepancies between our views and the market's views. Given the depth of industry experience and resources our sector heads have, it would be unusual for someone to call us with an idea that we don't already have some knowledge of. As a result, the vast majority of our ideas come from thinking through the ramifications of industry developments or the recognition of changes within a market as opposed to the one-off, "Here's an idea, let's chase it down" approach.

—Lee Ainslie, Maverick Capital

We like it when expectations are very low and we have a contrarian view on a broader issue impacting the company. Low expectations help limit the downside and can result in prices that leave you paying nothing for the upside if good things happen.

—Jeffrey Schwarz, Metropolitan Capital

The majority of our investments are originally driven from the top down. We'll identify an industry that has underperformed for the past 5 or 10 years that we believe is due for a cyclical regression up to the mean. From that, we systematically review the whole universe of microcaps in that industry, sorting them on the basis of financial measures and subjective assessments of management to identify the companies we'll bore into.

—David Nierenberg, D3 Family Funds

One thing Peter Lynch [of Fidelity Magellan fame] did really well was to figure out how else to make money on a good idea. Look right down the industry structure and figure out the other ways that this particular information can generate an edge. In our portfolio today, we identify a theme and then we try to figure out where all the opportunities are.

—Jeffrey Ubben, ValueAct Capital

You never know where your research will take you. Say you're interested in copper. You may start with the mining companies, then move to the refiners, then the intermediate processors, then the metal-bender manufacturers and on up the line. If one area of the business looks particularly lousy, you may want to look at the companies that buy from those people. You may look at the competitors or the alternatives to copper. Thirty-five companies down the road, you're likely to be in a completely different business and industry and you'll come across something that looks interesting.

—James Vanasek, VN Capital

It's hard to have unique insights in this business, but they often just come from working on something that leads you to something else. I work with two analysts and every once in a while we'll say, "Let's brainstorm about new ideas," but I can't say we've ever come up with an idea that way.

—*Ed Wachenheim, Greenhaven Associates*

It's kind of a bizarre conversation to have, but we actively discuss what isn't being talked about. Maybe an industry is at a low point in its cycle, where our favorite company would be one that is still making money and looking to expand while competitors are losing money and retrenching. If a commodity is trading at a multi-year low, we'll look at the producers of the commodity who may be suffering. If a commodity is at an all-time high, we'll look at companies that use the commodity as a raw material and are getting hurt as a result. This all becomes a starting point and then we wander around from there.

—*James Vanasek, VN Capital*

Not to be overly simplistic, but a lot of it comes down to following the news and reading. You never know what might jump off the page and say, "Look at this." As an example, years ago I was reading an article in *The Economist* in which someone was talking about emerging consumerism in Asia and there was a single line saying something about how this company, that company and Lotte Confectionery might be beneficiaries. I had never heard of Lotte Confectionery, but as I looked into it I found out not only that it was a large, global candy and sweets company based in South Korea, but also that it was cash-flow positive and its stock was trading at around net cash per share. You obviously end up hitting a lot of dead ends, but I've found plenty of things no one seems to be paying attention to in this way.

—*Chris Mittleman, Mittleman Brothers, LLC*

I think there are very few truly original ideas, so a lot of our [short] ideas come from what I call observational common sense. We talk a lot to people we respect in the business. We read everything, looking for patterns we've seen in the past that led to good ideas. It doesn't have to be negative news—often you read a bullish article or report and you can just tell the writer is missing it, that there's something wrong and it's worth a look. We're also avid observers of human behavior, looking for cases where people can collectively lose their minds for longer periods of time than you could imagine possible.

—James Chanos, Kynikos Associates

Many of our other ideas just come from having our eyes wide open. You read publications like yours. You talk to contacts you've developed in various industries. It's often just about paying attention to what's going on in the world.

—Ricky Sandler, Eminence Capital

We don't have a rigid process, but there are always linkages. My first investment 20 years ago was Fireman's Fund. Studying Jack Byrne's resuscitation of GEICO before going to Fireman's Fund led me to Berkshire Hathaway and this guy Warren Buffett. Then during the banking crisis in the early 1990s I looked at many banks, but chose Wells Fargo because Warren Buffett owned it.

—Bruce Berkowitz, Fairholme Capital

We have a disciplined idea-generation process, but it has to be open to serendipity—often it's the footnote in the trade journal where you see something interesting that eventually becomes an idea.

—Shawn Kravetz, Esplanade Capital

RELIABLE SOURCES

Each investor brings his or her own experience base, strategy, and acumen to the information-filtering process in looking for new ideas. Therefore it's not surprising that the information-gathering process in pursuing ideas, while often clever and creative, need not necessarily be that proprietary, sophisticated, or even original.

* * *

For the last 40 years I've been reading things like *Variety* and *Automotive News* and *Farm Journal* that give you an idea of what's going on around the world. A story that has always stuck in my mind since I first heard about it in high school is that in World

War II, an Allied intelligence analyst was reading the social papers and wondered why all these German generals were going to a particular location in the middle of nowhere. He figured out that it was the location of a factory making German V-1 bombs and sending them to England. The hard part is connecting all the dots, but you have to assemble plenty of dots to connect in the first place.

—*Mario Gabelli, GAMCO Investors*

I like to have information pushed at me, so I've set up keyword alerts on something like 3,000 companies, which results in 20 to 25 press releases a day announcing things like management changes, reorganizations or new dividends. Ideas come out of that all the time.

Another thing I've done in my personal account is to buy one share of probably 250 micro-cap companies, which is kind of my own customized research service. The daily mail delivery is kind of a Christmas grab bag—you never know when an annual or quarterly that arrives is going to catch your eye.

One last thing I'd mention as an idea generator is tracking new-lows lists. I always say margins of safety are created out of broken dreams, and there's a fresh list of those broken dreams published daily for us to hunt through.

—*Paul Sonkin, Hummingbird Value Fund*

We screen a lot on the metrics you'd expect for companies with a combination of low valuation and high business quality, but we also like to search article databases using keywords that indicate problems or big changes at a company—things like "profit warning," or "spin-off," or "restructuring."

—*David Samra, Artisan Partners*

We've over time built a number of systems and reports that enable us to track globally the movement of debt, equity and assets around on balance sheets. We follow in a disciplined way things like spinoffs, rights offerings, new equity issuance and buybacks.

—*James Crichton, Scout Capital*

You can usually only pay an undemanding price when there's fear or uncertainty associated with a name. If I was stranded on a desert island and was given only one way to come up with investment ideas, I'd want to see the daily list of biggest percentage decliners. There's no better indicator of fear and uncertainty.

—James Kieffer, Artisan Partners

We look at the new-lows list for long ideas and the new-highs list for short ideas. I look at the 13F filings of 20 to 25 other investors I respect to see what they're buying and selling. Bloomberg also on a monthly basis has the highest-ranked and lowest-ranked stocks by sell-side analysts. I look at the lowest-ranked for buying opportunities and the highest-ranked for selling opportunities.

—Jon Jacobson, Highfields Capital

We use a lot of grapevine ideas, asking people what they have finished buying that might be interesting. Why wouldn't you look at what other great investors have found?

—Bruce Berkowitz, Fairholme Capital

It's always interesting if those who have filed with the SEC as 5 percent owners are names we respect. Historically, if we've see Marty Whitman's name, we like it. If we see the T. Rowe Price Small-Cap Value Fund, we're happy.

—David Nierenberg, D3 Family Funds

We follow 13D and 13F filings of other people we respect. We read publications like yours. I'd much rather steal a good idea than generate a bad one myself.

—Steve Morrow, NewSouth Capital

We get a lot of ideas from studying what the people we respect are doing. We sit on panels, go to conferences, and regularly pick up the phone and talk to our friends in the business. As you get more experience, the network you've built becomes a resource that is difficult to replicate.

—John Rogers, Ariel Investments

We learn a lot from other investors. I go to idea dinners and regularly talk to a lot of people I respect in the business. I'm not afraid of ideas owned by other people, but you obviously need to do your own work and make sure they fit what you do.

There is no shortage of people trying to put ideas in front of us. We won't invest without doing our own research, but the give and take with other thoughtful analysts can spark ideas.

—James Rooney, Avenir Corp.

Probably half our ideas are generated internally in the normal course of business, from speaking with portfolio companies, their competitors, customers, and suppliers, or from the reading we do to research any given company and its industry. Another 25 percent or so of our ideas come from more niche brokerage and research firms with whom we've had a good experience. We get the balance of our ideas from other buy-side investors we know and respect. Other investors are particularly helpful for getting a quick take on the bull and bear case for any potential idea. That's not at all a replacement for doing our own work, but it helps focus our attention as we try to determine if something is worth a deeper dive.

—Robert Kirkpatrick, Cardinal Capital

I don't talk much to other fund managers, but I do have a network of investigative reporters I've gotten to know who call me from time to time to discuss long or short ideas they've come across, which can be helpful.

—Francois Parenteau, Defiance Capital

We find that Wall Street research does a fairly good job of describing the economics of any industry, but a bad job on reaching conclusions about companies. Most analysts just repeat what a company tells them. They're often more focused on protecting their relationships with management than on protecting the average investor from a potential loss.

—Robert Olstein, Olstein Capital Management

Building the Case

CHAPTER 6

Cutting Through the Noise

Professional investors are an exceedingly competitive lot, unsurprising
given that their chosen field is one where the score delineating winners and losers can be tallied at every market close. But as results-driven
as investors tend to be, the best money managers put equal emphasis on
the process they follow for conducting research and making portfolio
decisions. They have a clear understanding of the most important questions they want answered and how best to answer them. As we've stressed
many times already, the areas of focus and methods of discovery can vary
widely. Some investors put great emphasis on having macro views that
inform their decisions, while others firmly reject that approach. Some consider time spent with management critical to their research process, while
others consider it a waste of time. Some see industry specialization among
analysts as a benefit, others see it as a detriment. But nearly all successful
fundamental investors see their research and decision-making process as a
primary source of competitive advantage and should be able to explain in
detail why that's so.

Equity strategist James Montier, now at Boston investment firm GMO,
describes the importance of process this way:

> *As much as I'd like to be able to control the outcomes, I can't. The
> only thing I can do is maximize the probability of getting a good
> outcome by following what I've defined as the right process. A good
> process doesn't negate bad outcomes or bad judgments, it just tries
> to mitigate them.*
>
> *It's like a pilot's preflight checklist. Pilots do the same thing
> thousands and thousands of times in their lives, but they still go
> through the physical checklist to eliminate what could be a cata-
> strophic error if they try to circumvent it. Investors are well served
> by having similar types of checklists and sticking with them.*

The Baupost Group's Seth Klarman makes a similar point in a slightly different way:

> *Money managers must keep firmly in mind that the only things they really can control are their investment philosophy, investment process, and the nature of their client base. Controlling your process is absolutely crucial to long-term investment success in any market environment. James Montier recently pointed out that when athletes were asked what went through their minds just before competing in the Beijing Olympics, the consistent response was a focus on process, not outcome. The same ought to be true for investors.*

Just as the best and most rigorously followed process will at times yield bad outcomes, the most arbitrary and slipshod process can periodically produce a good outcome as well. But if you're looking for a way to bet, the manager with the superior process is far more likely to win out over time.

SECOND-LEVEL THINKING

In describing a key goal of their research and analysis, top investors focus on the necessity of having—and being able to justify—what hedge-fund pioneer Michael Steinhardt termed a *variant perception* about any given stock they're looking to buy. What have you uncovered and what do you believe that is at variance with what the market believes and is reflected in the share price? Without that, they say, how can you possibly expect to beat the market?

*   *   *

First-level thinking is simplistic and superficial, and just about everyone can do it (a bad sign for anything involving an attempt at superiority). All the first-level thinker needs is an opinion about the future, as in "The outlook for the company is favorable, meaning the stock will go up."

The second-level thinker takes many things into account: What is the range of likely future outcomes? Which outcome do I think will occur? What's the probability I'm right? What does the consensus think? How does my expectation differ from the consensus? How does the current price for the asset comport with the consensus view of the future and with mine? Is the consensus psychology incorporated in the price too bullish or bearish? What will happen to the asset's price if the consensus turns out to be right, and what if I'm right?

The difference in workload between first-level and second-level thinking is clearly massive, and the number of people capable of the latter is tiny compared to the number of people capable of the former.

—Howard Marks, Oaktree Capital

There's an old saying in poker that if you're not sure who the patsy is, you probably are. You cannot have an opinion about an investment unless you understand the consensus and can articulate why it's wrong. If you can't do that, you're most likely the patsy.

If you think what everybody else thinks, it's already priced in. Think about betting on the Super Bowl, why is Pittsburgh being a four-point favorite the wrong line if you want to bet on Seattle? You may not have to know if you're betting for fun on Sunday, but you sure better know if you're making decisions with $8 billion of your clients' money.

—Jon Jacobson, Highfields Capital

If you find a stock that you think is undervalued but you're unable to identify how your insights into the company differ from those the market is using to price the stock, it's probably not really undervalued.

—Steve Morrow, NewSouth Capital

This may sound obvious, but we work very hard to understand the fundamentals of a business and to identify the key drivers behind a company's potential success or failure. We end up focusing on many of the factors you'd expect—competitive positioning, returns on capital, organic growth, etc.—but always with an eye towards identifying the biggest differences between our view and the view of the market.

—Lee Ainslie, Maverick Capital

Why something is mispriced is too often ignored by value investors. The general thinking is that it doesn't really matter—if you're right that something is mispriced, it will eventually take care of itself. We think it matters because you can conceivably avoid a lot of pain waiting for truth to prevail if you have a good read on why it currently doesn't.

—*Curtis Macnguyen, Ivory Capital*

MACRO VERSUS MICRO

Prior to the 2008 financial crisis, it was rare for investors we interviewed to put much credence in applying informed macroeconomic views to buying stocks. Conventional value-investing wisdom had been that trying to forecast GDP growth or interest rates or the level of the overall market was excessively difficult and therefore unhelpful in assessing the attractiveness of any given stock. The 2008 crisis, in which individual stocks' relative merits were overwhelmed by horrible macro news that took all share prices down more or less together, modified that conventional view somewhat. That's not at all to say everyone switched to a focus on macroeconomic expertise, but its relevance to the research and analytical process is now subject to much livelier debate.

*   *   *

One conclusion I made from our 2008 and early 2009 experience being more unpleasant than I would have liked is that I needed to better incorporate my world view into individual security selection, with the goal of trying to minimize future unpleasantness. We're focused on better connecting the dots between the overall economic environment and the opportunities or pitfalls facing individual businesses. In 2008 we were looking at trees and didn't see the forest.

—*Chuck Akre, Akre Capital Management*

Most of the time [investing with less regard for macroeconomic forecasts] is the right approach, but in my experience there have been times when one or a handful of major factors—such as large waves of liquidity going in and going out—overwhelm traditional metrics of value to set market prices. In such times, ignoring those factors has proven to be dangerous.

—*Mohamed El-Erian, PIMCO*

We, like a lot of people, have been trained to be bottom-up stock pickers and not worry about the market. The fact is, however, that most of the risks we see today in our individual ideas are macro in nature, so as stewards of capital we ignore those risks at our peril.

Informing yourself on macro issues is not really any different than the work you do to inform yourself about a company or an industry. You read. You talk to people. You learn from the companies you own. You subscribe to the best services. It clearly takes time and energy to do it right, but to do otherwise today strikes us as a big mistake.

—Brian Feltzin, Sheffield Asset Management

One element to our process I have added in recent years is what I call "PEST" Control. I grew up in the business with the basic assumption that I didn't need to worry much about macro issues as long as I had enough margin of safety from a cheap stock price. That's no longer a safe assumption, so we force ourselves to more fully assess the risks of Political, Economic, Social and Technological changes that could derail our thesis.

—Jeffrey Bronchick, Cove Street Capital

In a market with all these potentially negative and serious macro factors, our gross and net exposures are likely to remain low. You don't want to be a sitting duck waiting for your fundamental catalysts to play out while all these macro factors might swing your stocks wildly and, in some cases, overwhelm any fundamental catalysts you're counting on.

—Curtis Macnguyen, Ivory Capital

I used to completely ignore the macro environment, but now I pay attention and try to have a basic view that informs how we look at everything. We're taking our cues on that from the companies and industries we research every day. That's more relevant to us than the transcript from the latest Federal Reserve meeting or some Bureau of Labor Statistics report.

—Ricky Sandler, Eminence Capital

If you're a hedge fund with the audacity to charge between 1 percent and 2 percent as a management fee and take 20 percent of the profits, your clients have the right to expect something more. One aspect of what I consider "more" is that when the market's overvalued, my clients expect me to figure it out and be hedged and out of harm's way. When the market's undervalued, they want me to be leveraged to the upside. We're not a slave to our market view, but the truth of the matter is that a rising tide does lift all boats and a falling tide lowers them.

—Leon Cooperman, Omega Advisors

Virtually all studies show that about 60 percent of the return and volatility of the average common stock is determined by the movement in the aggregate stock market. So while we're bottom-up stock pickers, we think it's important to have a view of the economy and the overall market to help us determine which industries and sectors to emphasize.

—Steven Einhorn, Omega Advisors

[Making reasoned macro calls] starts with having the best and longest-time-series data you can find. You may have to take some risks in terms of the quality of data sources, but it amazes me how people are often more willing to act based on little or no data than to use data that is a challenge to assemble.

—Robert Shiller, Yale University

I do fall in the camp of investors who now believe that blissfully ignoring macroeconomic trends is a mistake. Paying attention to macro issues is still probably a waste of effort 95 percent of the time, but that other 5 percent can be very important. One of my efforts in this regard is to better understand what's going on in credit markets and to figure out what those markets might be signaling that the equity markets aren't.

—Zeke Ashton, Centaur Capital

We're bottom-up stock pickers, so the main reason we concern ourselves with the macro environment is to pressure-test the companies we invest in. Using a nautical analogy, we're looking at the weather forecast to make sure our boat will be strong enough, not to pick the day to go sailing.

Even our macro views stem largely from bottom-up work. We were interested in Fannie Mae in 2007 but first wanted to understand their credit risk better. We spoke with the ratings agencies and asked them what would happen if house prices fell. "You mean a six-sigma event?" they asked. "No," I said, "just if prices fell 5 or 10 percent." They said, "That's six-sigma!" Well, if house prices going back to where they had been just 12 months earlier was considered six-sigma by the ratings agencies, I thought we were in trouble.

—Boykin Curry, Eagle Capital

We're not macro people, but you cannot be investing other people's money without thinking about the state of the world, much of which is unsettling.

Think about the U.S. government's debt level and what happens if interest rates increase. Think about housing values, the unemployment rate and the price of gasoline and what that means for consumer purchasing power. What's going to happen in the Middle East? What's going to happen in Japan? What's going to happen with the U.S. dollar? There are an unusual number of serious things to worry about.

When that's the case that all makes its way into the portfolio by our assessing the impact all of these things could have on each company we own and fully understanding the downside. We also think in times like these when there are so many imponderables out there, it's important to have a significant cash cushion in case something goes wrong.

—Dennis Delafield, Delafield Fund

We've always been dedicated, bottom-up investors, fully believing in that old line from Peter Lynch that if you spend 15 minutes a year studying the economy, you've wasted 10. While I'm not prepared to renounce that position, I do believe we need to do our bottom-up work with a greater appreciation for what's going on in the world.

—Jim Roumell, Roumell Asset Management

It's important not to get too caught up in the macroeconomic or political currents and just focus on the fundamentals of individual businesses. Bigger issues obviously matter, but they should just be a part of the many inputs you look at in assessing the quality of the business, its prospects and what you think it's worth. It doesn't matter how well you handicap the next presidential election if you can't discern a good business from a bad one.

—David Herro, Harris Associates

More people are saying, "Everything's macro, you've got to think in terms of risk on, risk off." I think that's really a nutty thing. I just don't believe you can be effective in trying to get those decisions right in the short term.

—Howard Marks, Oaktree Capital

I would argue that if macro factors are too big a determinant in your appraisal of a company's intrinsic value, you should just sit that out. Given all the issues in Europe, for example, we don't have to bet on European consumer companies whose fortunes are closely tied to how the debt crisis there plays out. In the U.S., we don't have to bet on healthcare stocks whose futures depend on macro healthcare legislation or the financial strength of government entities that pay a lot of the bills. We should just move on to where the micro is driving value.

—Staley Cates, Southeastern Asset Management

In general, we build the portfolio one stock at a time and don't really go offensive or go defensive based on what we think might happen in the macro environment. We'll always have things in the portfolio that will do better when times are tough or when times are good, but they tend to balance each other out. When you focus as much as we do on operating turnarounds, those kinds of stocks—if you're right—should do relatively well regardless of how healthy the economy is.

—Mariko Gordon, Daruma Capital Management

While it is always tempting to try to time the market and wait for the bottom to be reached (as if it would be obvious when it arrived), such a strategy has proven over the years to be deeply flawed. Historically, little volume transacts at the bottom or on the way back up and competition from other buyers will be much greater when the markets settle down and the economy begins to recover. Moreover, the price recovery from a bottom can be very swift. Therefore, an investor should put money to work amidst the throes of a bear market, appreciating that things will likely get worse before they get better.

—Seth Klarman, The Baupost Group

I gave a speech recently in which I borrowed [Oaktree Capital Chairman] Howard Marks' concept of the "I know" vs. the "I don't know" investor. The "I know" investor thinks knowledge of the future direction of economies, interest rates and markets is essential for investment success and is confident not only that he can have such knowledge, but that he'll have it first as well. These are people who are quite popular at dinner parties.

The "I don't know" investor doesn't believe that you need to know the future or even that you can, so spends most of his or her time on how big the margin of safety is and in assessing what risks can result in the permanent impairment of capital. This tends to be a contrarian lot and they aren't hugely popular at dinner parties.

—James Montier, GMO

We mostly have nothing to say about the market overall. Given that we maintain a disciplined range of net exposure, whether we get the market right or wrong doesn't make that much difference. If our net exposure is at 40 percent rather than 60 percent and the market makes a 10 percent move, that's a 200-basis-point impact. That's not nothing, but it has far less impact on how we do than individual stock selection.

—Adam Weiss, Scout Capital

In the end, I fall back on the fact that our process is meant to identify undervalued companies on an absolute basis, using conservative assumptions. If I can find them, I'll buy them. If I can't, I'll hold the cash until I can. That process is meant to work in any macro environment and so far it's held up pretty well.

—Eric Cinnamond, Intrepid Capital

I've always told people I have no idea what the market's going to do or when returns will appear in the portfolio. I don't think either of those is predictable. The best we can do today is to focus on companies with balance sheets to weather a credit-constrained world, business models that will be around for years to come and valuations that are cheap enough to make the wait for recovery worthwhile. That's what we can control—the rest of it takes care of itself.⸱

—Andrew Jones, North Star Partners

The first lesson [post-financial crisis] was that bottoms-up fundamental company analysis still matters quite a bit and that ignoring the experience of Graham, Buffett and our 35 years to become macro-driven "generals fighting the last war" would have probably left us on the sidelines at exactly the wrong time. Parking ourselves in cash in early 2009 to wait for clear signs the misery was over would have caused us to miss the best purchase point for equities in my lifetime.

—Staley Cates, Southeastern Asset Management

There's no question that getting the macro picture right is hugely valuable—I just wish I were capable of doing it. When it comes to macro events, you can either predict or react. I've proven time and again that my crystal ball is horrible, so my focus has to be on reacting to extremes in individual securities by selling at high valuations and buying at low valuations.

—Bruce Berkowitz, Fairholme Capital

Many of our peers seem to have concluded that bottom–up investing isn't good enough anymore, an opinion we don't share because the assumption is that it's easy to have a nonconsensus macro view that adds value. So many of the macro overlays you hear today talk about Europe having trouble restructuring its debt and the U.S. economy growing slower than it has historically. Could you be any more consensus than that?

With the five- to seven-year time horizon we think about, you're usually better off thinking that things are going to be sort of normal, as opposed to having a strong conviction about what the economy's going to look like that overrides all of your bottom-up work. Our view today that things normalize over five to seven years might be as anticonsensus as most of the macro overlays out there.

Bill Nygren, Harris Associates

I talk to investors who have just been in New York and who want to know my macro view and whether I think Japan is going to be a vortex that pulls the whole global economy down with it. Their eyes glaze over when I start talking instead about C.R. Bard's Foley catheters or the new BankFusion software at Misys. But that's what matters to us. Our goal is to find earnings streams that are defensible in good times and bad and that also demonstrate secular growth. It's frankly an advantage to not get overly distracted by macroeconomic concerns, which can make it hard to pull the trigger on a great business when the opportunity presents itself.

—Jeffrey Ubben, ValueAct Capital

BUSINESS FIRST

It's rare in speaking with accomplished investors that they say their initial effort in assessing an investment's viability is how cheap the stock is. That's obviously important in the end, but given that any credible assessment of a company's value relies in large part on judging the prospects for its business, most investors focus first on understanding the dynamics of the company's competitive environment, the secular trends affecting the industries in which it competes, and the impact all of the above has on the sustainability and profitability of its business model. As GAMCO Investors' Mario Gabelli puts it, simply, "Only after you understand the business can you understand the stock."

*   *   *

The biggest lesson learned from my father was that investing was all about businesses and people. He'd talk about McDonald's versus Burger King or the rise of Nike or how Steve Jobs started Apple, all in a way that was very interesting for a kid. There was nothing about P/E ratios or market caps—things he figured we could learn later. He wanted us to understand the essence of business and what made a business successful.

—*Christopher Davis, Davis Advisors*

One of the best lessons I learned early on was to look at companies as companies first—to understand what they want to achieve and the likelihood they can achieve it. People too often focus on stocks first and think they can generate an edge in how they're looking at valuation. In the end, static valuation is relatively efficient and it's what companies do that drives their futures.

—*Oliver Kratz, Deutsche Asset Management*

Before I even look at a financial statement, I try to find out as much as I can about the history of the company, to understand how it has arrived at its current predicament. (If we're looking at it, it's usually a predicament.) The Internet is very good for this type of research. I'm trying to find evidence of similar issues in the past and what happened, to help judge whether current problems are controllable and rectifiable. If a company loses dominant market share in a business, for example, in my experience it almost never recovers that share. If it retains dominant share but lets its costs get out of control, the probability of that problem being solved is very high. I want to know whatever I can to help me make those distinctions.

—*Murray Stahl, Horizon Asset Management*

We focus on companies with long competitive-advantage periods, which puts a premium on our truly understanding the business dynamics over time. As a result, features of businesses we're tempted by typically include stable market shares, stable margins, pricing power and long data series, so we can evaluate how the business has performed through good times and bad.

—*James Crichton, Scout Capital*

Our research is very focused on the context in which a company is operating and on understanding why the valuation is so low. If you're buying a house, you don't ask your real estate broker to blindfold you and take you to the cheapest house in town and just look at it from the inside. You have to stick your head out of the window and walk around the neighborhood to really understand what it's worth.

So when we look at banks, we want to know the leverage ratios for consumers in their primary markets. When we look at cement companies, we want to know where construction activity is historically relative to GDP in the relevant markets and what import prices are. Just buying cheap stocks without paying enough attention to those contextual issues can get value investors into trouble.

—Dan O'Keefe, Artisan Partners

We focus on industry structure. We like concentrated industries with two or three primary players. As value investors, we are typically buying the underperformer. There are issues to fix, but the customers are rooting for you and the leading competitor, with high margins and a high stock price, is probably not going to go for the jugular.

—Jeffrey Ubben, ValueAct Capital

The three primary drivers for a stock are the macro factors that influence the broader market, the dynamics of the industry in which the company participates, and the specific prospects for the company itself. We don't think we're particularly adept at predicting the broader market, but we're quite comfortable first analyzing an industry or sub-industry trend and then diving deeper into company-specific issues.

This "middle-down" approach, as we call it, keeps us from putting so much importance on a cheap valuation, a great company-specific story, or a particularly appealing management that we miss a broader industry trend that makes all that irrelevant. As Warren Buffett has said, when management with a great reputation takes on an industry with a bad one, it's the industry that usually comes out with its reputation intact.

We often find multiple ideas supported by common viewpoints. In general, we think it's easier to hit the side of the barn than one single spot on the barn.

—Michael Karsch, Karsch Capital

We spend a lot of time trying to figure out how competitors would attack the business of the company we're interested in. The harder that is, the more interested we are. We try to avoid markets per-ceived to be so attractive that capital could start pouring in at any time.

—Mario Cibelli, Marathon Partners

There are usually only a few things you have to get right about a company for it to be a successful investment. What are the key drivers of the business and how are they changing? What is the company doing to position itself for that future, and what is it doing to operate more efficiently and effectively? How are they redeploying capital? Our view is that if you can get 85 percent of the way there by answering the big questions, don't waste your time on the last 15 percent because the marginal utility isn't worth it.

—Steve Morrow, NewSouth Capital

The key questions we want to answer focus on assessing the basic attributes that to us make an interesting stock: Does the company generate structural free cash flows? Is there some element of defen-siveness in the business model that will hold off competitors from coming in and disrupting the economics? Is there some element of secular or company-specific growth potential? How capable is management? What is the catalyst to value creation?

—Matthew Berler, Osterweis Capital Management

[My daughter] was six or seven, so rather than try to explain money management and the stock market, I said I'd tell her how I spent my time. I told her that half the time I read things like newspapers and magazines and half the time I spent speaking with my colleagues. She said, "That's not work!" But that's what I do.

It's very common to drown in the details or be attracted to complexity, but what's most important to me is to know what three, four, or five major characteristics of the business really matter. We have a great team of analysts who find the ideas and do the investigative work and I see my job primarily as asking the right questions and focusing the analysis in order to make a decision.

—Jean-Marie Eveillard, First Eagle Funds

WHAT QUALITY MEANS

While not all value investors emphasize the quality of the businesses in which they invest, many follow Warren Buffett's lead in their preference for a great business at a fair price over a fair business at a great price. Those who emphasize quality also have a very refined sense of what they believe quality means when it comes to companies and their businesses.

*　　*　　*

Our ideal investments are in franchise businesses, the term we use to signify a right, a license, or a privilege that confers an economic advantage that will permit the company to earn above-average returns on capital over long periods of time. That generally manifests itself in some form of competitive barrier to entry, from brand strength, intellectual property, the regulatory environment, or scale. It also typically means the business is somewhat shielded from unpredictable macroeconomic forces and, even better, that it should grow in good times and bad. Companies with these characteristics are winners, and they tend to stay winners.

—Peter Keefe, Avenir Corp.

We start from the premise that we want to invest in great businesses that share common characteristics. They provide essential products and services, meaning they are more "have-to-have" than "nice-to-have." They have very satisfied and loyal customers. They have leadership positions and sustainable competitive advantages in attractive industries and markets. Financially, they earn high returns on capital—certainly above their cost of capital—and generate high after-tax free cash flow that can be used to invest, make acquisitions, pay down debt, buy back stock or pay dividends.

—Timothy Hartch, Brown Brothers Harriman

We like simple, predictable, free-cash-flow generative, resilient and sustainable businesses with strong profit-growth opportunities and/or scarcity value. The type of business Warren Buffett would say has a moat around it.

We've done almost nothing in energy or other cyclical business-es. We avoid healthcare because of all the regulatory uncertainty. We've done nothing active in financial services, except on the short side with MBIA. When you're putting 8%, 12% or 15% of your money in something, it's not a day trade. You have to focus first and foremost on high-quality businesses that can't blow up and should grow in value over time.

—*William Ackman, Pershing Square Capital Management*

What makes a high-quality business? At a basic level, the product or service being sold is critical to customers but is only a small part of their cost structure, and the customer relationship tends to be sticky and recurring. Generally, we end up in intellectual-property-based businesses that can price off of a value-add rather than some sort of cost basis.

—*Jeffrey Ubben, ValueAct Capital*

We're looking for businesses with low capital intensity, the abil-ity to generate high levels of free cash flow, and a privileged busi-ness model that enables the company to produce excess capital. We want the financial and business models to be transparent. In terms of competitive dynamics, we want to understand the value of the company's product or service to customers and the strength of its competitive moat. From an industry perspective, we ideally want to see long-term sustainable growth and secular tailwinds.

—*James Crichton, Scout Capital*

My favorite ideas tend to be companies that generate free cash flow, not cheap cyclicals or stocks trading at big discounts to book. One big advantage of investing in companies generating free cash flow is that you can be more patient because the intrinsic value tends to grow while you own it—they're adding cash to the balance sheet, paying down debt, buying back their stock. The stock price may not perform for a time, but the intrinsic-value growth will eventually be reflected in the market price. You're get-ting paid to wait.

—*Andrew Jones, North Star Partners*

High-return businesses have something special which allows them to earn above average rates on employed capital. That may be intellectual property, scale economies, a regulatory advantage, high customer switching costs, or some sort of network effect. We want to see evidence the business model produces unusual returns, to understand why and to believe that's likely to continue. Part of that is a function of the opportunity yet to be realized—we're always asking, "How wide and how long is the runway?"

—Chuck Akre, Akre Capital Management

An area on which we spend a lot of effort is to define how big the runway of opportunity is in the business. We're not looking for short-term or arbitrage opportunities, but cases where we can see a reasonable probability of a huge upside, which we're not paying for.

—Robert Jaffe, Force Capital Management

The most important thing that I figured out early on was the benefit when investing in turnarounds of focusing on companies that operate in growing markets. If a company has market growth as a tailwind, it's quite a bit easier for management to execute an operational turnaround.

—Kevin O'Boyle, Presidio Fund

It takes a lot to kill a strong, established franchise even if a company loses its way. Think IBM. Think McDonald's. The right management can make all the difference in whether the business comes back. The strength of the franchise and the quality of management are what I spend most of my time on.

—Lloyd Khaner, Khaner Capital

We're not usually looking for the scruffy cyclical or turnaround story, but for businesses with high market shares in their principal product or service lines, with long product cycles but short customer-repurchase cycles, and with relatively low capital requirements that allow the company to generate high cash returns on tangible assets while growing. We've always considered businesses requiring enormous amounts of capital for fixed assets, especially when they're economically sensitive, to be at a big disadvantage.

—Donald Yacktman, Yacktman Asset Management

One important aspect of business quality is how successful it will be in a less-buoyant economic period. Can they cut costs? Can they take market share? Will their balance sheet an asset? The answer to those questions can make a huge difference in the viability of any investment.

—David Samra, Artisan Partners

Since we often suggest that companies refocus on their core business, the majority of our research time is spent on determining the health and sustainability of that business. We need to fully stress test our assumptions on the core business—that's where something could go wrong if it were going to go wrong.

—Peter Feld, Starboard Value

In companies earning abnormal returns, there's something unique going on and we want to understand what it is, why it exists and whether it's sustainable. We're trying to find businesses that have great moats, which translates into great returns on capital. Moats are fairly rare but come from a variety of things, such as intellectual property, scale economies, a regulatory advantage, high customer switching costs, or some sort of network effect. True moats give you more confidence in projecting future performance.

—Chuck Akre, Akre Capital Management

To us, the definition of a good business is if you can specifically identify reasons why it should be able to earn a return in excess of its [cost of] capital. It could be anything: a competitive cost position, a franchise brand, an installed base of business, unique technology— some reason to believe that even if the current management fails to restore earnings, somebody else would want to try. Say, an acquirer of the assets. Or the board replacing management with other management. Or even the same management trying another plan, because it's worth trying and you can specifically understand why it's worth trying.

—*Richard Pzena, Pzena Investment Management*

CRUNCHING THE NUMBERS

While it's less common than you might think for successful investors to hold accounting-related degrees and credentials, that is not at all to say they're uninformed when it comes to the nuts and bolts of income statements, balance sheets, and cash flow statements. In fact, most top managers stress the importance of looking beyond the stated accounting numbers to draw insight that might give them an edge in analyzing a company and its stock.

* * *

The goal with all our accounting adjustments is to arrive at numbers that best reflect true economic reality. We'll increase earnings if depreciation charges are overstated, for example, which is often the case in countries where the tax code tends to govern reporting decisions. We'll decrease earnings if depreciation charges are understated, as often happens in countries like the United States where earnings per share and/or share prices matter greatly to the compensation of the top executives. We look at everything—pension liabilities, environmental liabilities, restructuring charges, etc.—and make adjustments to arrive at the "true" results. Sometimes those adjustments can make something much more attractive than the market seems to recognize.

—*Charles de Lardemelle, International Value Advisers*

We spend a lot of time accounting for the inefficiencies of generally accepted accounting principles, which are most prominent in longer-term assets.

That could be land held on the books at cost, which over time is worth something very different than cost. Any asset that can be depreciated is potentially valued at something materially different than current market value. When a company buys equipment or builds a building, it sets depreciation schedules based on useful lives and other accounting conventions, but those schedules know nothing about the future supply and demand for that equipment, or the occupancy levels and cap rates for that building. Over time as that asset is depreciated, there can be major discrepancies between book value and true market value.

—Ari Levy, Lakeview Investment Group

We primarily focus on understanding the unit economics of the business. In a retailer, for example, we have to understand how one store works: what are the capital requirements and maintenance spending, how does the lease work, how does the cash flow build? This is the way managers in the field think, and we find this approach helps us best understand the drivers of the business.

When we chose to pick a fight with the market—as we call it when we buy something—it's usually because of the work we do at this level. Wall Street is very top down, say, in looking at how much revenue at what overall margin equals how much EBITDA. We work from the bottom up, which we hope helps us understand better than the market how returns on capital can be improved.

Another advantage of knowing the unit economics is that we think it allows us to identify problems early. When we see a deterioration in unit-level returns on capital, that can give us a chance to respond before it's fully reported in the P&L.

—Joe Wolf, RS Investments

Our most important focus is on understanding a business' return on invested capital and, perhaps more importantly, its return on incremental invested capital [ROIC], which I've learned to appreciate more and more over the past 25 years. We scrub the financials to get a reliable picture of the company's historical full-cycle ROIC and want to see it significantly ahead of its weighted average cost of capital, which means the company is creating shareholder value. If a bad acquisition has been written off, for example, we'll evaluate whether some or all of that write-off should be added back to the capital base in assessing the return on capital. We're not just looking backwards, but also want to see that prospective returns— based on our estimates of earnings and the investments necessary to generate those earnings—are going to be attractive.

—Pat English, Fiduciary Management, Inc.

We analyze receivables and inventories to determine changes in each relative to changes in sales. Inventories and receivables increasing faster than sales can be early warning signs of future slowdowns. Inventories building in the right places, like raw materials and work-in-process, can be signs of future strength.

—Robert Olstein, Olstein Capital Management

One exercise we go through on all our most interesting ideas is what we call balance-sheet optimization. It's our term for debt recap. What can management do, fully under its control, with the capital structure to create value? Use Microsoft as an example. It has $60 billion of cash on hand, very little debt and throws off something like $30 billion in free cash flow per year. The equity has been trading at 8x to 10x earnings and the company can issue debt at less than 3.5%, so there's a huge difference between the cost of debt and the cost of equity. As an exercise, what would happen if it went to a net $60 billion debt position? Given the free cash flow, that's still a modest capital structure. They take the $120 billion in cash proceeds and buy back a significant amount of their equity. With a lowered cost of capital and shares outstanding cut in half, if we run that through our cash-flow model – assuming no growth – we come up with a share value in the low- to mid-$40s, versus around $28 today.

We look at this as our downside protection and also as a way to distinguish our analysis. It's difficult to out-predict the Street consistently on Microsoft's growth over the next five years, but very few analysts focus on value creation through the capital structure, so it can provide us with a different perspective on how to value the stock.

—Stephen Goddard, The London Company

The detail matters. It's one thing to say incremental margins are X percent, but we need to show all the detail used on things like pricing and fixed and variable costs to justify why that conclusion is accurate.

—James Crichton, Scout Capital

One reason we can find opportunities is that the market is pretty good at forecasting top-line growth, but then it gets a bit fuzzier as you go from sales growth to what earnings growth is going to be, and then most research gets really fuzzy when it comes to things like how much capital will be needed to support growth, where the capital will come from and how much excess cash will be generated—all of which feeds into ultimate business value.

—*Bill Nygren, Harris Associates*

I think the number one variable in the investing equation that Wall Street overlooks is margin leverage. Most investors focus on leverage from sales growth, which is relatively easy to figure out and everybody looks at that. But in the great organic growth stories, such as Starbucks, Home Depot, Wal-Mart, and Bed Bath & Beyond, a lot of the share price upside has come from these companies increasing operating and net margins as they grow. If you get this type of company early enough in the story, which is what I try to do, you will get a tremendous amount of appreciation from both sales and margin growth. That's the most overlooked source of big money gains I can think of.

—*Arne Alsin, Alsin Capital Management*

A predilection of mine that has caused problems at times is to favor stories or companies that are complicated or esoteric. The classic example for me was Novell, the software company, which provided probably the most painful investing experience we've had during my tenure here. It's a long story, but we bought the stock many years ago because it was very cheap on an enterprise value basis and it had a product, called Network Directory, that I thought was a real game-changer. The problem was that Novell had so discredited itself in the market through previous missteps that the target customers weren't willing to buy anything from them. I was so enamored with Network Directory's product specifications that I missed the forest from the trees on whether they could actually sell it.

—*Brian Barish, Cambiar Investors*

I should point out that we can go too far in our zeal to crunch numbers. We once missed a big run-up in Black & Decker because I docked them for some unfunded pension liabilities that took them something like 2 percent out of our buy range. We loved the company and loved the products and thought they were doing all the right things to turn around their business. So we missed a double by paying so much attention to detail that we missed the big picture.

—*Robert Olstein, Olstein Capital Management*

WHAT COULD GO WRONG?

As they analyze industries, business models and financial statements, value investors, in particular, place considerable emphasis on what can go wrong and the potential impacts those negative turns of event could have. They frequently repeat phrases, such as, "It's important to look down first before looking up," or "We're focused first on return *of* capital rather than return *on* capital." They take seriously the analysis of their mistakes, with the obvious goal of not repeating them. This obsession with the downside reflects a mindset captured nicely by Gotham Capital's Joel Greenblatt, who says, "If you don't lose money, most of the remaining alternatives are good ones!"

* * *

If you look at sports history, the champions have usually been the best defensive teams, not those with the most exciting offenses. I went to school at Michigan State when Woody Hayes was the football coach at Ohio State. Woody's philosophy was that a "three-yards-and-a-cloud-of-dust" offense was all you needed if you played great defense. We lost to him every year.

I've always believed that above-average, long-term performance in the stock market is highly correlated with avoiding serious errors, so I always focus on what can go wrong first. I want to know the downside risk potential before looking at the upside. While it isn't in real life, paranoia can be a virtue in the investment business.

—*Robert Olstein, Olstein Capital Management*

We are big fans of fear, and in investing it is clearly better to be scared than sorry.

—*Seth Klarman, The Baupost Group*

You're a product of your experience, so the fact that I came of age as an investor in the 1970s has basically made me scared of everything. I've found that abject fear and sound analysis can be a very healthy combination for an investor.

—*Susan Byrne, Westwood Management*

The very first thing we do when we start to analyze a company is to ask ourselves how far the stock price would fall if we were wrong. It's not some back-of-the-envelope calculation, but a full assessment looking at liquidation asset values and stressing the business model and valuation levels under any number of bad scenarios. If the downside is more than 30 percent from today's price, it's unlikely we'll invest, regardless of the upside potential. If we can't establish a concrete downside number—which probably means it isn't far from 100 percent—we absolutely won't buy the stock.

Going through this first sets the tone we want to set in our research. Rather than start out looking to convince ourselves why we should buy something, we start out trying to prove why we shouldn't buy it. We try to keep that level of skepticism alive throughout the process.

—*Ragen Stienke, Westwood Management*

We believe in the power of compounding and the simple math is that you can't compound very well if you suffer too much on the downside. I don't understand why people who can go on at length about why this or that company will grow and prosper often spend little time on what can go wrong and the impact it could have on the share price. It's not as if defining the downside is more difficult – it's probably easier than estimating the upside.

—*Tom Perkins, Perkins Investment Management*

Top of mind for us in identifying potential investments is a notion borrowed from Warren Buffett that we call the five-year rule. If we hold a stock and the market closes for five years, will we sleep well at night with it in the portfolio? We find answering that question is a great line of defense against big mistakes. If you'd find yourself needing regular market feedback to be comfortable with your estimate of value, maybe it doesn't really have the margin of safety you think it does.

—*Mitchell Kovitz, Kovitz Investment Group*

We always ask before buying whether we'd be comfortable putting the stock in a lockbox for five years and not touching it. If we're not, we shouldn't buy it. That's not an argument for putting your head in the sand, but we think you need that level of confidence in the business to think most clearly when things go temporarily awry and clients are questioning you.

—_Pat English, Fiduciary Management, Inc._

You can't take a long-term view without confidence that the company's financial condition will allow it to meet out-of-left-field macro or micro challenges. There's an old saying that the balance sheet doesn't matter until it's all that matters, so we want to be ahead of that. That's particularly important in smaller companies, which are generally built on more fragile foundations than big, diversified ones.

We measure leverage fairly broadly by looking at the ratio of assets to stockholders' equity. This allows us to see risk items that might not otherwise show up if we were primarily focused on long-term debt, like higher-than-usual levels of receivables, or bulging inventories, or increasing short-term bank lines of credit that may have a way of turning into more permanent debt. Our general rule of thumb, for non-financials, is to look for a 2:1 ratio of assets to stockholders' equity, which we consider a reasonable margin of safety.

—_Whitney George, Royce & Associates_

If you've looked at tens of thousands of balance sheets, as I have, you know what to look for in each situation. Generally, though, we look at debt-to-equity ratios, liquidity, depreciation rates, accounting practices, pension and healthcare liabilities, and hidden assets and liabilities. The overriding question is if something goes wrong, what's our protection?

—_Ed Wachenheim, Greenhaven Associates_

One [of my more common mistakes] would be ignoring the potential impact of leverage. I know the effect goes both ways, but say you do a sum-of-the-parts analysis and think the assets of a company are worth $100. If the company has $70 of debt, overstating the asset value by only $10 makes the equity value go from

$30 to $20. In the grand scheme of things, being 10 percent off isn't that big a mistake, but when there's heavy leverage, it is.

—Jean-Marie Eveillard, First Eagle Funds

To some extent, balance sheet risk is a character issue for us. The CEO whose company has a great balance sheet probably isn't going to make the big, dumb acquisition that will kill the company. He's probably not the guy throwing $2 million birthday parties for his third wife at company expense. Other investors like the leverage that having debt gives you on the upside, but we generally try to look down before we look up—leverage doesn't look so great from that perspective.

—James Clarke, Clarke Bennitt LLC

Value investors' advantage usually comes from having a time horizon longer than most investors, over which the issues that might be making something cheap either cycle away or are fixed. In companies with strong financial positions, it can take longer than you think for things to work out, but you always get to come back and play another day. If you start with a bad balance sheet, the clock is ticking loudly right out of the chute and you may never get the chance to prove how smart your long-term analysis really is.

—Jay Kaplan, Royce & Associates

One thing we are very conscious of is the degree of leverage in a business. That can be financial leverage, which is reflected on the balance sheet. It can be operational leverage, where you look at how much of the cost base is fixed or variable. It can also be the degree of leverage to a particular industry or geography. In general, I'm uncomfortable with companies that are vulnerable to more than one of those kinds of leverage going against them at the same time. A cyclical business that has a lot of fixed costs, for example, should not have a lot of financial leverage or be too levered to one geography or industry. If things go the wrong way, management has its hands tied in trying to get out of trouble. This is a big reason we rarely find opportunity in more commodity-type businesses.

—David Herro, Harris Associates

What we try to do with each potential investment is mark to market the assets and liabilities that have been reported on the balance sheet using generally accepted accounting principles. The underlying goal is to determine what the company would be worth if the assets were sold and the liabilities were paid off, providing us with a direct assessment of downside protection.

—Matthew Swaim, Advisory Research, Inc.

The most direct influence on my strategy was my time working for Advisory Research, where the first emphasis is on marking assets and liabilities to market and determining the true net asset value supporting any potential investment. But behind that is a great deal of empirical research from people like Graham and Dodd, Roger Ibbotson, and Fama and French showing the long-term outperformance of value strategies focused on smaller-cap companies that trade cheaply versus book value. The idea that as a starting point as an investor you look to pay no more—and ideally a lot less—than what you could realize if you sold all the assets and paid back all the liabilities has always been a powerful concept to me.

—Ari Levy, Lakeview Investment Group

We're probably more focused than the typical equity investor on staying power. Spreadsheets make everything look linear and controlled, but the real world oscillates, overshoots, collapses, and rebounds. A company with operational and financial flexibility—what we mean by staying power—is able to exercise options that are quite valuable at different points in the cycle. Without the firm handle on that flexibility that credit analysis provides, we'd argue you can't fully understand the wealth-creation process as an equity investor.

—Mitchell Julis, Canyon Capital

MBAs learn all about optimizing capital structures, but I've been quite content sticking with companies that have extra-safe balance sheets. I'll trade return on equity for safety any day.

—Jim Roumell, Roumell Asset Management

One general defense against value traps is to by and large avoid product-cycle businesses. You can have faith that Nokia gets its act together in smartphones, or that Motorola returns to prominence in handsets, or that the latest device from Nintendo is a big hit, but we think that's very tricky. For a company caught in the headwind of a business cycle, we can make assumptions about recovery that we consider to be well founded. We believe we're much less able to make similar assumptions about future product cycles.

We're also leery of industries with excess capacity independent of the business cycle. We're being very careful today in the automobile industry, for example, where there's still a lot of excess capacity and stepped-up competition is coming from China and elsewhere in Asia.

—Sarah Ketterer, Causeway Capital

I do tend to stay away from companies overly dependent on raising capital and the good opinion of the securities markets. Mark Twain used to say he was a good writer because he could "remember everything, whether it happened or not." I'm leery of situations where management has too much temptation to report great earnings, whether they really happened or not.

—Thomas Gayner, Markel Corp.

Over the years we have also become very leery, based on experience, of companies that need to raise capital in order to survive and prosper. It's not a good thing to be vulnerable to the whims of the capital markets, which can close rapidly and surprisingly.

—Jeffrey Tannenbaum, Fir Tree Partners

I've learned from experience to avoid acquisition-driven stories during the actual acquisition-growth phase—big problems always come of that.

—Jeffrey Ubben, ValueAct Capital

The biggest mistakes we ever made involved a few investments in highly acquisitive companies that had balance sheet leverage. The big lesson is that when you mix financial risk, in the form of leverage, with operating risk, from having to integrate acquisitions, you compound the overall risk dramatically. If we come across a levered acquisitive company today, we're most likely to short it, hedge it or pass on it.

—Jeffrey Tannenbaum, Fir Tree Partners

We've made mistakes in recent years investing in secularly challenged businesses, including newspapers, yellow-pages publishers, printing companies, and bookstores. The pace of change has accelerated in many of these types of businesses and it's proven challenging for us to stay ahead of that. We've essentially concluded that the simplest way to avoid mistakes in secularly challenged industries is to just not invest in them.

—Eugene Fox, Cardinal Capital

We're very unlikely to make the bet that a secular decline in an industry or that a company just won't be as bad as the market expects. You can make tempting valuation arguments at certain points for businesses with secular headwinds, but modeling the trajectory of the decline is very difficult. In the late 1990s if you were first starting to model the decline in consumer photo film for Kodak, you likely assumed a slow single-digit annual percentage decline over time. That's what happened for a few years, but then it started declining by 20–30–40 percent per year, which had a large impact on profitability. We've also found in these types of companies that the risk of misallocation of capital is high. Management may have a lot of free cash flow at their disposal, they're anxiously looking for ways to grow, and they often end up paying too much for acquisitions when they find them.

—Canon Coleman, Invesco

A bubble is a logical impossibility, when people are investing on a premise that not only won't happen, it can't happen. The tech bubble in 2000 wasn't because stock prices were high, it was because stock prices incorporated the belief that many companies in the same industry were all going to have 20 percent market shares and high margins. That can't happen, so you better recognize it when that's the expectation.

—Murray Stahl, Horizon Asset Management

I can't tell you how many times I heard [during the Internet bubble] "You just don't get it." I'd say things like, "Let's compare Kennametal to Cisco. I buy Kennametal and every year it makes 25 percent more money. Yes, I know the market is telling you it doesn't want to put a high multiple on it, but I still have that money at the end of the year. And I'll have more money at the end of the next year. Why wouldn't I want to get that return?" And then I'd say, "Let's compare that to Cisco. Cisco's market cap is $500 billion. Say you're happy with a 15 percent return, so Cisco needs to make $75 billion for you to be happy. They're making $1 billion. Not in your wildest dream can they get to $75 billion—the size of the industry doesn't support it, nothing supports it." But people would still say, "You just don't get it," and I'd finally say, "You're right, I just don't get it."

—Richard Pzena, Pzena Investment Management

One element we've added to the tail end of our analytical process in recent years is to consider scenarios that could send the stock down 30 percent or more and we would *not* want to add substantially to our position. Common examples would be things like the loss of a giant customer, or market incursions from a powerful competitor. Given the outsized positions we take, we want in a disciplined way to contemplate those scenarios up front and pass on the investment if they're even somewhat likely.

—Kian Ghazi, Hawkshaw Capital

One lesson reinforced by the financial crisis is that if you own common stocks, they will periodically go down 50 percent. We've heard Warren Buffett and Charlie Munger talk about that and I've reminded my clients of it from time to time, but I'd have to say it wasn't particularly top-of-mind before the trouble hit. When making bets on what will happen, it's very important to consider all that can happen.

—Chuck Akre, Akre Capital Management

It's hard to get away from truisms and clichés, but things that appear too good to be true—investments or otherwise—usually are.

—Thomas Gayner, Markel Corp.

FROM THE TOP

While they won't always admit it, most investors hold a special place in their hearts for successful and honest corporate managers. That's primarily driven by the significant role strong management can play in increasing share value—the surest way into an investor's heart—but it also reflects respect for the difficult job top managers have. As The Fairholme Fund's Bruce Berkowitz says of the best CEOs: "These are people who are great operators and managers, with excellent people skills—not qualities value investors are generally known for."

Investors similarly hold a special enmity for corrupt or inept management, who waste shareholders money, line their own pockets at the expense of the company's true owners or otherwise breach the trust put in them. "Investors face a variety of risks, which we can more or less address in how we conduct our analysis and make our investment choices," says Thomas Russo of Gardner Russo & Gardner. "But the risk that can really set you back— and that is more difficult to control—is if you have a management that takes these great cash flows and wastes them or expropriates them more for their own benefit than for the benefit of the company. That, I think, is the biggest risk public equity owners face."

Researching people may be one of the more difficult tasks investors face, requiring more subjective judgment than needed when parsing a balance sheet, for instance. While some top investors downplay the importance they put on assessing management capability, a greater number spend considerable time and use a variety of methods to learn about top managers' track records, their skills, their thought processes, and their motivations.

How Important Is Management?

Warren Buffett has famously noted when talking about management that, "I try to buy stock in businesses that are so wonderful that an idiot can run them. Because sooner or later, one will." This says more about Buffett's emphasis on business quality and sustainability than his disinterest in top managers' talent. In fact, his own management style in running Berkshire Hathaway puts primary emphasis on identifying first-class managers to run his businesses and getting out of their way in letting them do it. This emphasis on knowing as much as possible about top managers' skills, aspirations, and motivations in running their companies is widely shared among the best investors.

* * *

Making judgments about management is important to us and something I think value managers tend to underweight. You can analyze something statistically, but if you expect to own it for 10 years, management is going to make thousands of decisions you can't predict and may never even know about, which collectively make earnings compound at a rate more or less than they would have otherwise. Those things can add up over time to the difference between a great performer and an also-ran.

—Boykin Curry, Eagle Capital

Julian Robertson [of Tiger Management] was maniacal on the importance of management: "Have you done your work on management?" Yes, sir. "Where did the CFO go to college?" Umm, umm. "I thought you did your work?" He wanted you to know everything there was to know about the people running the companies you invested in.

—Lee Ainslie, Maverick Capital

We've looked carefully at why we so often sell investments too early. People tend to give you a pass on that, saying you invested in the safest part of the profit cycle. But I have to say, people have made a lot of money buying stocks from me. Over an investment career, that's not a good thing. What I discovered is that the investments that have done much better than I expected—after I sold—are consistently those in superior businesses and/or with superior managements. That's why we now spend so much time analyzing management's prior actions and their results in creating shareholder value.

—Ken Shubin Stein, Spencer Capital

I'm at a stage in my career where I'd say human behavior is the most important determinant of a business's long-term success. I don't care how smart an analyst you are, you can't really know what's going on inside a business. We want to invest not only in highly capable managers, but also those with clear track records of integrity and acting in shareholders' best interest.

—Chuck Akre, Akre Capital Management

Our entire investment team has had training in interview techniques and lie detection. I don't think you can spend too much effort trying to understand the quality of management—at the end of the day, it's the most important investment criterion. I've learned over time that great management teams deliver positive surprises and bad ones deliver negative surprises.

What's important? Integrity, intelligence, competitive drive and a proven desire to create value for all shareholders. We just find the odds of success to be too low in situations where we have to fight to get management to work on our behalf. We'd much rather work as partners.

—Lee Ainslie, Maverick Capital

The importance we put on management really depends on the type of investment we're making. If a company is underearning against its industry or historical levels and the challenge is to get things back to normal, my perspective is that if current management isn't up to the challenge, a new one will be. But in a situation where the business is growing and management's ability to reinvest capital is critical to the thesis, knowing and believing in management is very important.

—Alan Fournier, Pennant Capital

We sometimes buy companies with bad management, if that fact is more than accounted for in the price. At a cheap enough price on a decent business, I'm willing to ride out any problems until somebody, if not current management, figures out how to turn things around.

—Robert Olstein, Olstein Capital Management

Handicapping the Jockeys

As anyone who has ever been in a hiring position knows, even the most rigorous and reasoned selection process can result in situations in which only days after a new employee's arrival you recognize that the hire was a mistake. Such mistakes in assessing a CEO can be particularly costly for an investor. So it's no surprise that top money managers have clear and detailed views on what they want to know about management and exactly how they will go about finding it out.

*   *   *

We only want to invest in management teams with equal measures of talent and integrity, because one without the other is worthless. The talent part largely speaks for itself through an objective look at performance, especially over time. Integrity is a bit harder to judge, but it's one of those things that you know when you see. Think about how you decided whom you were going to marry. You spent lots of time together. You met her family. You met her friends. You learned what she cared about and her basic value structure. We do the same types of things to get to know management of the companies we invest in. It's imperfect, but to our way of thinking nothing is more important.

—*Thomas Gayner, Markel Corp.*

We haven't tried to evaluate, before they have a record, who will be the superstar managers. Instead, we find people who have batted .350 for 10 to 50 years. We just assume we won't screw it up by hiring them. We take people who play the game very well and allow them to play.

—*Warren Buffett, 2005 Berkshire Hathaway Annual Meeting*

One key benefit of experience is that we've heard it all from management teams over the years and have developed a pretty refined sense of what's important and what to look for. We want to hear from management why the company has historically been successful and how in the current competitive environment they expect it to remain so. We want to understand how they make decisions, both to see if there's a clear discipline and to assess whether they're focused on building long-term shareholder value. We want to hear their goals and judge whether they're realistic. When the new CEO of a steady grower all of the sudden wants to double revenues in two years, watch out.

—*Whitney George, Royce & Associates*

What are we looking for in leadership? Intellectual honesty is probably first. I want the person who is going to address the elephant in the room. It drives me crazy when you meet with management and there are real issues and they act like they aren't there.

Also important is a contrarian bent, a confidence to go against the prevailing trend. You generally don't want people who are saying this is what we should do because this is what others are doing. You want people who are spending when others are not, and taking chits off the table when everybody else is putting them on.

—Jeffrey Ubben, ValueAct Capital

We tell management that the idea is not for them to get investors to buy their stock, but to give them reasons never to sell it. When they get that, we're interested.

—James Rooney, Avenir Corp.

It's certainly not an exact science, but we want to be convinced the people running the company are knowledgeable, capable, trustworthy and energetic. If times are tough we want them to be upfront about it, and if times are good we want them to always be looking around the next corner for trouble. We believe getting to know management over time builds a rapport that allows us to pick up subtle clues about the company's prospects that others are likely to miss.

—Scott Hood, First Wilshire Securities

In addition to the capacity to invest behind growth, it's equally vital in our companies that corporate leadership has the will to do so even when such investments burden current reported profits. Jean-Marie Eveillard used to talk about the importance for investors to have the "capacity to suffer," and I'd argue that same capacity to accept short-term pain for long-term gain is critical in management. The market often doesn't like any burden on reported profits, so adequate levels of investment often invite scorn and ridicule that leaders have to be able and willing to endure.

—Thomas Russo, Gardner Russo & Gardner

Access to management is very important to us. Our starting point is usually disappointment and decimated stock prices, so we need to understand fully what the problems are, how they arose, whether management recognizes them, what they're doing to fix them, and how consistently the fixes are being applied. All of that requires regular interaction with management. We don't at all consider it a one-way conversation—we have ideas for what they should be doing and think a real back-and-forth dialogue better brings out their true intentions.

—Andrew Jones, North Star Partners

If I've concluded there's an issue that can be solved, I then want to know management's plan to solve it. If there's a lot of orchestration involved, meaning they can't accomplish much in the next year or two despite their willingness, that's all the better. That means management can and will do things to ameliorate the situation, but the market won't care because the results are still two, three, or four years out.

—Murray Stahl, Horizon Asset Management

We're putting increased importance on our senior portfolio managers being fully engaged in the ongoing dialog with management. That's not something to delegate and then read a report on. I have to be visiting people face to face, attending conferences, and sitting in on the conference calls. Successful investing, especially during times of stress, requires conviction, which is hard to truly have unless you're really out there yourself.

—John Rogers, Ariel Investments

Our models don't just regurgitate what the company says. When we visit a company, we have little interest in what they think they're going to earn next quarter or next year. We're more focused on understanding their business, how they operate, how they view the world. I think the companies appreciate that.

—Mario Cibelli, Marathon Partners

Spending time with management isn't important in the early stages of the research process. We'd rather analyze the company, its opportunities and issues, and how it has allocated capital in the past, without first being fed the party line. When we do meet with management, it should be an educated discussion between two knowledgeable parties.

—Charles de Vaulx, International Value Advisers

We obviously prefer to invest with good management than not, but our assessment there isn't central to our process. We fully develop our investment thesis before we meet with management and then look to confirm whether their ideas for creating value are aligned with ours. If they aren't, we're unlikely to buy in the hope that they or their replacements eventually come around. Our experience is that you can wait a very long time for that to happen.

—Ragen Stienke, Westwood Management

I think I've been in the top five percent of my age cohort almost all my adult life in understanding the power of incentives, and yet I've always underestimated that power.

—Charlie Munger, Poor Charlie's Almanack

The first thing I do [in researching a company] is look at the proxy for the annual meeting. I want to see what management has done before, how reasonable compensation arrangements are, who's on the board of directors and what their backgrounds are. Red flags include things like somebody's son-in-law being on the payroll, other related-party transactions, compensation systems that aren't adequately performance-related and board seats occupied by the company's lawyer and CPA.

What's good is management with a pedigree of accomplishment in well-run companies where they may have learned something. When base salaries are reasonable and the preponderance of executive compensation is long-term and performance-driven.

—David Nierenberg, D3 Family Funds

Character today is best judged in the proxy statement—what do they pay themselves and how? Is their financial self-interest truly aligned with mine as a shareholder? I have absolutely no problem with the people running huge, complicated, global businesses making a lot of money. The big problem we have now is that you're seeing a lot of superstar compensation for only minor-league performance.

—Thomas Gayner, Markel Corp.

I don't think you can overstate how careful we have to be about the incentives of people who make decisions that affect us or who give us advice. When you see conflicts of interest, it's a very good indicator that something is going to go very wrong, very soon. One of the best remedies here is transparency—but it only helps if people actually care about the conflicts of interest that might be exposed.

—Dan Ariely, Duke University

The ideal turnaround CEO is in the first-time CEO, between the ages of 48 and 52. They have 25 to 30 years of experience, but have never had a number one spot. They're seeking out a challenge, have everything to prove, and—while they've surely done very well—probably haven't yet had the huge payday, which they badly want.

The CEOs I invest in attract the best talent and have that magic combination of creativity and business acumen. That's who you want to align yourself with in this business—or in any business, for that matter.

—Lloyd Khaner, Khaner Capital

We're looking for managers who have demonstrated they are killers at business execution, and who have a history of always acting in the best interests of all shareholders. I'm not interested, for example, in CEOs who appear personally greedy. I frequently ask CEOs how they measure success. They often speak about meeting the needs of their various constituencies, including shareholders, employees, customers, and the community. Many have said they measure their success by the rise in the share price. The closer they get to saying they measure success by growth in the company's real economic value per share, the more interested I am.

—Chuck Akre, Akre Capital Management

The historical record on how management allocates capital—acquisitions, divestitures, buying and selling of shares, etc.—is ultimately most important to shareholder value, but we also pay attention to the level of management and director share ownership and whether they're buying or selling. We mean real share ownership, not just options. It's rare to see excellent capital allocation without significant share ownership.

—Clyde McGregor, Harris Associates

If I was stuck on a desert island and had to make a decision on management talent, I'd chose a summary of past returns on capital over a cell phone to call people.

—Jeffrey Bronchick, Reed, Conner & Birdwell

Because we're looking for companies generating substantial free cash flow, we put a significant premium on managers who are first-rate capital allocators and who have our interests at heart. If we find a great business, the only way it becomes a great investment is if management directs the marginal dollar of free cash flow to its highest-return purpose. That's how intrinsic value gets compounded over long periods of time.

—James Rooney, Avenir Corp.

The most important aspect of analyzing management is how well they've invested cash in the past, not what they say they are going to do. Because we typically own companies generating a lot of free cash flow, we're in trouble if management doesn't allocate that cash wisely.

—Donald Yacktman, Yacktman Asset Management

If the stocks we own are as beaten down as we think they are, we better see management and the board acting on the same premise.

—Staley Cates, Southeastern Asset Management

We think management's reinvestment acumen is something Wall Street doesn't adequately value. Most analysts are capable of developing linear earnings models, multiples, and price targets, but they're very likely to miss the extent to which smart capital allocation can compound value over a 5- or 10-year period.

—Peter Keefe, Avenir Corp.

There are five ways for company management to spend money: dividends, paying down debt, internal investment, acquisitions, and share repurchases. When we see excess cash on a balance sheet we don't go in with a knee-jerk response like, "You better buy back your stock," because that's limiting and can be stupid if done at the wrong time or for the wrong reasons. We focus on whether they have clear disciplines and processes for determining which of those five things they choose at any given time, and whether it makes sense in the context of the growth/return tradeoff. It's amazing how often companies say, "We like a balance of each," which is meaningless. Others say, "We buy back enough shares to offset the dilution of our stock-option grants." This betrays a fundamental misunderstanding of financial management. How the shares were issued is irrelevant—you first have to know if the repurchase is attractive in the context of all potential uses of the capital. We have what we consider a best-practice model for making these decisions, which we make a point to communicate early and often.

—Ralph Whitworth, Relational Investors

The preference by many investors for dividends is understandable, given that it's a value-agnostic way to return capital and it dummy-proofs the allocation of capital. If you look at corporate share-repurchase activity over the past 10 years, it was very high in 2006 and 2007, and very low in 2008 and 2009. That's the opposite of what it should have been. So I get the argument, "Give me the money and I'll allocate it myself," but smart corporate capital allocators can and should create value by using the money to buy back shares at a discount. If you owned 50 percent of a business with a partner and he offered to sell you his stock at half what you thought it was worth, you'd do that in a second. Since you have the best information on your own company, there's value to create in buying back shares in such situations.

—Brad Singer, ValueAct Capital

The most important discussion we have with management is when we ask how they allocate capital. You can usually pick out the empire builders with that question alone—they tend to have a hard time zeroing in on a concrete answer. The best managers can usually say clearly and with confidence where they see the highest return-on-invested-capital opportunities and what they expect those returns to be. They also are typically smart about buying back their shares—not just on some systematic basis, but opportunistically when they believe the shares are cheap.

—Robert Williamson, Williamson McAree Investment Partners

Probably the most important part of our discipline is keeping in constant touch with management. My assistant gives me an updated list of every company I haven't spoken with in five weeks and I just dial them up: "Hi John, this is Candy Weir, I'm curious whether the retail traffic we spoke about last month has picked up." Or, "We've been working on your numbers and believe you can do a 20 percent gross margin this year. What do you think about that?" Or, more important recently, "I see you have a debt issue coming due in May 2010, what are your plans to deal with that?" We take copious notes and transcribe our conversations, so that the four analysts I have cranking out earnings models keep a running record of what we've learned and incorporate it into the models, with my input.

I always tell people I'm not looking for inside information, just for insight into how they run their business. If I'm investing at least $10 to $20 million in their company, I'm not really doing my job if I'm just reading press releases. There are always ways to ask questions of management that provide you with some insight into whether the assumptions you're making are the right ones. We either eventually get enough information to be comfortable or we don't.

—Candace Weir, Paradigm Capital

We don't ascribe to the view you shouldn't meet with management to avoid being "sold." A personal connection gives us a better understanding of what's going on, allows us to judge management more directly and even can give us some influence—all of which we consider necessary to invest with conviction.

—Randall Abramson, Trapeze Asset Management

My style is to meet with management each quarter and basically ask the same questions. There can be good reasons for different answers, but I want to see a consistency of answers. Also critical is a passion for the business—a will to win—which you can only judge by sitting across the desk.

—Thomas Brown, Second Curve Capital

Red Flags

Few things are as frustrating for an investor as the sense of being misled by management and subsequently caught off guard by what appears to be value-destroying behavior. As a result, top investors can be a skeptical lot when dealing with management and are particularly sensitive to red flags that may signal management's propensity for non-shareholder-friendly behavior.

* * *

I started my career doing criminal defense work and learned a lot from having my clients lie to me and having to see through that. That's been invaluable in dealing with corporate America.

—*Edward Studzinski, Harris Associates*

There's just a huge amount of skill in exposition. Part of being a wise person is resisting the other person's expository—to know nonsense when you see it. If you're like me, you can conceal your contempt for the person even as they speak.

—*Charlie Munger, 2006 Wesco Annual Meeting*

When I started in research, I had one of the worst character traits an investor can have—I was a "believer." I was too often seduced by charismatic CEOs and by concept stocks, where the product or service made a lot of sense but there turned out to be cost, competitive or other reasons it would never succeed. I learned the hard way to be a skeptic about management's—and my own—ability to forecast with precision well into the future.

—*François Parenteau, Defiance Capital*

Meetings [with management] tend to be promotional and I'm a sucker for a charismatic CEO. Early in my career I met with Dave Thomas, the founder and CEO of Wendy's. He was an incredibly nice guy and he told me over lunch all about this pita-sandwich concept they were rolling out. I came back to my portfolio manager and said, "You have to buy Wendy's, this pita thing is going to be big." This was in 1996 or 1997 and the launch was a flop. That's one of the last times I went to meet management.

We do develop an in-depth list of questions for management as part of our research, focused on getting direct answers that help us understand the mechanics and personality of the business. I also find earnings-call transcripts quite useful, particularly the Q&A

sections. Reading a lot of them, across an industry and over time, can give you a decent sense of what's really going on.

—_Eric Cinnamond, Intrepid Capital_

One acid test I use is simply whether in talking about their business and the external environment in which they operate, are they describing reality as I perceive it? There's surprisingly often a disconnect there, where they either aren't owning up to potential missteps or recognizing external challenges. When that happens, you just cannot give them your capital to manage.

—_Matthew Berler, Osterweis Capital Management_

Several years ago I made an investment in Cannondale, the bike company. I'm a cyclist, so I knew and liked the product. I went to visit the company around the time they had decided they needed to diversify by manufacturing all-terrain vehicles (ATVs). The CEO then was a pilot, as am I, so I find myself with him flying the company's plane to visit the new ATV plant. I test-ride the ATVs and fall in love with the product. I was so impressed by everything that I wasn't as careful as I should have been in analyzing whether getting into the ATV business was even a good idea. It wasn't. Not long thereafter the company ended up being taken private, the CEO got kicked out and the equity ended up being worthless. I tell that story because it's always important to remember the risk that your judgment can be compromised when you get too close to management.

—_François Parenteau, Defiance Capital_

I've been fooled many times by being too impressed by executives who are articulate and have done well in the past. I've learned to be humble about my own opinions and rely more on the opinions of people who aren't biased and have known the management personally or professionally for a long time.

—_Ed Wachenheim, Greenhaven Associates_

We look for certain behavior patterns in management that are consistent with an efficient and prudent guardianship of our assets. If we visit a fan manufacturer in Texas and the CEO meets us at the airport in his Lexus, spends five hours with us, and then takes us out to an expensive restaurant and buys $300 bottles of wine, that is suggestive of somebody who isn't as prudent as we would like.

We try to meet management of all the companies we own, but I must say that over the years I've become more skeptical and less believing of people. I don't really want to know or like these people any more than I need to. We generally think it's more interesting to talk to industry salespeople, ex-salespeople, and customers of the company's products to truly understand what's going on.

—Carlo Cannell, Cannell Capital

One red flag is when management sits down with us and right off asks, "What do you think is wrong with our share price?" Any implicit or explicit focus on the share price rather than the business is a bad sign. This may sound funny coming from an investor, but we also don't like to see managements spending an inordinate amount of time at investor conferences. The value-add to the business is likely to be much higher by spending the time with customers and their own employees.

We're also not fans of the lavish executive office suite. It's not their money. We basically want the capital we as shareholders have entrusted to management to be treated with as much respect as we treat the capital that has been entrusted to us.

—Edward Studzinski, Harris Associates

We care a lot more about what management is doing, which is very well documented, than what they are saying. I can learn everything I need to know about management by looking at the numbers. I can see how conservative they are. I can compare three years of shareholder letters and see if they are discussing problems openly and addressing them. If a company isn't discussing any problems, I don't believe what they're saying. I can see if disclosure is complete and easy to understand. If I have to call to get something important explained, there's something wrong.

I have yet to hear a management team warn of an existing problem, that if not resolved would result in a dramatic drop in the share price. Given that that's exactly what I most care about, I better do a lot more than listen to management to form my opinions.

—Robert Olstein, Olstein Capital Management

Management is clearly a potential resource, but you always have to consider the source—it can be like asking a bartender if you need a drink or a barber if you need a haircut.

—*Carlo Cannell, Cannell Capital*

It comes down to doing business with people you trust. We pay careful attention to all management communication. Does the CEO write the shareholder letter himself or herself? Do they tell you when they've been right and when they've been wrong? Do they talk about what's difficult about the business? Do they articulate how they allocate free cash flow, and do so with an owner mentality? Are the key benchmarks consistent? We worry about companies that one year focus you on adjusted net operating EPS, then the next year on EBITDA margin and the year after that on something else.

—*Adam Weiss, Scout Capital*

We put a lot of emphasis on how management communicates. All shareholders are entitled to candid, timely communication from management and when it's lacking, it's pretty obvious. You can be two-thirds of the way through a shareholder letter and it may be so full of consultant-speak that you have no idea what company it is or what industry it's in. That leads us to wonder whether management is really thinking about shareholders as owners of the business, who deserve clear and complete information so they can make important decisions as owners.

We're also leery of mission statements that get sidetracked talking about various stakeholders and obligations a company has to the community. Those things are important, but only in the context of maximizing the long-term business value. If you don't treat employees fairly, you're not going to have the labor force you need to maximize business value. If you don't treat customers fairly, you can't maximize business value. We get concerned when those types of things are laid out as independent objectives rather than just part of what management should do to build long-term value.

How management communicates about mistakes is very important. No one is mistake-free—as investment managers, about 40 percent of the stocks we buy end up underperforming the market—and I'd be concerned about any company where shareholder communication doesn't include a candid assessment of mistakes.

—Bill Nygren, Harris Associates

I'm particularly averse to the gobbledygook that passes as communication for some managers. Are they thinking clearly and logically about problems, or just repeating buzzwords?

—John Osterweis, Osterweis Capital Management

We hope to add some value is in assessing the coherence of management's strategy, how they're making capital allocation decisions, where they're putting specific emphasis and how they're measuring success. An inability or unwillingness to articulate all that is a red flag, as is a focus on the ends rather than the means. You want to be confident that decisions are being made out of the good analysis of a set of probabilistic outcomes, not hope or ambition.

—Brad Singer, ValueAct Capital

Some of my biggest drubbings have come from not responding quickly to inconsistencies in what management is saying over time or in different forums. Changing stories are a huge red flag.

—Robert Lietzow, Lakeway Capital

Most turnarounds involve making tough decisions about the portfolio of businesses. We spend a lot of time looking at each business within a company and how we think its value can be maximized. We're suspicious of management saying they can fix everything.

—Lloyd Khaner, Khaner Capital

I have made the point in the past with Coca-Cola about the danger of having management that knows the business side cold but doesn't understand the product and its relationship to consumers. The best managers bring both skill sets to the table.

—Morris Mark, Mark Asset Management

The hardest thing is to find management that actually objectively behaves in shareholders' interest as opposed to their own long-term interest. It's not what they say, it's what they actually do. A lot of people tell a good story on shareholder value, but their behavior belies that. Take SPX Corp., the industrial company that came out with this elaborate description on how they were focused on EVA [Economic Value Added] . . . until they didn't hit their targets and then the board changed the criteria and gave management their bonuses anyway, saying "it wasn't their fault, the economy was bad, why should they get penalized for that?" So you're looking for managements and boards that actually act in shareholders' interest, and there aren't many of them.

—Bill Miller, Legg Mason Funds

Whether we're investing in New York, Zurich, or Kuala Lumpur, we do everything we can to insure that the people to whom we've entrusted our capital wake up in the morning focused on how to make money for all shareholders and that they're good at it. A lot of that is just seeing what they've accomplished and how they've behaved in the past, but their incentives are also critical. You want to see management own real equity in the business, without the "heads I win, tails I win bigger" types of compensation packages that have been handed out over the years.

—David Winters, Wintergreen Fund

There is no way to make a good deal with a bad person. It's the character of the people you go into business with that will fundamentally determine your investment returns and your ability to sleep well and eat well in the meantime. If you're not comfortable with the people involved because of their prior conduct and how they've treated shareholders, you're probably not going to be comfortable with your investment results. I take it to heart and use it as a screen for potential investments.

—Thomas Russo, Gardner Russo & Gardner

When a company has integrity issues, there's no firm ground. If somebody is willing to do the medium-size crime you know about, there's no particular reason they wouldn't have done the bigger crime you haven't found out about yet.

—Wally Weitz, Weitz Funds

There's really no substitute for direct communication—looking people in the eye, gauging the tone of their voice, trying to read the level of energy and enthusiasm they have. We spoke not long ago with management of one company and asked if they were still on target with their profitability goals and the answer started, "Welll, yeahhhh . . . .", which clearly didn't sound good.

—*Amelia Weir, Paradigm Capital*

CATALYSTS

Almost as important as identifying the extent to which a stock is undervalued is assessing what can make that misjudgment by the market go away. After all, the proverbial "50-cent-dollar" that value investors seek will produce a very different investment result if the gap between price and value closes within one year, or if it takes 10 years. For that reason, most—but not all—successful investors put emphasis in their analysis on the potential catalysts that can trigger an enhanced market appreciation for a company's business and its shares.

* * *

Our strategy goes under the general category of event-driven. We're value investors looking for mispriced securities—at any level of the capital structure—with specific catalysts that should help trigger a narrowing of the gap between the market price and our estimate of intrinsic value.

The basic idea, which has probably been best articulated by Seth Klarman, is that if your investment is more predicated on an event occurring, that transfers risk away from the vagaries of the market to the specifics of the particular investment. That doesn't mean you'll always make a lot of money if you're right about the event, but it helps clarify the analysis and allows you to arrive at firm conclusions.

We do have traditional investments based more on a broad-based analysis of the business, but even in those we like to have specific catalysts to track. In the case of Wal-Mart, for example, we were focused mostly on the company slowing down expansion—reducing spending on new stores and acquisitions and giving that money back to shareholders. It can be a bit fuzzy to determine exactly when an event like that has "occurred," but our judgment that it has occurred is usually what starts us down the road to selling.

—Timothy Mullen, VNBTrust

Since the crisis there are fewer fundamental long-term investors in the market. It's bots, or traders, playing a game on the next quarter's earnings, or people making thematic macro bets. As a result, the market is assigning less value to the durability and consistent growth of cash flow, which is why quality stocks have increasingly become cheap. For most of your readers investing in a high-quality company that is 30 percent undervalued and can compound value at 15 percent over a three-year time horizon is a great investment, but for your typical trader it's more like kissing your sister.

That has also caused a change in the market dynamic. The playbook for fundamental investors has been to value businesses based on expectations for growth and profitability and buy them when that value is much higher than the current stock price. There were guardrails in the form of lots of other investors doing the same thing that kept valuations in check while you were patiently waiting to be proven right. Without enough of those types of investors, however, the guardrails have been blown out. That means the quality-value stock working through some negative fundamental development can trade way through what you could imagine on the downside, and the low-quality stock still doing okay can blast way beyond your assumption of economic fair value on the upside.

You could say, "Gee, doesn't that just create greater opportunity?" Yes, but it can extend the time it takes to get paid and creates much more risk to shorter-term performance. That's been a challenge for us. We've had to ask ourselves if our job as a hedge-fund manager is to figure out the value of businesses, or to figure out where they trade in a year. I know we're good at the former. The latter is difficult and requires a different skill set in judging things like near-term earnings versus expectations and changes in investor perceptions.

On the long side, we're paying more attention than before to the presence of things that can create a change in investor perception. We're then overweighting the stocks with the quality value we've always emphasized, but where we also have the highest confidence we'll see a change in investor perception over the next 18 months.

Those highest-conviction ideas will be 4 to 8 percent positions, while the good business with a cheap stock but we have no idea when it works, that's probably a 2 percent position. Too high a weighting of those latter types of positions can make you really underperform for longer than we or are investors are comfortable.

—Ricky Sandler, Eminence Capital

The catalysts we look for can be company-specific or more macro. It could be any number of things—new management, a reorganization, buying back stock, a new product launch, the resolution of litigation. It could also be a call on a specific sector turning up.

We're just trying to push back against the natural propensity of value investors to be early—there's just no way around the fact that if you're way too early, you're wrong.

—William Nasgovitz, Heartland Advisors

We're generally of the school that "a bargain that stays a bargain is not a bargain." We may buy something just because it's cheap, but it's very unlikely to be a core position without a data point or two—like earnings exceeding expectations or an asset sale—that we think should move the stock.

—Curtis Macnguyen, Ivory Capital

We're selecting for companies that are entering episodes of their public lives in which they're going to be transformed. We do both the fundamental valuation work as well as an analysis of the probabilities of successful, value-unlocking outcomes. We tend not to focus on short-term opportunities in which we may have no real edge, or on very long-term, buy-and- hold-forever investment themes. There's a medium term where the risk/reward can be quite high if we stick to our value-plus-catalyst discipline.

—Gary Claar, JANA Partners

Given our emphasis on improving valuations, catalysts tend to be important us. The catalysts can be things like a successful new-product introduction, the onset of a new product cycle, a change in senior management, the divestiture of an underperforming division, or simply better financial performance. There must be identifiable events that would cause rational expectations for the business to improve, resulting in a higher valuation.

—Brian Barish, Cambiar Investors

We think it's difficult to have a reliable view of events beyond 12 to 18 months, so we focus on specific investment catalysts that can move stocks toward their warranted target prices over the next 12 to 18 months. We've identified five primary catalysts—management, restructuring, problem fixing, new products, and pricing flexibility—that we believe can consistently take advantage of pockets of inefficiency in the market. Larger-cap stocks are usually priced relatively efficiently, but we've found this focus on catalysts helps us identify when they aren't.

—Jerry Senser, Institutional Capital LLC

With large caps, regression to the mean seems to work often enough after things have gone bad, but in small caps we believe identifiable catalysts—like management changes, restructurings, or maybe industry consolidation—increase the odds of winning.

—Preston Athey, T. Rowe Price

For lower-quality businesses, we put more emphasis on whether there is a catalyst or not. If something is cheap but the business dynamics aren't great, time can be your enemy unless you see a clear catalyst for value to be recognized.

—Jeffrey Tannenbaum, Fir Tree Partners

We sometimes make a distinction here between blue-chip companies and less-than-blue-chip companies. For example, our purchases of Google and Johnson & Johnson were probably a bit catalyst-light and had more to do with our view that negative perceptions of each would turn out not to be as negative or long-lasting as the market seemed to fear. With somewhat lesser-quality names, we typically want more definition around the catalyst or inflection point. It's one thing to sit awhile with J&J in your portfolio than it is some lesser-quality company.

—John Osterweis, Osterweis Capital Management

If there's a disparity between price and value, we like to know when that might close up so we can figure out our expected rate of return. Having said that, some situations are just out-of-favor and cheap and there is no catalyst other than a change in people's perceptions, which usually happens within two or three years. When we find a cheap situation with no catalyst, we'll likely want it to be available at a lower price than one that does have a catalyst.

—Joel Greenblatt, Gotham Capital

In general we're not obsessed with seeing near-term catalysts—if those are clear, the stock is probably 30 percent higher. But it obviously matters when things return to normal, so we judge everything based on an internal rate of return. If we can't reasonably expect a return to normal in both earnings and the multiple paid on those earnings over a period that produces an IRR from today's price of at least 20 percent, we typically consider the risk of it being a value trap too high.

—Lee Atzil, Pennant Capital

We rarely count on the catalysts most people like to talk about; one, because you set yourself up for disappointment if they don't materialize, and two, you can get too caught up in a stock's "story" and be less driven by the numbers.

—Jeff Kautz, Perkins Investment Management

There's the perception that having specific catalysts for all your positions mitigates risk, when in fact we believe the opposite is true. If there's an obvious catalyst, there's an excellent chance that it's at least partially priced into the stock, which increases your risk in the event it never shows up. As long as the potential return in an investment is significant enough, and the potential downside is limited, we're okay with dead money.

—Tucker Golden, Solas Capital

We really don't pay that much attention to why something is undervalued. If we buy companies in which shareholders' capital compounds at a 20 percent rate of return over a reasonable time period and we pay a below-average multiple for it, our investors will do extremely well.

—Chuck Akre, Akre Capital Management

We focus first on good businesses, with high returns on capital, barriers to entry and significant free cash flow generation over a cycle. If you're right about the business, time should be your friend, so catalysts are not important.

—Charles de Vaulx, International Value Advisers

In our experience, it can take a lot longer than for value to be realized than we expect, but that it's taking longer doesn't mean we've made a mistake. If the market hasn't recognized the value we see and the company is continuing to increase its intrinsic value, that's when we'd be buying more.

—Ric Dillon, Diamond Hill Investments

GETTING IT DONE

Sometimes lost in the discussion of the vast quantities of information an investor can look at in researching an investment is an appreciation for the effort, diligence, and creativity required to unearth that information. Knowing what you need to know to make a decision is obviously important, but equally important is that the information you acquire is complete and accurate. This doesn't just happen, and many investors look to distinguish themselves by the breadth and depth of their information-gathering process. How credibly they make that case, and deliver on that premise, is a valuable indicator of how successful they are likely to be.

*   *   *

We're big believers in that Peter Lynch quote, that "the person who turns over the most rocks wins the game." We always say that people who know what they're doing can get 80 percent of the story in no time, just by looking through the financials. But it's that last 20 percent that requires tremendous effort and that is going to set you apart, or not. That's the detective work, the site visits, the channel checks, the background checks, the legal research—all the things that may or may not give you unique insight, but which you have to do well to get any kind of edge.

—Scott Hood, First Wilshire Securities

We take all the computer screening we do very seriously, but that's the easy part. The harder part is going through the public documents, reading call earnings transcripts, and speaking with management and people outside of the company who can shed light on the business—all in an effort to make conclusions about the sustainability of the business and its cash flow. How leveraged is the income statement to ups and downs? Does the company have much control over its pricing? Is there margin upside versus peers or are margins threatened by new competition? Is there technology risk? How does EBITDA cover interest expense in a downturn?

All of this is the hard work of securities research, for which there's no substitute for rolling up your sleeves and going at it. [Company co-founder] Howard Browne was fond of saying, "No one ever learned anything by talking," and we still try to take that to heart in how we approach our research.

—John Spears, Tweedy, Browne Co.

I learned early that you should never cut corners in research, even when you think you can. It's like remembering to bend your knees in tennis.

—Timothy Mullen, VNBTrust

In the field research we do, we're not trying to assess whether sales are going to be up 6 percent rather than 4 percent next quarter, but focus more on things like the quality of the company's products or services relative to the competition, how they conduct themselves, the pricing trends in the industry, and whether there are material shifts going on in market share.

Everyone probably says this, but we just don't think you can underestimate the importance of speaking to not just a few, but a lot of customers, suppliers, competitors, and people in all levels of the company. We're constantly trying to triangulate and confirm what we hear or see elsewhere. If returns on invested capital tell us it's a great business, we also want to hear from customers about why they value the company as a supplier and expect to continue to do so. If the company expects to increase market share, we want to hear directly from competitors why they don't think that will happen. Taking short cuts in due diligence, for whatever seemingly decent reason, is just a recipe for disaster in our view.

—*Robert Williamson, Williamson McAree Investment Partners*

Often there are specific issues central to our thesis that we need to better understand. To own Oracle, for example, we needed to believe that it was integrating its many acquisitions in a more customer-friendly way than just ramming its own products down acquired customers' throats, which was a concern of the Street's. We also had to believe that its maintenance-revenue stream was sustainable, which if so, made it possibly the single most defensive business I've ever looked at. These are the types of things you can only really address in the field and we wouldn't have been comfortable owning the stock in volume without doing so.

—*Ricky Sandler, Eminence Capital*

I want to talk directly to people installing solar panels, or buying and selling a certain kind of shoe, or taking classes at a for-profit college at night. It's one thing to read a sell-side report or go to a conference, but it's another to understand first-hand how decisions are really being made about the products and services sold by companies in which you want to invest. I want to do that type of thing myself rather than read notes from someone two years out of business school.

—*Shawn Kravetz, Esplanade Capital*

I'm still amazed by the things you'll hear or see on a company visit. We visited one company in Florida that made simulators for pilot training and amusement rides and heard all about the long lead time between the start of contract negotiations and product delivery, including nine months or so for manufacturing. Later on in the day we toured the manufacturing facility and of the 12 assembly bays, only two had anything going on. That wasn't a big endorsement of the company's prospects.

—*Scott Hood, First Wilshire Securities*

We want to learn from personal experience. Every spring I give everyone in my firm $500 to open two accounts at local banks and then report back on the experience. I'm a big believer that a company's success is about execution and the hundreds of little things that one company does better than another. We want to understand that for the companies we invest in—is the party line we're hearing actually what's taking place in the branches? In the bad companies, there's an enormous difference.

—Thomas Brown, Second Curve Capital

This is an old story, but a great example of when we did learn something was when Bill Smithburg of Quaker Oats bought Stokely-Van Camp, which owned by Gatorade. We couldn't understand the price he was paying, which seemed completely out of bounds. When we finally got an audience with him, he explained that the economics worked for Quaker to pay 1x revenues for any strong regional brand that it could flow through its national distribution system. It was obvious and simple to him, but we hadn't figured that out. That changed the whole way we looked at branded food companies and led us to invest in Nabisco, which got bought out, General Foods, which also got bought out, and others.

The lesson there is how important it is to get out there are talk to people. If you spend all your time with your models and spreadsheets, you're likely to miss something important. You need to understand how the economics work for the people who are making the actual decisions and when you come across something you didn't know that has broad application, it can be very useful.

—Clyde McGregor, Harris Associates

Peter Lynch's greatest influence, which still pervades Fidelity, is that you pick up the phone and call companies. At the end of the day, if you haven't spoken to a few companies in existing positions or on new ideas, you go home a failure. That's a good discipline—you should spend your day talking to operators, not to Wall Street.

—Jeffrey Ubben, ValueAct Capital

We spend time speaking with competitors, the one group with a vested interest in telling us why our thesis is wrong. Before we bought [used-car retailer] CarMax in 2001, we went through

Sunday newspapers from every market they're in and visited car dealers advertising against them in the paper. We'd describe how CarMax was going to inexorably take market share and the local dealer was eager to argue why that was wrong. I'd much rather hear why our thesis might be wrong at this point than for the market to tell us after we own the stock.

—Boykin Curry, Eagle Capital

One thing we try to do in industry due diligence is to find the "guru." Getting to the truth can really be accelerated by finding the handful of folks who truly understand a business or industry. A deep database of relationships with industry experts is a key value-add to that process.

—Jeffrey Tannenbaum, Fir Tree Partners

Because of digital technology, information flows much faster and in greater volume. That doesn't mean the information is better—misinformation travels faster too—but there's more to digest and synthesize.

—Morris Mark, Mark Asset Management

We work very hard to get as much information as possible, but it's hard to win the information arms race. There are always people who will know things you don't. Investing is about the conclusions you draw from the information you have. Just because someone speaks to seven store managers instead of the five we speak to doesn't mean they'll make a better investment decision. People in industries have as many or more biases than investors do, and often draw circular conclusions—for example, the company is bad because the stock is bad.

We focus on uncovering information that helps us understand the probabilities of what can happen. Beyond that, too many opinions can often confuse things more than help.

—Brian Gaines, Springhouse Capital

We've had bad experiences where we've tried to do scuttlebutt research, such as overweighting anecdotal evidence given to us by someone in the value chain. We've also overweighted a toxic response to the current management team when we shouldn't have.

For us, and for most people, it's very hard not to overvalue information that you think you get from some kind of specialized source. We try to keep that in perspective.

When the investment decision hinges on one or two critical questions, and you can get those questions answered if you make some phone calls, we'll clearly make the calls. But most of our ideas aren't like that.

—Zeke Ashton, Centaur Capital

As the saying goes, the plural of anecdote is not evidence.

—Michael Mauboussin, Legg Mason Funds

I love the intellectual challenge of investing—there are always new questions to try to answer. But it's important to remember that you don't actually have to answer all the questions you ask yourself. It's like being able to take a test in school where you can answer any 10 questions of your choice on a 100-question test. You answer only those you know well and ignore those that are very difficult to answer. That's what investing is all about.

—Murray Stahl, Horizon Asset Management

ORGANIZING PRINCIPLES

While they spend much of their time critiquing how other businesses are run, money managers have their own businesses to run as well. Not surprisingly, they typically have strong views on how best to organize and manage their research and analytical functions. One common decision point is the extent to which research analysts are generalists who look everywhere for ideas, or specialists focused on specific industry sectors. Also frequently addressed is the environment created around the research and analytical process, how team members are selected, and how they're meant to interact.

* * *

We break the world into geographic regions, but within those regions we want our analysts to be generalists looking across all industries. Part of that is so people can apply a broad knowledge of business models, industries and markets to every company they analyze. It also allows people to more naturally gravitate to where the opportunity is right now. If you're a generalist you can more easily ignore banks if they don't look interesting, while the bank expert will inevitably find one bank or another they want to buy. As Charlie Munger says, "To the man with a hammer, everything looks like a nail."

—David Samra, Artisan Partners

We like being generalists. We haven't owned any healthcare for more than a year, but nobody feels like they have to push healthcare ideas, or that their bonus is threatened, because they're the person focused on healthcare. Ideas rise to the top only on their merits.

—Christopher Grisanti, Grisanti Brown & Partners

Given that what we're looking for is clear and has been consistently applied, we can give our analysts a great deal of freedom in identifying and pursuing ideas. They know that if they can't explain why something is at a discount to value, why that value is going to grow, and why we should be comfortable with management, they just don't bring the idea to the table. While what we're looking for is tightly constrained, we don't constrain where analysts can look. If two people want to pursue an idea, regardless of the industry, that's fine. Is it a waste of resources when two people find something interesting, when that probably means it actually is interesting and the two of them working it out together makes it more likely we arrive at the right conclusion?

—Bill Nygren, Harris Associates

We have a total of seven analysts, including myself, and we believe when investment teams have more than 10 people they start to break down. Egos get in the way, people start to specialize, and you just can't have the quality of collective discussion we think is necessary.

—Pat English, Fiduciary Management, Inc.

Our portfolio managers are also analysts, with all coverage responsibility segmented by industry, up and down the market-cap spectrum. There's leverage in bringing what you already know to an incremental new idea. If I'm looking at a small-cap software firm, I should have a good sense of the competitive environment, for example, including what Microsoft, Oracle, and SAP are doing in the area. If I'm looking at Microsoft, I should know its strengths and weaknesses as well as the new technologies it's up against in any given market. A generalist having to learn things like that for the first time may not recognize change and opportunity as quickly.

We're cognizant of the risk that people lose sight of the forest from the trees, so each analyst covers two very different industries. I cover software and machinery. Someone else follows healthcare and energy. This should make us less likely to lock onto one way of thinking and less apt to recommend the best house in a bad neighborhood just because it's where we live.

—Ragen Stienke, Westwood Management

In an ideal world, I'd like to be more selective in the U.S. and take advantage of more opportunities outside the U.S. That will only happen if we have the bottom-up ideas that warrant a place in the portfolio. To increase our chances of finding those, we've changed how we organize our international efforts. I used to think it was more important to have individual sector team members in the same office, so they could more easily learn from each other and compare notes. Now we're putting more people on the ground, closer to the companies they track, in order to improve the quality and frequency of their external relationships.

—Lee Ainslie, Maverick Capital

An extensive knowledge of a business improves your ability to recognize patterns and draw useful insights, a prerequisite to having an investment edge. Beyond that, I'd argue that expertise is critical when things inevitably happen and you either need the conviction to stick with your thesis or the wisdom to recognize that it's changed and react accordingly. Stepping outside of areas we know well just seems too much like dancing through a minefield.

—Shawn Kravetz, Esplanade Capital

If I believed having 10 people rather than 52 would allow us to be more successful, we'd quickly make that transition. But with the specialization of the people we're competing against today, I think it's very difficult to have a meaningful edge without significant depth and expertise. We should know more about every one of the companies in which we invest than any other non-insider. Consistently picking winners and losers requires extremely in-depth knowledge of operating businesses and the industry dynamics. That takes work.

—Lee Ainslie, Maverick Capital

We recently read *Groupthink*, Irving Janis' classic study of how small, cohesive groups of very smart people can make really bad decisions, such as getting deeper into Korea, the Bay of Pigs, and Vietnam. The main point is to make sure you have a culture that questions everything and vets out all the decision alternatives before zeroing in on one of them.

One of the personal insights I gained from the book is the value of playing one's cards a bit closer to the vest early in the decision-making process. I have a habit of speaking my mind all the time, but in the earlier stages of research that can set a direction that I and others may unconsciously anchor on, closing off a fuller exploration of alternatives. The last thing you want to do is shut down people's initiative.

—Adam Weiss, Scout Capital

My analysts are now saying, "I know you're going to hate this, but …". That's a great thing. If my initial reaction is to hate it, so is the market's, and that probably means it's something we should look at more closely.

—Jeffrey Bronchick, Cove Street Capital

There's a virtuous cycle in people having to defend challenges to their ideas. Any gaps in thinking or analysis become clear pretty quickly when smart people ask good, logical questions. You can't be a good value investor without being an independent thinker—you're seeing valuations that the market is not appreciating. But it's critical that you understand why the market isn't seeing the value you do. The back and forth that goes on in the investment process helps you get at that.

—Joel Greenblatt, Gotham Capital

At our Tuesday meeting an analyst will give a short summary of why he believes the idea meets our criteria and then everyone around the table tries to shoot holes in it and prove that he's wrong. You have no friends in that meeting—everyone is trying to prove that you're making a mistake. We're trying to identify as high a percentage of our errors as possible, before we've lost any money on them.

—Bill Nygren, Harris Associates

I refer to our investment committee meetings as "Fight Club," but there's a respectful way of valuing your colleagues while at the same time questioning every word that comes out of their mouths.

—Adam Weiss, Scout Capital

We have three analysts, including myself, and for every idea we pursue in depth, two of us will make the purchase case and one makes the case for selling the stock short. There are behavioral biases that can kick in when you pursue what you think is a good long idea, and by expressly tasking one person with developing what the intelligence community calls the "alternative competing hypothesis," we're looking to minimize the risk of missing something. We want to be clear upfront about what could go wrong, the probabilities attached to those scenarios and the resulting downside to the stock as a result.

—Jeffrey Bronchick, Cove Street Capital

A major risk-management step in our research process is a peer review within our research groups. After an analyst works up an idea he or she presents it to the others in the group, who evaluate and challenge all the downside and upside assumptions being made. While they may not know the specific industry or company, they will likely be quite current on the business models and fundamental drivers of the business. We like to say it's a lot easier to crawl out of hole if you stop digging early—here we're bringing as much collective wisdom to bear as we can to keep us from even picking up the shovel.

—Ragen Stienke, Westwood Management

The risk among any group of investors is that they only pay attention to what they already agree with. That's limiting and dangerous.

—Michael Mauboussin, Legg Mason Funds

Always ask yourself what are the arguments on the other side. It's bad to have an opinion you're proud of if you can't state the arguments for the other side better than your opponents. This is a great mental discipline.

—Charlie Munger, 2006 Wesco Annual Meeting

[Tiger Management founder] Julian Robertson was always adamant about seeking out the opposite point of view and then being completely honest with yourself in deciding whether your analysis overrides that. That's something we try to practice every day.

—Robert Williamson, Williamson McAree Investment Partners

In markets, everyone tends to see the same things, read the same newspapers and get the same data feeds. The only way to arrive at a different answer from everybody else is to organize the data in different ways, or bring to the analytic process things that are not typically present. One research source of ours is a firm in Hong Kong called GaveKal, which has a regular feature they publish called, "What we see and what we don't see." They say. "Here is what we see, namely all the data everybody else sees, but now here's a systematic look at relevant things people are not talking about, what they're not thinking about, what the other side of the issue might be." That's very important.

—Bill Miller, Legg Mason Funds

We pay a lot of attention to dotting our i's and crossing our t's when it comes to the fundamentals of finding opportunities that are "safe, cheap and good," because we think it makes it easier to reframe things in new, flexible ways. One problem with value investors is that they can often become ideologues. But there's a big difference between focusing on the basics and being an ideologue. We've found that you have to constantly challenge your ways of thinking and re-educate yourself to remain successful as an investor.

—Mitchell Julis, Canyon Capital

The last step in our research process is to invite in a Wall Street analyst who is a bear, and they come in and make a pitch why we shouldn't buy this stock. We want to see if the reason they don't like it is if they see a real structural flaw in the business that we didn't pick up on, or if it's just that they don't know what's happening. Most of the time they're negative just because of "no earnings visibility," which is Wall Street language for "I don't really have a clue what's going to happen next."

—*Richard Pzena, Pzena Investment Management*

I guess it was my good fortune to work with several egomaniacs during my career, and I promised myself that when I started my own business that I'd create a much different environment than what I'd experienced. It wasn't going to be all about me and we weren't going to treat people like commodities. We try to have an inclusive environment and treat people well and with great respect.

—*Barry Rosenstein, JANA Partners*

It's important to realize that the brain isn't programmed like a computer, and that every individual can approach problems and issues in a unique way. Even at my age, I try to remain flexible and open to new ideas and ways of approaching things. That keeps me from being a frustrated pedagogue and also allows me to get more from the individual strengths of the people who work for me.

—*Spencer Davidson, General American Investors*

We evaluate ourselves on rolling five-year periods. If a portfolio manager has one great year, it doesn't factor *at all* into how he or she is paid. That could just be a random event. I think it's actually a stretch to say five years is long enough to be relevant, but I realize not everyone has the same time frames.

—*Ric Dillon, Diamond Hill Investments*

I do not hire people I would not want as friends or as neighbors. I work with people who make my life easier. You can't work with people who make your stomach grind.

—*Warren Buffett, 2005 meeting with Wharton students*

I really think that we benefited from starting with good young people, who begat more good young people. We eventually devised testing that all applicants had to take. We still give that test, which takes about three or four hours. It is part aptitude, but also psychological. It sort of emanated from our having a few people over time who just didn't have the firepower to do the job—it's tragic when that happens, because it's not their fault. So we designed these tests to better avoid that.

The test was also designed to show what kind of team player the person was and their competitiveness. I've found that most good money managers are great competitors. I think that all helped us pick good people. Whether it helped as much as having great young people recommending more great young people, I don't know.

—Julian Robertson, Tiger Management

It's important to hire people with diverse experiences and viewpoints, which you don't necessarily get if you just hire straight-A Harvard MBAs. Getting good grades and having courage are not the same thing. Being really smart and having good judgment are not the same thing. No one should be winnowed out so early in life.

—Susan Byrne, Westwood Management

We have in the past hired smart young analysts right out of business school, but have concluded that's not for us. We're looking for people who have been around long enough to know who they are as investors and the type of environment in which they do their best work—they're not still trying different approaches on for size. If you want to maintain a research-driven, collegial and long-term-oriented culture, there's no better way than by only hiring people who share those values.

—Whitney George, Royce & Associates

It's wonderful to be trusted. Some think if we just had more compliance checks and process, virtue would be maximized. At Berkshire Hathaway, we have a subnormal process. We try to operate in a web of seamless trust, deserved trust, and try to be careful whom we let in.

—Charles Munger, 2007 Wesco Annual Meeting

CHAPTER 7

Getting to Yes

A long-ago mentor, in a business other than investing, used to like to make one of his favorite points by describing how he could create the most popular restaurant in New York City. He would hire the best real estate experts to identify the ideal location and then pay whatever it took to acquire the property. He'd spare no expense in hiring world-class architects and designers to build out the space with only the highest-quality materials, fittings and furnishings. He would staff and outfit the kitchen under the direction of chefs who he had poached from the world's finest restaurants by allowing them to name their price to come onboard. Once the doors opened, he'd offer four-course *prix-fixe* menus, including wine, for $9.99 each, with tips and valet parking included. "Voilà, New York's hottest restaurant is born," he'd say.

An extreme example, to be sure, but the point stuck: Business is all about what you pay for what you get. If costs to produce are too high relative to what you're paid—no matter how sublime the product or service—you will ultimately fail.

This same basic principle applies to investing. Through creative and diligent research you may uncover fascinating companies in wonderful industries. Through brilliant and incisive analysis you may see unfolding for a company positive events that mere mortals would miss. But all of that is for naught if you pay too much for a stock relative to what you get. Price obviously matters—the cheaper it is relative to what you believe a company is worth, the better.

This section is about how smart investors conclude whether the price they're paying for a stock is sufficiently cheap relative to the value they believe they will receive through their resulting partial ownership stake in the company. While there are clearly common elements in how investors ascribe value, we've been struck over time by the variety of valuation measures they utilize and how they approach and answer the question, "What's cheap enough?"

CASH (FLOW) IS KING

There are some prevalent themes in how smart investors approach valuation, the primary one being their focus on the future stream of actual cash that the company is expected to generate after taking in all revenues and paying out all expenses.

* * *

It has always made sense to me to rely far more on cash flow than reported earnings. When I was in graduate school, my brother-in-law hired me to do some temporary work at a canning company. One project was to go through a pile of invoices and pull out anything that looked at all like a capital purchase, even for things like tires and other pretty basic recurring expenses. I finally asked why I was doing that and he said the CFO wanted to capitalize anything that remotely looked like capital spending so they could write it off over time.

The lesson in that for me was that a clever accountant can make financial statements say whatever he wants in the short term. That conclusion has only been reinforced over time, especially as the differing tax regimes and accounting conventions you see overseas can make comparisons based on reported net income even more meaningless.

—*David Herro, Harris Associates*

Earnings are basically a negotiated number between management and the auditors, subject to considerable manipulation. Cash flow—earnings before depreciation and amortization and after working-capital changes and either maintenance or total capital spending—is much less subject to manipulation and just a much better measure of corporate profitability.

At the same time, free cash flow is what allows companies to increase the value of the business—from making capital investments, to making acquisitions, to paying down debt, to buying back stock or paying dividends. Companies that produce free cash flow also attract potential buyers, either financial or strategic.

—*John Osterweis, Osterweis Capital Management*

We ask what our expected rate of return would be if we owned the whole business, which is essentially taking pretax free cash flow and dividing it by the current enterprise value. For pretax free cash flow we look at normal earnings before interest, taxes, depreciation and amortization, less maintenance capital spending. In the denominator, we adjust enterprise value by adding contingent liabilities and subtracting any kinds of hidden assets we find. If after all adjustments we can see a mid-teens rate of return, we're very interested.

—Steven Romick, First Pacific Advisors

We've always done very well when we can use sixth-grade math on the back of a postcard to show how inexpensive something is relative to its free cash. Once we start getting more sophisticated— trying to prove something rather than see if we can disprove it by killing the business—we get into trouble.

We're looking to pay 10x free cash flow or less, period. If you find those and you can't kill the business, you should be buying all day long.

—Bruce Berkowitz, Fairholme Capital

We want to see at least a 10 percent free-cash-flow yield and a 6x or less multiple of enterprise value to next year's earnings before interest, taxes, depreciation and amortization [EBITDA]. For enterprise value we use the current market value plus the estimated net debt 12 months out.

Most of the companies in our universe generally live within a range of 6x to 8x EBITDA. The idea is to identify companies having some earnings or other trouble that leave them trading at the low end of the valuation range. If our analysis is right that the difficulties are temporary, we get two boosts: from earnings recovering and from the market reacting to the earnings recovering and moving the multiple to the higher end of the range. We believe that dynamic gives all our core positions a very high probability of at least a 50 percent return within two years.

At the end of the day we're trying to buy companies as if we were buying a $10 million office building across the street. We do our homework on the tenants and the leases in place and make sure it's financed in a way that produces a 10 percent free-cash-flow yield. The idea is to increase equity by paying down debt with the free cash flow and also to benefit from the asset appreciating over time. With stocks, if you focus on companies with around 10 percent free cash flow yields and highly predictable, sustainable franchises, you protect your downside and set yourself up for nice capital appreciation.

—Alexander Roepers, Atlantic Investment Management

Our valuations are based on estimated EBITDA 12 to 18 months out. We don't look out further because we have little confidence in our ability to forecast beyond that and because we're most interested in what the business is worth today. The art in the valuation is arriving at the appropriate multiple to put on the cash flow. We look at private-market transactions and public comps, adjusting up or down from those based on things like the profitability of the business, its predictability, the prospects for growth, and the amount of leverage.

—James Shircliff, River Road Asset Management

We look at the securities analysis part of what we do in the way people look at valuing a bond. Ignoring the maturity date, what you need to know is the price, the coupon, and the reinvestment rate. It would be crazy to value a bond knowing only two of those things and we look at stocks the same way.

For price, we look at enterprise value, because you need to take into consideration all the calls on the earnings that are senior to you as an equity holder. We also try to mark the balance sheet to market by adjusting for things like underfunded pensions or real estate on the books at cost.

As a coupon, we're looking at owner earnings, which adjusts GAAP earnings to arrive at the cash flow you'd have at your disposal as an owner. There are many adjustments to make, but the most important is accounting for the difference between the inflation-adjusted amount of capital a company spends to maintain its competitive position compared to its reported depreciation levels.

The third key item is the rate at which owner earnings can be reinvested. This is the hard part, but obviously enormously important to any investment thesis. If you look out 5 to 10 years, as we typically do, that return on incremental capital is going to be far more important than the earnings yield you get in year one. That's why the business analysis is so important.

—Christopher Davis, Davis Advisors

What gets our interest is when a target company's share price goes down to the point where the free-cash-flow yield—EBITDA minus real capital spending, minus incremental working capital, divided by enterprise value—is at least 10 percent.

The reason we have do at least cursory work on 100 companies per year is that it is really hard to find the three or four that in addition to the 10 percent free-cash-flow coupon, can also generate growth in free cash flow of at least 10 percent per year. In most value situations, too much of the company's revenue is tied to mature and oftentimes declining product lines. But when we can see 6 to 8 percent organic growth combined with margin gains producing double-digit free cash flow growth, that's interesting.

If we can buy 10 percent current coupons and if the coupon grows at 10 percent, the math says we will generate an annual 20 percent unlevered return. That's the target for each position we hold and it's what we expect out of the entire portfolio.

—Jeffrey Ubben, ValueAct Capital

We're trying to own things that look like value stocks when we buy them, but which turn out to be growth stocks. So we try to build a portfolio of businesses with two primary characteristics. The first is that, even in times of stress, the underlying income-producing assets are strong enough to maintain a value floor for the investment. In other words, the company is cheap based on what we can be fairly certain of now. The second characteristic is some change going on that is unrecognized by the market and likely to be very valuable in the out years—a free call option.

We generally want to invest at a price where if our growth thesis is totally wrong, we can still expect to earn at least an 8 percent nominal cash-on-cash return. That's roughly in line with what the overall market is likely to return, so we should match that even if none of the free options pay off.

—Boykin Curry, Eagle Capital

The first thing we do is normalize what we think the company's earnings power is. A lot goes into that, but it essentially means looking at what the business has traditionally been able to generate over time and adjusting for various factors that might make it more or less attractive going forward. We then estimate the percentage of those normal earnings that the company will keep after things like capital spending and investments in working capital, resulting in a free cash flow number we can divide by the current market value to get a free cash flow yield. On top of that we'll add inflation and the annual growth in free cash flow we expect in order to arrive at our estimated rate of return, which we typically want to be at least in the teens.

By focusing on forward rates of return, it keeps us more centered on the fundamentals of the business and its cash flows. We aren't counting on or trying to figure out what someone else might pay as a P/E or cash flow multiple down the road.

—Stephen Yacktman, Yacktman Asset Management

The metric we care most about is what we call reinvestment cash flow, which is essentially earnings before interest and taxes, plus depreciation and amortization, minus maintenance capital spending. We look out three years and want to see the reinvestment yield the company earns increasing relative to its enterprise value. Then using a discounted cash flow model, we calculate a warranted value that has to be at least 50 percent greater than the current market price.

—Joe Wolf, RS Investments

We're primarily focused on free cash flow yield, which, after taxes and maintenance capital spending, we want to be at least 8 to 10 percent. For faster-growing companies we accept a bit less, but that's the general guideline. We tend to look at valuation in layers. The first layer is sort of a no-growth, as-is valuation, based on historical performance and how we believe free cash flow will respond going forward to a few key variables. The second layer looks at the free cash flow yield after incorporating operational improvements we expect that don't require top-line growth. Finally, we build in the opportunities for revenue growth we see. Our goal is to be satisfied with the yield we'd get based on the first layer, but obviously the thicker the other layers are, the better the opportunity. Good things can happen when competent people are working every day to improve a high-quality company's performance, which we usually look at as free options on the upside. It's maybe a bit boring, but our objective is to compound at a minimum of 10 percent per year. You do that over 20 years and you increase capital by almost seven times. That's rare enough that when people actually do it, you're likely to hear about it.

—*Patrick McNeill, Alatus Capital*

We're essentially willing to pay for the current cash earnings power. It varies, but if we're paying a price that results in at least a 7 percent maintenance free cash flow yield, we believe we're paying only for what's being generated today, getting for free the ability of the business model to grow free cash flow at a rate significantly ahead of the market. We look to make money in a couple of ways. The first is through compounding of the company's intrinsic equity value at 20 percent or more per year. Secondly, if we're right in identifying this type of business earlier than other investors, we should get paid over time from multiple expansion as well.

—*Joerg Diedrich, Pennant Capital*

It's not exactly reducible to a bumper sticker, but the key to our approach is free-cash-flow total return. We look at free cash flow yield plus expected growth in free cash flow, compared to the market-implied rate of return. Take Amazon: the free cash flow yield is around 5 percent, but the free cash flow growth rate is 20 to 25 percent easy. So that's a 30 percent free cash flow total return versus, at most, the 8 to 10 percent you'll get on the overall market. Our view is that it doesn't take a mathematical genius to figure out that 30 percent is going to beat 10 percent if you have any time on your side.

—*Bill Miller, Legg Mason Funds*

Basically we have to answer three questions: Is the stock mispriced, why is it mispriced, and what's going to make the mispricing go away? If we can't adequately answer those questions, we either haven't done enough work or it's probably not a great idea. To answer the first question, we arrive at a fundamental value for each company we analyze, which is essentially the price at which its cash flows or asset values provide an adequate, risk-adjusted, cash-on-cash return. For a moderate-growth business with moderate leverage in a normal interest rate environment, that return over time would be roughly 15 percent per year. Against that fundamental value, we typically want our shorts to be at least 30 percent overvalued and our longs to trade at a 30 percent discount or higher.

—*Curtis Macnguyen, Ivory Capital*

I've always believed that as an investor you have to be comfortable with a number of different valuation approaches and methodologies, and that part of the art of investing is to recognize which approach is most appropriate in different situations. The metric we tend to look at most frequently is sustainable free cash flow yield— in other words, free cash flow after the capital spending necessary to maintain a company's competitive position relative to the current market price. Across most businesses we consider that a consistent, important measure of value.

—*Lee Ainslie, Maverick Capital*

MULTIPLE ANGLES

While some measure of cash flow relative to the current market price is the most common valuation metric used by leading value investors, they frequently utilize a number of additional measures of value in forming their judgments. This approach has strong research support, including that of *What Works on Wall Street* author and money manager James O'Shaughnessy, whose multi-decade research indicates that stocks that screen well on a composite of value-based factors—including price-to-book, price-to-earnings, and price-to-cash-flow—perform much better over time than those screening well on any one individual factor.

*   *   *

We try to use multiple methodologies to establish a company's intrinsic value—discounted cash flow models, private market values, and market-based multiples compared to peers and the company's own history. We think coming at it from multiple directions can give us a higher level of confidence in our ultimate estimate of value.

—*Timothy Beyer, Sterling Capital Management*

We won't buy if we don't see a 35 percent discount to our current estimate of intrinsic value, which we arrive at in a variety of different ways depending on the company. Ideally we're running a discounted cash flow model, cross-checked against where we believe something should trade based on other metrics like price to earnings, price to cash flow, price to net asset value or a sum of the parts. We think at least a 35 percent discount gives us enough margin of safety that we can be wrong and not get killed.

—*Steve Morrow, NewSouth Capital*

The metrics we use to determine value are pretty much what you'd expect. We do private-market-value analysis using discounted future cash flows and by looking at breakup values. At the same time we like stocks that are statistically cheap on a traditional price/earnings basis. We focus on companies trading at a 40 percent or greater discount to our private market value or no more than 13x our estimate of next year's earnings. We have to have one or the other to buy.

—*John Rogers, Ariel Investments*

We like looking at multisegment businesses where it's a bit more complicated to analyze all the parts and there's not an obvious answer to the question of what the entire company is worth. In this context, we pay a lot of attention to private-market values of each segment and trying to understand how underperforming segments should be valued.

—*Peter Langerman, Mutual Series Funds*

We'll estimate what we think earnings can be four to five years out, apply the current multiple to those earnings, and then see what the price would be if discounted back to today using a 20 percent annual rate. If the price today implies a discount rate of more than 20 percent per year, we're interested. We're not even looking at what we think can happen next year, because that's already fairly accurately built into the stock price. We also don't usually count on multiple expansion—although it would be great if it happened—because you really can't estimate a multiple five years out unless you have a good idea what interest rates will be then, which is not something I know anything about.

—*Murray Stahl, Horizon Asset Management*

THE INFORMED BUYER

Value investors from Benjamin Graham on down have stressed the importance of looking at equity ownership not as the shuffling of papers to be traded, but as a partial ownership interest in an ongoing business enterprise. A logical extension of that in arriving at what a stock is worth is the frequent focus among accomplished investors on what they believe a knowledgeable buyer would pay for the entire business.

*   *   *

In ballpark terms, we like to be a buyer when the current share price is no more than 60 percent of our estimate of business value, which is the highest price a cash acquirer could pay for the entire business and still earn an adequate return on their investment. The words are all important. By focusing on a cash buyer, we're trying to separate people who are paying real money from those who might overpay with their own overvalued shares. The focus on adequate returns allows for the possibility that the buyer has some way to extract synergy from the purchase. Especially when you're looking at small- to mid-cap companies, the maximum value may come from a buyer who will integrate the business into a larger organization. We're not just looking at the maximum price of a given company in its current corporate form as a public entity.

Why 60 cents on the dollar to buy rather than 50 or 40? Over long periods of time stocks tend to perform better than other assets do, and the more stringent you are about what you'll accept the more difficult it becomes to field a portfolio. We've found over our history that at 60 cents on a dollar, we've been able at any given time to field a relatively full and well-diversified portfolio of ideas. If we buy right, the discount closes, and the value of the $1 we buy today goes to $1.20 or so over the next two or three years, we have the potential to double our money. That kind of makes sense to us.

—Bill Nygren, Harris Associates

Intrinsic value to us means the price that a knowledgeable buyer would pay for a business in its entirety in cash today. Any knowledgeable buyer will recognize and take into consideration whether current earnings are too high or too low, based on the cyclicality of the business and where it is in the cycle. Similarly, we don't want to capitalize earnings streams that are too high or too low, but focus in valuation on what the cash flow of the business is somewhere between the extremes. Because the future is uncertain, we don't exaggerate the precision of the values we come up with.

—Abhay Deshpande, First Eagle Funds

We try to figure out what a rational, informed buyer would pay for the whole business. We'd expect that kind of buyer to base the price on how much cash the business would generate over the next 15 to 20 years in excess of what's needed to run the business, so true free cash flow. We use a standard 12 percent discount rate as the hurdle rate that buyer would want to earn.

—Wally Weitz, Weitz Funds

In general we want to see a 35 to 40 percent discount from what a prudent man making an acquisition would pay for the entire business. We put it that way because sometimes, such as in 2006 and 2007, acquisitions are being done at levels we consider imprudent, so we don't use them in calculating intrinsic values. If you're fairly conservative in valuing the business and then demand a 40 percent haircut off of that, you should have a pretty healthy margin of safety.

—Robert Wyckoff, Tweedy, Browne Co.

We basically focus on what a somewhat knowledgeable buyer, expecting a reasonable return, would be willing to pay in cash for the entire business. We put a lot of emphasis on comparable transaction and market values, crosschecked against valuation measures like enterprise value to EBIT. We'll generally only invest when the EV/EBIT multiple is in the range of 8× to 15×—the low end for businesses, using Warren Buffett's terminology, that might be more questionable, while the high end is for businesses that are more comfortable.

—Jean-Marie Eveillard, First Eagle Funds

We're not P/E buyers. We're not P/E-to-growth-rate buyers. And we're not EV/EBITDA buyers because we think over time that the D and A in EBITDA are real expenses you need to account for.

We look at current operating income divided by enterprise value as our "cap rate," and we want to buy when that's 15 percent or more and sell when it goes to 7 to 8 percent. I'm trying not to buy hopes and dreams, but the here and now. The layman's way to think about it is if you could buy the whole company and—before financing and paying taxes—earn 15 cents on a dollar invested, that's a pretty good deal. If the hopes and dreams come true, all the better.

—*Jay Kaplan, Royce & Associates*

The underlying principle is what someone would pay in an arm's-length transaction for the entire business. We usually arrive at that by applying what we consider to be the appropriate multiple to estimated EBITDA one year out, adjusted for the balance sheet. To enter a position, we want to see a 30 to 40 percent discount to our intrinsic-value estimate. We try not to fool ourselves that just because we built a spreadsheet that all of this is very precise—we're making estimates and thinking about things that are unknown. But there are cases in which our level of confidence in the estimated earnings or in the multiple is higher. The more confident we are, the more likely we'll find a 30 percent discount sufficient. The less confident we are, the higher the discount required. In our experience a portfolio of stocks with those types of entry points will generate an attractive return over time. We will not be right on every stock, we just need to be right on average.

—*Andrew Jones, North Star Partners*

MODEL BEHAVIOR

In the investing world writ large, there is an extremely wide variance in the extent to which money managers automate their valuation, assessment, buying and selling decisions. At one end of the spectrum are those who rely heavily on discounted-cash-flow models and other defined valuation parameters to drive portfolio decisions executed by computer algorithms that respond to changes in market prices. At the other end of the spectrum are investors with a decidedly healthy skepticism of computer models and the certainty and precision that they imply exists. Most of the investors we've interviewed fall somewhere in the middle—rigorous in their use of models to assess valuation and make trading decisions, but also relying on experience and intuition to overrule the system when they believe it's warranted. As we've said many times, there is no one right approach, but every successful investor we've come across is quite adept at describing where automation ends and intuition begins in his or her approach.

* * *

Models beat human forecasters because they reliably and consistently apply the same criteria time after time. Models never vary. They are never moody, never fight with their spouse, are never hung over from a night on the town, and never get bored. They don't favor vivid, interesting stories over reams of statistical data. They never take anything personally. They don't have egos. They're not out to prove anything. If they were people, they'd be the death of any party.

People on the other hand, are far more interesting. It's far more natural to react emotionally or to personalize a problem than it is to dispassionately review broad statistical occurrences—and so much more fun! It's much more natural for us to look at the limited set of our personal experiences and then generalize from this small sample to create a rule-of-thumb heuristic. We are a bundle of inconsistencies, and although this tends to make us interesting, it plays havoc with our ability to successfully invest.

—James O'Shaughnessy, O'Shaughnessy Asset Management

An ideal stock according to our model would be inexpensive on an absolute basis, relative to its peers and relative to its history. It would be supported by high-quality earnings, as measured by things such as cash flow relative to net income, capital spending relative to depreciation and earnings-estimate dispersion. It would be financially secure, as measured by things like the levels of cash and operating cash flow versus liabilities, the operating return on assets, and the ratio of shareholders' equity to total assets. Finally, it would be in the midst of an upswing in business operating momentum and investor sentiment, as indicated by, say, share-price momentum and earnings-estimate revisions.

—Paul VeZolles, WEDGE Capital

We have a sophisticated, proprietary model that we have shown to be a source of alpha by valuing companies and judging where they are in their earnings cycles. That's the science of what we do and is quite systematic and repeatable.

The art of what we do is in the interpretation of that data and deciding what to actually buy and sell. Here you need to rely on experience, judgment and continuous learning. Is that repeatable as the people change? If you pick the right people, teach them well, and give them the experience necessary to act on their own, we think so.

—Ronald Mushock, Systematic Financial Management

With our quantitative and more automated approach to buying, we're just trying to take as many of the behavioral foibles off the table as possible. Think about it in terms of the S&P 500 index, which is actually a not-so-great investing strategy because all it says is "Buy big stocks." The reason it beats 70 to 80 percent of conventionally managed funds is not because it's a good strategy, but because it's a strategy that's religiously adhered to. It doesn't panic, have second thoughts, or become jealous of what its next-door-neighbor index owns. The key to its long-term success is an unwavering implementation of an investment strategy. We're using the same logic, but with what we believe are better strategies.

—James O'Shaughnessy, O'Shaughnessy Asset Management

To arrive at an intrinsic value we forecast cash flows out five years, and then discount the first four years back to the present and add to that the present value of the fifth year's cash flow after applying a multiple to it. The setting of that multiple, of course, is very important and is where we have the most debates in our approval process. There are quantitative and qualitative aspects to it. We'll maybe start with peer multiples or the multiples at which deals have been done, for example, but that's not the only input because every company is different. We also take into consideration things like the consistency of the business, its financial strength, and the operating prowess of the management team.

—David Herro, Harris Associates

We're trying to find 20 to 30 long investments, run by management teams that truly understand the cost of capital and capital allocation, where we believe based on a dividend-discount model that we're paying 60 to 70 cents on the dollar today and that that dollar can grow at an equity rate of return. If you can buy a 60-cent dollar and over three years that dollar appreciates 10 percent per year and the discount closes, the stock will more than double. You obviously won't do that on every position, but if you hit that on half your positions on average and don't lose any money on the other half, you'll earn 13 to 14 percent per year.

—Jon Jacobson, Highfields Capital

Our discounted-cash-flow calculation then produces two prices. Our buy price is the price at which the cash flows are being discounted to produce our required real return of 8 percent. Basically, the company is priced low enough to allow us to earn in excess of the market's expected return. Our sell price is the one that discounts future cash flows at 6 percent, meaning the valuation no longer allows us to earn an expected return greater than the market's.

—Bernard Horn, Polaris Capital

Our goal is to create a detailed financial model that estimates cash flow available to shareholders over the next five years. With that model we're able to calculate the present value of both the five-year cash flows and a terminal share value, calculated by applying an estimated terminal multiple to our year-five cash flow estimate. We discount both those values back to the present using a required rate of return, which reflects the riskiness of the cash flows due to things like industry cyclicality, competitive threats and the rate of technological change. In today's interest-rate environment, required rates of return for most companies we analyze are from 8 percent to 12 percent.

—Chris Bingaman, Diamond Hill Investments

We do the same discounted cash flow analysis everyone does, but the most important variable—and the one that most impacts the answer—is the growth rate you assume for the business. Lee Cooperman always used to say that if you got that right, you were 90 percent there. I've always considered that to be true.

—Morris Mark, Mark Asset Management

If you're buying high-quality businesses at what you think are discounted prices, you can be a little bit wrong on your intrinsic-value estimates and still make money. If you've ever done a DCF analysis, you know how variable the results can be with small adjustments in things like operating leverage or discount rates. We want to buy only when the share price is 50 to 60 percent of our calculation of intrinsic value, but our qualitative judgment of the business, management, and risk involved will play a bigger role in the positions we take than whether this stock is at 58 percent of intrinsic value and this other one is at 54 percent.

—*Brian Bares, Bares Capital*

We're not big fans of DCF models because of the garbage-in, garbage-out risk. I don't know if lunch will be good later on today, so how am I going to forecast a company's earnings five or ten years out?

Most of our valuation work focuses on what a company would be worth today in an arm's-length transaction. The best sources for that, of course, are comparable recent deals. We also look at how valuation multiples on a given company or the sum of its parts match up against historical and competitive comps.

—*David Winters, Wintergreen Fund*

We try to avoid false precision when we do our valuation work. We don't know what earnings are going to be next year and we don't believe management teams themselves can know that with any great precision either. What we can try to do is estimate the normalized economic earnings power of a business and then put a reasonable multiple on those earnings, based on the characteristics of the business—i.e. growth, need for capital, competitive position—and relative to what's happening out there in the real world of mergers and acquisitions.

—*Curtis Jensen, Third Avenue Management*

I'm still more back-of-the-envelope when it comes to valuation. To me it all comes down to the assumptions you're making. If they're correct, a back-of-the-envelope calculation works perfectly well. If they're not, sophisticated modeling isn't going to help.

—*Robert Kleinschmidt, Tocqueville Asset Management*

I was brought up in the business to be skeptical of big, long-term discounted cash flow models, so that's not an important part of how we invest.

—Steven Tananbaum, GoldenTree Asset Management

Discounted cash flow to us is sort of like the Hubble telescope—you turn it a fraction of an inch and you're in a different galaxy. There are just so many variables in this kind of an analysis—that's not for us.

—Curtis Jensen, Third Avenue Management

PLAYING THE ODDS

Consistent with value investors' emphasis on what can go wrong with any given investment, they typically in their valuation work assess a variety of possible upside and downside value scenarios and, implicitly or explicitly, assign probabilities to each before making any final judgments.

*　*　*

We're very focused on how much money we can lose. What's the hard asset value? What protection does the balance sheet provide? We stress test the business using draconian assumptions and compare the worst-case scenario with what we predict will actually happen. We want $4 to $5 of upside for every $1 of downside. We've found over time that if you marry improving returns on invested capital with an asymmetric risk profile, the odds of losing money are low.

—Joe Wolf, RS Investments

I'll say it in a way that implies more precision and rigidity than we use, but we also want to see potential upside versus downside of at least 3:1. If at normalized earnings levels in two years or so we see an upside that is three times the downside we could imagine in the next year or so, we're usually comfortable going forward.

—Steven Romick, First Pacific Advisors

The prospective return must always be generous relative to the risk incurred. For riskier investments, the upside potential must be many multiples of any potential loss. We believe there is room for a few of these potential five and ten baggers in a diversified, low-risk portfolio.

—*Seth Klarman, The Baupost Group*

One lesson from 2008 was that we were guilty of having a failure of imagination on the downside. We develop a base, high, and low case for each business we analyze and one practical adjustment we've made is to make our low cases somewhat more draconian. That comes into play in what we're willing to pay. We're more reluctant to buy a stock that might look attractive relative to the base case if the downside from the low case is too great. That's always been true—if the range of outcomes is wide, that probably means the cash flows aren't as predictable as we'd like and we require a bigger discount—but it's even more of a focus now.

—*Wally Weitz, Weitz Funds*

In valuing companies, we're putting more emphasis on the relationship between the current price and the worst-case scenario and—regardless of the potential upside—are more likely to sit and wait if that downside is material. In a sideways market, cash is not trash.

—*David Nierenberg, D3 Family Funds*

It isn't human nature to view the future in terms of a wide range of possibilities. We naturally think in terms of what is most likely to occur and implicitly assess the probability of that scenario occurring at 100 percent. That may sound reckless, but it's what most people do and isn't a bad way to think as long as less likely, but still plausible, scenarios don't have vastly different outcomes. In the investment world, however, they often do, so making decisions solely on the most likely outcome can cause severe damage.

In addition to what might be the business-as-usual case, we also want to identify four or five scenarios that are different from the recent past and analyze the present value of likely future cash generation under each. We calculate an intrinsic value and apply a probability to each scenario. Our final estimate of value is the value under each scenario weighted by its probability of occurring. A key is to capture low-probability but high-impact scenarios, primarily to see where the vulnerabilities are.

—Bryan Jacoboski, Abingdon Capital

We come at valuation in a variety of ways, but the primary one is to assign probabilities to three or four different scenarios to arrive at an expected outcome, which we compare to the current share price in looking for a margin of safety.

—Michael Karsch, Karsch Capital

At the end of every quarter we get a report showing the holdings we had in each portfolio five years ago and how those stocks have performed over the ensuing five years. The goal is to assess the decisions we made and whether the estimates of intrinsic value upon which those decisions were based were properly done.

One thing we've learned is that we often don't give companies enough credit for the fundamental strength or weakness of their competitive positions and business models. That has resulted in selling winners too soon, and in holding losers too long because we haven't had the imagination to see how bad things could get. You can never eradicate those kinds of mistakes completely, but it has made us more sensitive to both best-case and worst-case scenarios in our valuation analysis.

—Chris Welch, Diamond Hill Investments

We look back as far as possible to inform what would be the worst-case levels of revenues and margins, and then apply what we think are trough multiples to the resulting worst-case earnings. If the worst case is more than 20 percent below the existing share price we won't buy it, no matter how much the discount is to our intrinsic value.

—Charles de Lardemelle, International Value Advisers

We don't invest in things that could be a coin flip between doubling or going to zero. We want the downside of every holding to be no more than 10 to 15 percent and the upside to be at least 50 percent. The key for us is to not be wrong about the downside.

—Jon Jacobson, Highfields Capital

We don't invest in binary win/lose situations. A deep-value manager can quite openly accept that some of his holdings may go to zero, assuming that big winners will more than offset the occasional big loser. We don't contemplate losing too terribly much on any investment.

—Brian Barish, Cambiar Investors

One mistake value investors can make is to focus too literally on the absolute difference between an estimate of intrinsic value and the stock price as the valuation cushion. If the range of potential outcomes is very wide, you may have much less of a cushion than you think. One big reason we focus on better-quality businesses with great balance sheets is that the variability in outcomes—and therefore the risk of blowing through the valuation cushion—is lower.

—Dan O'Keefe, Artisan Partners

THEORIES OF RELATIVITY

An investor's attitude towards absolute versus relative measures of valuation is often a function of how fully invested he or she expects to be. If holding a decent amount of cash is not an option, for example, a focus on relative valuation against other stocks is more likely. When cash is allowed to build, managers are more apt to wait for absolute valuation criteria to be met before acting. But even holding one's cash strategy constant, views on what constitutes actual value at any given time can vary widely.

*   *   *

Here's how we think about it: Say the S&P 500 companies sell at 15× next year's earnings, 3× book value, 11× cash flow, 1.5× revenues, have an ROE of 17 to18 percent and have anticipated trend earnings growth of 8 percent. We're looking for companies with equal or superior growth characteristics that sell at discounts to the market valuation.

—Leon Cooperman, Omega Advisors

We're basically willing to pay average or below-average valuations for companies we believe will continue to have better-than-average performance. Relative to more elaborate valuation disciplines you may hear about from others, ours is relatively simple. Only a small amount of our returns are from being clever on valuation when we buy.

—*Eric Ende, First Pacific Advisors*

We've developed a quantitative model that's designed to reflect the attractiveness of every company in our 1,000-company database based on three factors: expected earnings growth relative to the P/E multiple (the higher the better), valuation relative the company's past history (the lower the better), and the trend in consensus Wall Street estimates (upward movement gives us more confidence).

—*Philip Tasho, TAMRO Capital*

We rely on companies' historic valuation ranges and/or peer group valuations on traditional measures like price-to earnings, price-to-book, and price-to-sales to identify investment targets and then project future valuation ranges. The basic discipline is to buy in the lower quartile of the valuation range and sell towards the upper end of the long-term range.

You do have to recognize if a disruptive technological or structural industry change is underway or relative value will point you to a lot of value traps. We're always asking whether there's a transitory disruption to a business or whether there's a point of discontinuity, as was the case with Eastman Kodak. There are also analytical checks to do on past valuation levels. If there have been periods of hyper-normal valuations, such as technology and telecom in the 1990s, you have to ignore those data points.

—*Brian Barish, Cambiar Investors*

One of the big mistakes value investors can make is to be too enamored with absolute cheapness. If you focus on statistical cheapness, you're often driven to businesses serving shrinking markets or that have developed structural disadvantages that make it more likely they're going to lose market share.

—*Bill Nygren, Harris Associates*

We generally avoid the most deeply discounted stocks. In a normal market, companies trading at half of intrinsic value or less often do so because there is some significant risk in the business. It may be a low-probability risk, but we'll steer clear of high-severity, low-probability risks. In our portfolio today we only have one or two holdings that—after the fact—have been shown to face more of a binary outcome.

—Timothy Hartch, Brown Brothers Harriman

When I look at mistakes I've made—like buying the best sub-prime mortgage lender in late 2006—they've primarily been when I thought I was getting a great deal on a house, only to find out later there had been a fire smoldering in the basement. The obvious lesson is that things that look cheap aren't necessarily so.

—Jed Nussdorf, Soapstone Capital

One distinction we generally try to make when betting more on industry cycles is that something should be cheap based on the current numbers, not just on what is considered normalized earnings. That makes it a more conservative investment with even more upside when the cycle eventually comes back.

—Andrew Jones, North Star Partners

We focus on absolute value, trying to resist reaching for relative-value justifications just because we have the cash. Relying on relative valuation is how you end up paying silly prices for houses, Internet stocks, and anything else in life.

—Peter Keefe, Avenir Corp.

I try to own businesses that are inexpensive in an absolute rather than relative sense. No position I own today trades at more than 15× my estimate of the next 12 months' earnings. The only companies I own at more than 12× earnings are in businesses that I think are among the best in the world.

The problem I've found in paying higher multiples is that you can have a differentiated view on the business fundamentals and be absolutely right, but the risk is higher that the multiple contracts and takes away your positive return. That doesn't have to happen, of course, but I want to credibly believe the multiple trajectory is biased upwards, even if that's not the primary reason I'm investing.

—Jed Nussdorf, Soapstone Capital

We firmly believe no investment is so wonderful that it can't be ruined by a too-high entry price, so on our discount-to-cash-flow stocks we will not pay more than the market multiple on forward earnings. We want to avoid the temptation of making relative valuation bets—say, finding a software company attractive because it's only 30× earnings when the group sells at 40×.

—Christopher Grisanti, Grisanti Brown & Partners,

What you're unlikely to see us invest in is something like The Cheesecake Factory when it's at 30× earnings. At that level everybody knows it's a great story and, when it comes down to it, the bet you're making is whether or not the business grows a little faster or for a little longer than people expect. Those are not the types of calls we look to make.

—Brian Gaines, Springhouse Capital

A fair price today is one that should allow us over time to realize on our investment the same level of compound annual growth we expect in per-share book value, earnings or cash flow—whichever is most appropriate for the company at hand. What that tries desperately to preclude is paying so much that the business can do extremely well but the stock price goes nowhere, which can happen as businesses inevitably mature and valuation multiples shrink.

What that means practically to us is that if we find a business that meets all our criteria and we pay no more than 14 to 15× trailing earnings, we're not going to be wildly off on price. For any number of market, industry, or company-specific reasons, it's been my experience that we'll episodically get opportunities to pay these kinds of prices.

—Thomas Gayner, Markel Corp.

We look out two to three years at what a company can earn in a normal economy if our expectations for change play out. We don't look at a shorter period because so many other investors are doing that that it's much more competitive. Looking out much further than that, the uncertainties go up and thus our ability to predict goes down.

We then apply a valuation multiple anchored on the average S&P 500 P/E over the last five decades of around 15.8×. We consider that a fair valuation for an average company. Taking into consideration things like the balance sheet, re- turns on capital, growth, barriers to entry and management quality, we'll go up and down from 15.8× to come up with what we believe is an appropriate multiple and apply it to our EPS estimate. For a stock to be interesting, we want to see at least 50 percent upside from today's price to that fair value.

—*Ed Wachenheim, Greenhaven Associates*

I'm amazed at how common the relative valuation argument is. But you shouldn't forget that all that argument may be telling you is that bonds or another asset class might suck, not that equities are great. It's like going to Cinderella's house and meeting the two ugly stepsisters and being told you should be happy to date one of them. Personally, I'd rather wait for Cinderella.

None of that stops people who want you to buy equities from talking about how much better they are today than bonds. "What else am I going to do?" is not the most compelling reason for doing something. If there's nothing to do, do nothing. It's not that difficult.

Absolute standards of valuation get you away from the idea that you have to be doing something, which goes all the way back to Ben Graham. He was looking at all elements of the capital structure in a very unconstrained fashion, but was fully prepared to hold cash when there were no opportunities. Today with the rise of specialist mandates and passive indexing, so many people want to be fully invested all the time. I'd argue that has caused our industry a lot of problems.

—*James Montier, GMO*

PULLING THE TRIGGER

Timing may not be everything, but it's certainly of keen importance in making the ultimate decision to buy a stock. That decision can engender any number of caught-up-in-the-moment types of emotions—exactly what reasoned, rational investors try hard to avoid—and the vast majority of the time will be deemed in hindsight as having been excessively early or late. In making the final buy call, the best investors strive mightily to maintain the same patient and careful process that got them to that point in the first place. Some find virtue in a team-based approach to pulling the trigger, others argue that too many cooks spoil the broth.

* * *

One of my favorite investing quotes of all time is from Joe Rosenberg, Loews Corp.'s chief investment strategist for many years, who said the secret to outperformance is to "have opinions at extremes, and wait for extreme moments." We're willing to wait for the perfect pitch rather than swing at things that look pretty good. It's not that hard to find pretty good values, it's much harder to be patient and only buy the great ones.

—Chris Mittleman, Mittleman Brothers, LLC

Once we act, we forfeit the option of waiting until new information comes along. As a result, not acting has value. The more uncertain the outcome, the greater may be the value of procrastination.

—Peter Bernstein, in Against the Gods

In a world in which most investors appear interested in figuring out how to make money every second and chase the idea *du jour*, there's also something validating about the value-investing message that it's okay to do nothing and wait for opportunities to present themselves or to pay off. That's lonely and contrary a lot of the time, but reminding yourself that that's what it takes is quite helpful.

—Seth Klarman, The Baupost Group

Much of our research and analysis involves identifying companies we're willing to buy and the prices at which we'll buy them. If the market isn't offering up those companies at those prices, we sit and wait. Clients sometimes get anxious about that, but we try to remind them we get paid for results, not activity.

—Steve Leonard, Pacifica Capital

You obviously have to get your analysis right to be a great investor, but success also comes down to patience. We think of ourselves a bit like a lion lying in wait. There are plenty of gazelles running around, but we can't run after them all, so we wait for one to get within 125 feet before we go. Not 150 feet or 200 feet, but no more than 125. Sometimes the market offers up those great kills and we try our best to be ready and to take advantage when they come along.

—François Parenteau, Defiance Capital

In a typical year, the average large-cap stock fluctuates about 50 percent from its low to its high. If you've done your homework and you're patient, more than enough opportunities to buy will come along.

—Donald Yacktman, Yacktman Asset Management

As Graham, Dodd, and Buffett have all said, you should always remember that you don't have to swing at every pitch. You can wait for opportunities that fit your criteria and if you don't find them, patiently wait. Deciding not to panic is still a decision.

—Seth Klarman, The Baupost Group

I've never considered it a legitimate goal to say you're going to invest at the bottom. There is no price other than zero that can't be exceeded on the downside, so you can't really know where the bottom is, other than in retrospect. That means you have to invest at other times. If you wait until the bottom has passed, when the dust has settled and uncertainty has been resolved, demand starts to outstrip supply and you end up competing with too many other buyers. So if you can't expect to buy at the bottom and it's hard to buy on the way up after the bottom, that means you have to be willing to buy on the way down. It's our job as value investors, whatever the asset class, to try to catch falling knives as skillfully as possible.

—Howard Marks, Oaktree Capital

You must buy on the way down. There is far more volume on the way down than on the way back up, and far less competition among buyers. It is almost always better to be too early than too late, but you must be prepared for price markdowns on what you buy.

—*Seth Klarman, The Baupost Group*

[SAC Capital's] Steve Cohen thought it was the silliest thing in the world to try to capture the first and last part of a stock's move—those were the most dangerous parts of investing. For me, I'd like to capture more of the early part of the move and leave the latter part for somebody else. In general, if you're right on the fundamentals and can capture the big, fat middle portion of a stock's move, you're going to make a lot of money.

—*Robert Jaffe, Force Capital Management*

I'm a value guy at heart, so would rather buy early than late. The problem with being late is that you're already paying for the turnaround itself, so you have to count much more on the turnaround resulting in sustained revenue and profit growth.

—*Kevin O'Boyle, Presidio Fund*

A common expression we use around here is the Chinese one, "to have known and not to have acted, is not to have known." We try to fight against statements like "this would be a great investment if it was 10 percent cheaper." That's a wussy conclusion because you can't be wrong: If it goes down, you can say you knew it was too expensive. If it goes up, you can say you knew it was a great investment. But if you know it's a great investment you should buy it.

—*Christopher Davis, Davis Advisors*

When we were buying Coca-Cola years ago, I'd lay out for other investors one part of our thesis—that enormous demand in emerging markets could eventually turn Coke into a growth stock again—but many of them just weren't interested. "Tell me again in a couple of years," they said. If we're comfortable that value will compound over a long period of time, we think it's not productive to try to time so precisely when to get in. It's too hard and you often end up missing out.

—*Boykin Curry, Eagle Capital*

Sir John Templeton, who always argued for buying during periods of maximum pessimism, had one of the best methods for keeping emotion out of the process. He used to do his calculations of intrinsic value when there wasn't a lot going on in the market. He'd then place a margin of safety on those intrinsic values and place buy orders with his broker at, say, 40 percent below the current market price. I'm sure a fair amount of those orders never got filled, but if there was an enormous dislocation in the market or in an individual stock, the order would fill. Psychologically, that kind of precommitment is a very powerful tool to help us in periods of emotional turmoil. If you look at something when it's just gone down 40 percent, you're probably not going to want to touch it because it just warned on earnings or something similar.

—James Montier, Société Générale

In general, we try to constantly remind ourselves that when an industry goes south, things often get worse than you expect and stay bad longer—there's usually plenty of time to find the bottom.

—John Dorfman, Thunderstorm Capital

Our primary mistake in 2008 was buying too soon when the market started cracking in September. My takeaway: Sometimes it's best to let the other guy try to pick the bottom. In selloffs like that, there will be plenty of room to get in on the upside.

—Carlo Cannell, Cannell Capital

Many value investors will buy the cheap company when there's just a turnaround story attached to it, but we patiently wait for the fundamentals to improve first. The philosophy works because investors underreact to both positive and negative changes in fundamentals. If a company has chronically underperformed, investors dislike it, don't trust management, and won't give them the benefit of the doubt. When things improve, it takes a long time for people to believe it and incorporate the improvement fully into expectations and valuations.

If we see all the ingredients of a sustainable turnaround, we'll buy after one quarter of good earnings, allowing our clients to benefit from the slow rebuilding of confidence that will be reflected in the stock price over time.

—Kevin McCreesh, Systematic Financial Management

You have to be reasonably early and we of course love to get in at the absolute bottom, but so long as our valuation work indicates enough upside and we're confident in management's ability to execute, we'll initiate a position even after a restructuring is well underway or a problem is already on its way to being fixed.

—Jerry Senser, Institutional Capital LLC

The potential efficacy of combining value and momentum factors has always been a consistent theme of my research. Our Trending Value strategy still identifies the best values in the market, with the added twist that it then chooses from that narrow list the stocks that have increased the most in price over the past six months. In other words, we're looking at stocks that are still really cheap, but the market has started to take notice. I wasn't surprised that it worked—incorporating an element of price momentum can counteract value investors' tendency to buy too early and fall into value traps—but I'll admit that I was surprised how well it worked.

—James O'Shaughnessy, O'Shaughnessy Asset Management

Valuation predominates in our models, but we do believe value managers underweight positive [share price] momentum in their portfolios. The obvious reason is that stocks with positive momentum are often overpriced, but when they're not, we think its presence helps us avoid value traps. We'll ignore momentum if there's sufficient value-based justification, but if our awareness of the effect of momentum indicates we should buy later rather than sooner, we will.

—Paul VeZolles, WEDGE Capital

One thing we may do a bit differently from others is that once we've identified a stock as something in which we're interested, my two partners and I will all separately look at the valuation and arrive independently at what we think we ought to pay, based on the potential upside and, as importantly, the potential risk. When we reach different conclusions, that leads to a very important back-and-forth as we try to find a meeting of the minds. We absolutely believe the end decision is better as a result.

—Jonathan Shapiro, Kovitz Investment Group

We have three people in charge of the portfolio and we require unanimity on a stock in order to buy. That's not to say we have to feel equally strongly about something, but a great thing about having different intuition is that we're less apt to skim over something important because we're looking at things the same way.

—*Christopher Grisanti, Grisanti, Brown & Partners*

We've never thought it was a good idea to demand unanimous agreement in making a buy decisions because the best investment ideas tend to be somewhat controversial. The risk in forcing unanimous agreement in any committee structure is that you too often weed out your better ideas.

—*Bill Nygren, Harris Associates*

I've sat on buy-list committees where everyone had to agree, and while it sounds comfortable and prudent, it doesn't work. Every good idea with a creative or provocative angle, somebody's not going to like it. You end up with ideas that don't offend anyone, which aren't likely to be very good.

—*Scott Satterwhite, Artisan Partners*

Active Management

CHAPTER 8

The Portfolio

The majority of the popular discussion about stock investing focuses on "What are you buying today?" There's no question, of course, that intelligent buying decisions are a prerequisite to successful investing. But there's also no question that smart buying isn't at all sufficient to insure success. Equally important are the less-sexy aspects of equity investing involved in portfolio construction and management. How are positions sized? How many positions are held? How actively are holdings traded? How are portfolio risks assessed and what efforts are made to mitigate them? Is hedging a part of the strategy? Is shareholder activism? Finally, among the most vexing topics an investor must address: How do I decide when to sell?

These more nitty-gritty aspects of equity investing again highlight the variety of strategies and methods employed by otherwise like-minded investors. While the specifics will differ, what shouldn't vary is the investor's ability to articulate in detail how the portfolio is managed and why. Based on our experience, fuzziness here—relative, say, to describing one's buying discipline—is a warning sign.

CONCENTRATION VERSUS DIVERSIFICATION

One of the most basic elements of portfolio strategy is determining the number of positions to hold. While the subject of much analytical research over the years—about which accomplished investors are typically well-versed—the question of how concentrated or diversified one's portfolio is often appears driven as much by personal experience, comfort level, and "feel" than anything else.

*   *   *

When Warren lectures at business schools, he says, "I could improve your ultimate financial welfare by giving you a ticket with only 20 slots in it so that you had twenty punches—representing all the investments that you got to make in a lifetime. And once you'd punched through the card, you couldn't make any more investments at all." He says, "Under those rules, you'd think carefully about what you did, and you'd be forced to load up on what you'd really thought about. So you'd do so much better."

It's not given to human beings to have such talent that they can just know everything about everything all the time. But it is given to human beings who work hard at it—who look and sift the world for a mispriced bet—that they can occasionally find one. And the wise ones bet heavily when the world offers them that opportunity. They bet big when they have the odds. And the rest of the time, they don't. It's just that simple.

—Charlie Munger, Poor Charlie's Almanack

The strategy we've adopted precludes our following standard diversification dogma. Many pundits would therefore say the strategy must be riskier than that employed by more conventional investors. We disagree. We believe that a policy of portfolio concentration may well decrease risk if it raises, as it should, both the intensity with which an investor thinks about a business and the comfort level he must feel with its economic characteristics before buying into it.

—Warren Buffett, 1993 Berkshire Hathaway Shareholder Letter

Value investors should concentrate their holdings in their best ideas; if you can tell a good investment from a bad one, you can also distinguish a great one from a good one.

—Seth Klarman, The Baupost Group

In our separate accounts we typically hold 10 to 15 securities. In our partnership we're typically more concentrated, with the top five positions making up about 65 percent of the portfolio.

If I didn't have partners, our concentration would be even higher. You know how much of Warren Buffett's partnership held in American Express when he bought it after the DeAngelis salad-oil scandal? 40 percent or so.

A company compounding capital at way above-average rates, when I have great confidence that will continue and the valuation is modest, I want to hold it at a size where it can have a material impact on the portfolio. The rationale is that simple.

—*Chuck Akre, Akre Capital Management*

We typically have 15 to 20 positions. Our general feeling is that if we don't like something enough to own a 5 percent position in it, we should wait to find something else. Put another way, if the only way you can feel comfortable about an idea is to own less of it, to my mind that tells you something about the quality of the idea.

—*Andrew Jones, North Star Partners*

We're deliberately concentrated on 10 to 14 investments, for two reasons related to time. First, it takes considerable time to learn enough about a company, its people, and its industry to develop and maintain a proprietary level of insight information, or knowing more than the Street. The second relates to our focus on activism: pushing for change at companies takes a lot of time.

I will say that I have in the past fallen into what I call time traps, where I've spent too much time trying to resolve problem investments. We will pick our battles, but usually we're better off helping our best investments maximize opportunities than trying to perform brain surgery on dogs.

—*David Nierenberg, D3 Family Funds*

Owning fewer than 15 stocks I'd have more risk of being wrong with one company than I'd like. At the same time, if I owned 30 to 40 stocks, experience tells me that roughly half would be my favorites and other half would either have less upside potential or more risk. Rather than force myself to make that choice between less upside and more risk, I would rather just limit the number of individual holdings to 15 to 20. Most managers would buy the stocks with more risk rather than give away upside, which can often offset whatever benefit they think they are getting from greater diversification.

—*Ed Wachenheim, Greenhaven Associates*

We're not playing a probability game, where you invest in 100 businesses and do fine if 70 of them succeed and 30 do poorly. We're trying to select 25 to 30 businesses to own and we count on all of them doing well over a five-year period.

—Timothy Hartch, Brown Brothers Harriman

We think there are profound research advantages in concentration. This is a world of very smart people and you can't enter that marketplace without a profoundly humble view about how you're going to win. For us, concentration and depth of research allows us to go to bed at night and feel like we have a defensible source of our returns.

—Adam Weiss, Scout Capital

We ideally hold 25 to 35 positions, with a core holding at around 5 percent. That gives us most of the free lunch of diversification and allows us to maximize return by owning only our best ideas.

There's also a human element to limiting our number of positions. With 25 to 35 stocks, our entire investment team knows every company and can have a clear opinion on it. With 100 stocks, you can't do that. The portfolio manager can only know how well each individual analyst is doing by the performance of his or her picks, as opposed to evaluating the decision inputs. Suddenly, the reality of reviews and compensation force you to look at that performance over shorter time periods than you should. The analyst knows that, of course, so then starts worrying about whether Wal-Mart's same-store sales next month are going to disappoint, rather than whether the company is creating long-term value. So we think a long-term strategy just works best with no more than 35 stocks.

—Boykin Curry, Eagle Capital

We typically hold 30 to 35 stocks. We cap any one position at no more than 6 percent of the portfolio, but we won't put anything in the portfolio at less than a 2 percent position. Setting things up this way keeps us from being distracted, makes us dig that much harder for truly interesting ideas, and forces us to make active decisions. Any one holding is too important to let slide if it's not working, and there's always healthy pressure on existing holdings from new ideas. We want to take away the drag of inertia, which can be very strong in human psychology.

—Mariko Gordon, Daruma Capital Management

We're fairly concentrated, with about 70 to 75 percent of our capital in our top 20 positions, so we know what we own and don't need a lot of statistical analysis to figure out where we're exposed. We think concentration is the key to big performance, but we also have no desire to have our year depend on one or two things working out, so we have generally kept our largest positions at 5 to 8 percent of total capital and make sure those big positions are not particularly speculative or highly levered.

—Gary Claar, JANA Partners

Our view is that too much diversification in many cases reflects the fact that the portfolio manager isn't doing the work to fully understand the businesses. If you do the work and find a great business run by great managers at a great price, that ought to express itself in the size of the holding within your portfolio. It's uncommon for us to go above 10 percent on cost in a given name, but we've held appreciated positions as high as 20 percent of the portfolio. We generally don't think you can have too much of a good thing.

—Peter Keefe, Avenir Corp.

When we see competitors holding 75 to 100 positions, with 75 to 100 percent annual turnover, we're either very impressed with their ability to keep track of 150 or more companies . . . or we're skeptical of their ability to credibly follow that many companies. We don't have anywhere near that many good ideas in a year.

—Eric Ende, First Pacific Advisors

Given that our funds are concentrated both in the absolute number of positions we hold and in the number of industries that are represented, it's natural for our performance to be lumpy. If the alternative is being consistent but mediocre, we would much prefer to be streaky but good.

—Wally Weitz, Weitz Funds

Diversification is an important part of our risk management. Average individual positions range from 1 to 2 percent, with the largest core positions at 4 to 5 percent. In 15 years, we've had three positions that got as high as 8 percent, two that worked out very well and one, Tyco, that was a disaster at the time.

An important percentage of the firm's total capital is our own money and we're just trying to do what we think is intelligent in a highly uncertain world. I don't know how some of these young hedge fund guys do it, being 160 percent gross long and 40 percent net long. I'm not questioning anybody, but if you're running a lot of capital, to be that gross long you have to either have enormous positions where you give up liquidity or you have to have an incredible number of positions, too many to follow effectively. Our level of diversification reflects our unwillingness to make such giant bets or to give up liquidity. We could liquidate our portfolio in 48 hours.

—Leon Cooperman, Omega Advisors

With six analysts and the amount of money we have, [50 to 60 positions] has turned out to be what we feel we can best manage. It's not more concentrated out of prudence and humility. There's always a chance we'll be wrong on any given idea.

—Spencer Davidson, General American Investors

Part of our rationale [for holding more than 300 positions at a time] is just the practical reality of running $8 billion in a small-cap strategy—with that much money, you can't hold 50 stocks without moving well out of small-cap range for many of them.

Another practical consideration is our investor base, which is retail investors and large institutions. Performance obviously matters when they choose T. Rowe Price to run their small-cap assets, but they also want to be comfortable that the portfolio isn't going to blow up. For many investors volatility is the enemy of rational investment decisions, so the less volatile we are, the more likely our investors won't sell at the bottom and buy at the top. Running with the level of diversification we have, the standard deviation of our returns has been lower than that of our benchmark Russell index.

Philosophically, I find broad diversification makes it easier to be a contrarian. We made the mistake in 2007 of buying some housing, recreational vehicle, and mobile home stocks after they fell 50 percent, which clearly turned out to be too early.

But because of the way we run the portfolio and our recognition of the risks involved, we never made those holdings, in aggregate, more than 3 percent of the portfolio. While that particular out-of-favor bet hasn't paid off, it hasn't hurt us much either. As long as the potential upside is high, we should be making those types of investments and they can make a real difference when they work.

—Preston Athey, T. Rowe Price

Small-cap stocks by definition are more fragile, more likely to have one dominant product or one key executive or one big customer. Strange things happen, so you have to diversify no matter how much you may love individual names.

When something strange happens in one of Johnson & Johnson's or GE's businesses, it's a rounding error to the overall company. In a small-cap it can blow it up, so you don't want to be overly exposed in any one name.

—Whitney George, Royce & Associates

Concentration and micro caps don't mix well, so we typically own around 100 names, with a big position being 3 to 4 percent of the portfolio. Tiny companies are by definition more vulnerable to catastrophe if something goes wrong, so we try to limit the potential damage from that by owning a lot of them.

I've had people ask if we're spreading ourselves too thin by owning so many positions at a time. What I answer is that there's an enormous difference in the effort required to follow a big company than a small company. I'd argue that a portfolio of 20 large-cap companies, each of which is in five or six distinct businesses, is more difficult to keep track of than 100 small companies that typically operate in a single niche. An IBM or a Disney can have a single footnote longer than a lot of the entire annual reports I look at.

—Paul Sonkin, Hummingbird Value Fund

Our level of diversification [130–140 positions] is just spreading the risk. It serves us well during downturns, which was certainly reinforced in 2008. I think it also makes us less emotionally attached to ideas and more willing to admit we're wrong, which is important for any investor.

—Tom Perkins, Perkins Investment Management

Our flagship mutual fund today has 300 stocks. Buying things when they meet the valuation characteristics that have worked for us in the past is our selection methodology, period. It's not about picking the best 5 percent, 10 percent, or 20 percent of those—I don't know which ones those are.

We've done a distribution analysis of our winners and losers: 18 percent of our stocks have lost 50 percent or more, while 25 percent have made 250 percent percent or more. The math has worked in our favor by exposing ourselves to as many multibaggers as possible that meet our valuation criteria at the outset, and then patiently waiting.

—John Buckingham, Al Frank Asset Management

While we've generally avoided being hurt by underhanded executives, that risk is always there and it's far more pronounced if you're running a concentrated global portfolio. A second reason we're more diversified [with up to 150 stocks] is because I believe a lot of our alpha comes from being in the right sets of companies rather than the right specific companies. If we get the themes right, we'll do as well, with lower volatility, owning more names rather than fewer.

—Oliver Kratz, Deutsche Asset Management

The knock on funds as diversified as ours is that they're index-huggers, which given the geographic breadth of where we invest, is not at all the case for us. I know the argument that you should only own your best 30 or 40 ideas, but I've never proven over time that I actually know in advance what those are.

—Jean-Marie Eveillard, First Eagle Funds

THE SIZE THAT FITS

A corollary to the determination of how many positions generally to hold is how to size those positions relative to each other. Tolerance levels for larger position sizes obviously vary, but even the most concentrated investors at some point typically respect the admonition to not put too many eggs in one basket.

* * *

We believe in constructing the portfolio so that we put our biggest amount of money in our highest-conviction idea, and then we view the other ideas relative to that. We find things that we think are exceptional only occasionally. So if we find something that is really set up, where we think it's mispriced, where we have a good understanding of why it's mispriced, where we think the mispricing is very large and the overall risk is very small, we take an outsized position to make sure we give ourselves the chance to be well compensated for getting it right.

—*David Einhorn, Greenlight Capital*

We're in the camp that there just aren't that many good ideas and when we identify one, we want to make sure it can have a meaningful impact on performance. The biggest holdings are those in which we have the most conviction, which is a function of several things: the size of the discount, the potential for intrinsic-value growth, having a clear and strongly held variant view, identifying a meaningful catalyst or catalysts, liquidity, and the extent of the positive impact on portfolio diversification.

—*Steve Morrow, NewSouth Capital*

Perfect investments have three layers of return. The first layer is the short-term return to what I'd call static intrinsic value. The second one is when the business, strategy, and management turn out to be what you think they are and there's real value creation. The third layer, if you're really lucky, is when the market gets so excited that it discounts more and more of the future into the present. The big homeruns are usually there.

I always try to find at least two layers of potential, but it's also important to recognize when you put something in your portfolio whether it's a one-layer or a two-layer name. You should make a two-layer name a bigger position.

—*Lisa Rapuano, Matador Capital Management*

We're looking for a total annual return of at least 25 percent, with position sizes adjusted for the degree of difficulty. For a given expected internal rate of return, the lower the outcome's expected volatility, the higher the position size. We create an estimated risk-adjusted Internal Rate of Return for everything and then allocate the portfolio based on that.

—Steven Tananbaum, GoldenTree Asset Management

In holding around 40 stocks at a time, we're trying to get the appropriate balance between diversification and putting most of our dollars in the names we like the best. As a practical matter, it's difficult to find 40 names that you really like. The lion's share of your excess returns will come from a few names—the trick is identifying which those will be and placing bigger bets on them. Our clients typically require we limit maximum position sizes to 4 percent, but even with that restriction it makes a big difference in results over time if your largest positions outperform.

—Paul VeZolles, WEDGE Capital

Our position sizes are set based on how well each company fits our three investment criteria [valuation, business quality, and balance sheet strength]. If it clears each hurdle with flying colors, it will be at the top end of the portfolio in terms of position size. If, say, it's cheap and the business economics are fine, but it just clears the hurdle on financial soundness, it will be at the bottom end. That gives a risk/reward profile to the entire portfolio—it's perfectly fine that our deepest-discount stocks may not be our biggest positions.

—George Sertl, Artisan Partners

Our positions tend to be equally weighted. We know there are potential errors in the portfolio, which we'd obviously avoid if we could predict what they were. Since we can't, we assume the future errors are randomly distributed, which is a primary reason we equally weight the positions.

—Bernard Horn, Polaris Capital

My view is that whatever edge I have comes more from knowing where to shop than knowing specifically which of the items I buy will be the best. So I maintain roughly equal stakes to reflect that.

—Ralph Shive, Wasatch Advisors

For each position we define a downside price at which the stock would trade if everything about our thesis turned out to be wrong. In deciding whether to put something into the portfolio, we'll assign probabilities and look at the expected value, but the downside is particularly important in sizing the position. We don't want to lose more than 100 basis points in return in any one position, so if our downside is 20 percent below the current price, say, we'd put on no more than a 5 percent position.

—Curtis Macnguyen, Ivory Capital

Our calculated downside price is extremely important in how we size positions. We limit each position to a maximum risk, measured in basis points, to our downside price. In other words, if a stock went to its downside price, we don't expect the fund to lose any more than the maximum risk we've defined for that particular position.

—Jeffrey Smith, Starboard Value

Being concentrated doesn't mean we'll just take the 15 best ideas we have and plug them into our portfolio. Because of that level of concentration, the companies we choose will overall likely be less cyclical, with more stable underlying business models. We at the margin will be less apt to hold names with higher expected values if that coincides with much larger downside risk.

—Lee Atzil, Pennant Capital

In periods of rapid change in liquidity and economic conditions, the odds that we're simply wrong about our estimates of companies' near-term fundamentals are higher than average. As a result, we're more focused then on maintaining flexibility—through cash levels and buying power—and in sizing our bets according to the medium- to lower-confidence environment we're in. We won't necessarily make fewer bets, but they'll be smaller in size.

—Larry Robbins, Glenview Capital

What tends to happen is that as the market gets more expensive we take on more, less discounted names, and when the market is less expensive, we'll have fewer names trading at bigger discounts. At the market peak in 2007, for example, we held about 40 names in our large-cap portfolio and the overall price-to-value ratio based on our estimates got to 82 percent. The other extreme was March 2009, when our weighted-average price-to-value ratio got down to 40 percent and we concentrated the portfolio in 18 names.

—*C.T. Fitzpatrick, Vulcan Value Partners*

Our fund usually has 40 to 60 positions. The actual number at any time is usually a function of how pricey the market is: When discounts are larger, the full weights tend to be 2 to 4 percent; when discounts aren't as large, position sizes are more like 1 to 3 percent.

—*Eric Cinnamond, Intrepid Capital*

I will not put more than 5 percent of the portfolio in any stock, and we usually don't have more than 2.5 percent. Early in my career I had 20 percent of my portfolio in Johnson & Johnson just before Tylenol was laced with poison. My objective is to produce an above-average, long-term return, and I think I can do that without taking that kind of concentration risk. Things happen.

If I really knew the best stock in my portfolio I'd put 100 percent of the portfolio in it, but I don't. [Financial columnist] Dan Dorfman once asked me in an interview what the best and worst stocks were in my portfolio. I told him the worst stock was Converse, the shoe company, which he dutifully reported in his column. It got taken over two days later, up 50 percent.

—*Robert Olstein, Olstein Capital Management*

Our not letting single positions get to more than 5 percent of the portfolio is a function of having seen the stocks of too many good companies fall off a cliff as a result of something out of left field. One example I like to use is when Merck announced it was pulling Vioxx off the market in 2004. You went to bed with the stock at $45 and woke up with it 25 percent lower. I'll give up some of the upside you might get from an outsized position in order to be better protected from a risk you couldn't possibly foresee.

—*Robert Kleinschmidt, Tocqueville Asset Management*

COGNIZANCE OF CORRELATION

A portfolio's level of concentration or diversification can clearly go beyond just the number of stocks held, also encompassing how apt holdings are to move in concert as a result of market moves or broader macroeconomic and industry trends. To some investors this is critical input into the portfolio's risk/return profile, while to others it's only a passing reference.

*　　*　　*

We have what we call a risk-bucket model. We look at the sensitivity of each of our holdings to several macroeconomic factors: Is it economically sensitive or recession resistant? Is it hurt or helped by increases in energy prices or interest rates or the dollar? Does it have political or regulatory risk? By assigning positions to any appropriate buckets, we can better understand the extent of the risks we're taking on a portfolio level. There aren't any triggers or limits, but we need to know our exposure to things like widening credit spreads or a higher dollar's impact on exports, and then be comfortable with that exposure. This comes most into practice when we're considering a new buy and want to know its potential impact on portfolio risk and diversification.

—*Steve Morrow, NewSouth Capital*

We tag every stock in our portfolio for more than 40 possible spread-risk factors on which stock prices can diverge dramatically. The factors include common ones like sector exposure, market cap, liquidity, leverage, and dividend rates, and maybe less obvious ones like exposure to China or the constitution of the shareholder base. At any given time, for example, we'll know that 16 percent of our longs and 13 percent of our shorts are in highly leveraged companies. We'll know our exposure to companies that should perform well in an inflationary environment versus those that won't.

We focus on managing the spread risks between our longs and shorts so that we don't have significant exposure to unintended bets. We want our returns to derive from our skill as analysts and not from all the other factors that can create price volatility.

In other words, the goal is for our longs and shorts to move relatively in sync with each other while we wait for fundamental catalysts to revalue our longs upward and our shorts downward.

—Curtis Macnguyen, Ivory Capital

We're keenly focused on how our holdings line up as cyclical or noncyclical. We have a lot of macro concerns, but it's difficult to translate those into an investment strategy when our investment horizon for individual stocks doesn't match up particularly well with how the macro issues may play out. Our base-case position is that the U.S. economy will sustain tepid growth through the dramatic deleveraging process the country is going through. But that may play out in a relatively organized fashion over 20 years (witness Japan), or it may cause a severe crisis in one to two years (witness what's going on in Europe). Our approach in the face of all that has been to keep the portfolio somewhat balanced between cyclical and noncyclical exposures, while being tactical in moving toward or away from either.

—Timothy Beyer, Sterling Capital Management

I never pay attention to sector or industry concentrations—I don't believe it's a reliable tool for diversification. Enron and the banks that lent to Enron were in entirely different sectors, but their fortunes were tied by that relationship. If I own Nestle, am I geographically diversified by holding a company that has its headquarters in Switzerland but earns almost none of its revenue there?

I do pay attention to codependencies of outcomes between companies and think true risk reduction comes from purchasing securities that are inversely or noncorrelated. For example, owning natural gas producers, which benefit from a rise in natural gas prices, and also holding natural-gas-based utilities that benefit from a price fall would reflect hedging for inversely correlating outcomes. An example of noncorrelation is the relationship that mostly exists between the economic climate and the volume of securities traded on exchanges. While the economic climate may impact many securities we hold, the success of the publicly traded exchanges we own is largely independent of it.

—Murray Stahl, Horizon Asset Management

We pay attention to end-market diversification, within our companies and across the portfolio. One large holding in a company with five separate global financial businesses is probably more diversified than five holdings in similar regional bank stocks. Our goal is to own businesses with uncorrelated enough end markets that we can continue growing the intrinsic value of the portfolio in any kind of market.

—*Brian Bares, Bares Capital*

Long/short funds typically don't blow up because they made a bunch of wrong fundamental stock picks. They blow up because they're overexposed to correlated sectors, or they own too many leveraged companies, or they have too many illiquid positions. These are explanations you see all the time in funds' letters to investors. That's exactly what we try to avoid.

——*Curtis Macnguyen, Ivory Capital*

Our rule is to own something in every sector, in part to avoid missing something important because it's out-of-sight, out-of- mind. We're not a slave to our benchmark—the Russell 2000 Value Index—but I typically don't go much below half, or much above twice, the index weighting in any sector. I've found that gives us plenty of room to beat the index, while avoiding the type of relative volatility that makes most investors nervous.

—*Preston Athey, T. Rowe Price*

We have sector limits, at plus or minus 10 percentage points from the percentage weighting of the 10 S&P 500 industry sectors. That gives us the flexibility to zero out sectors that are less than 10 percent of the index—like utilities and telecom today—or overweight fairly heavily in sectors we find attractive, such as energy. But it does put limits on how under- or overweighted we can be, which we think provides prudent diversification and risk management.

—*Daniel Bubis, Tetrem Capital*

One of our biggest mistakes was ten years ago, going too heavily into emerging market closed-end funds, which were selling at 25 to 30 percent discounts. When the Russian debt crisis hit, the NAVs got hammered. It's one of the first lessons you learn: be diversified enough that if that 1-in-100 event happens, you don't blow up.

—Phillip Goldstein, Bulldog Investors

In our flagship domestic and international products we do not hold individual positions over 5 percent and will not have more than 30 percent in any one sector. Historically, whether it was energy in the 1980s, technology in the late 1990s, or financials more recently, when a single sector approaches 30 percent of our portfolio or of the market that signals the end rather than the beginning of great investment performance.

—Jerry Senser, Institutional Capital LLC

We cap a given industry's exposure at 25 percent of the portfolio, which is a check on the innate lack of humility we often have as investment managers. Owning five or six 4 percent positions in an industry is a good, strong bet, but also isn't betting the house on how smart we are relative to everyone else.

—Jeffrey Bronchick, Reed, Conner & Birdwell

People tend to assume that the only form of active portfolio management is through relatively concentrated portfolios. We think there's an equally legitimate form of active money management in running a diversified portfolio that has nothing to do with the benchmark.

—Charles de Vaulx, International Value Advisers

We don't benchmark at all. I don't care if we own almost no financials and I don't care if we own an excess amount of energy. We'll go where we think the value is and let the weightings fall where they may.

—Steven Romick, First Pacific Advisors

We've purposely avoided basing our bonuses on performance against benchmarks. We're always running into managers who say they're unable to look at certain stocks because they don't fall within a prescribed benchmark. They tell us, "I can't take the risk.

If I buy it and it goes down, I'll have to write all sorts of memos explaining it, and I'll get less bonus because my portfolio went down more than the benchmark."

—*Bernard Horn, Polaris Capital*

You can understand why many succumb to the pressure to hug the index, so to speak. But we believe if you go down the road of trying to make sure you'll never do much worse than the index, you're almost insuring that you'll never do well enough to justify your compensation as an active manager.

—*Bill Nygren, Harris Associates*

The only way to add value as an active manager is to be persistently different than the index. We tell prospective clients that if their main goal is to minimize standard deviation around the index, save money and buy an index fund.

—*Jeffrey Bronchick, Reed, Conner & Birdwell*

CHAPTER 9

Playing the Hand

Fundamental value investors will aggregate toward the lower end of the activity range when it comes to day-to-day trading in their portfolios. The primary reasons the stocks they favor are undervalued—market neglect, company-specific operating troubles, an out-of-favor industry—tend to be situations that work themselves out over longer periods of time, making patience a virtue.

That said, the embrace of a traditional buy-and-hold mentality—particularly in a market that in recent years has been characterized by high share-price volatility—is by no means universal. As much as we all would love for subsequent events to conform beautifully with our original expectations, that rarely happens, and the best investors can well articulate how they prepare and execute their responses. Some, through activism, look to take the resolution of outstanding or evolving issues that impact shareholder value more into their own hands.

TRADING MENTALITY

We don't know what kind of investor poker legend Amarillo Slim (born Thomas Austin Preston) was, but we have often found investing insight in his musings. One of our favorite quotes: "The result of one particular game doesn't mean a damn thing, and that's why one of my mantras has always been 'Decisions, not results.' Do the right thing enough times and the results will take care of themselves in the long run." As important as the decision to buy a stock is, events dictate that a variety of new decisions be made about that stock during your ownership of it. While many investors' frequently conclude as those events unfold that doing nothing is the right decision, others see actively trading around positions as central to their success.

* * *

Our turnover is usually in the low teens—last year it was 8 percent, versus an average for small-cap value funds followed by Morningstar of around 70 percent. This is driven by the belief that if you've truly done your upfront research well, you should have the patience and courage to let ideas work. I don't believe you can explain 70 percent turnover or more without assuming people are buying many things they don't really know and dumping them when they get a negative surprise. We're not immune to missing things, but its rare that unexpected risks come up so quickly that we reverse course before the thesis has had a chance to play out. This obviously only works if you pay the right price going in, to the point where the downside is truly low.

—Preston Athey, T. Rowe Price

Our turnover is typically in the single digits. It's great when something goes up 50 percent in a year, but if you sell it you've got transaction costs and taxes and then need to find an incrementally better use for the money. We've never been very good at trimming and adding and, if we're right about buying the long-term compounding machines we want to buy, it doesn't make much difference. In general, we think a lot of trading around positions overvalues what you think you can know.

—Christopher Davis, Davis Advisors

It's just very hard to trade in and out of positions successfully over the long-term. It's only possible when you can have unusually high confidence in the precision of your intrinsic-value estimate. The most common reason we sell is when we find a better opportunity—that naturally takes us out of some higher-valued stocks that might be most prone to a correction.

—Brian Bares, Bares Capital

We try to take a page from the Weizmann Institute, a leading scientific research center based in Israel. Weizmann has a world-class reputation, a result of their having the largest patent and royalty stream of any academic institution in the world. If you talk to the scientists there, they believe very strongly that their success comes from being able to do their work without having to worry about how their science will translate to commercial profit—even though in the end it quite often does. By focusing on long-term goals, they eliminate day-to-day distractions and are more likely to work through problems that inevitably arise.

We want to have a similar mindset. We know our investors are going to worry about their portfolios over short time periods, but we explain to them that we won't. We try to look at short-term market gyrations as nothing more than opportunities to smartly enter or exit a position, subject to valuation and fundamentals.

—Steven Romick, First Pacific Advisors

We practice the Taoist *wei wu wei*, the "doing not doing' as regards our portfolio. We are mostly inert when it comes to shuffling the portfolio around, with turnover that has averaged in the 15 to 20 percent range. Many funds have turnover in excess of 100 percent per year, as they constantly react to events or try to take advantage of short-term price moves. We usually do neither. We believe successful investing involves anticipating change, not reacting to it.

—Bill Miller, Legg Mason Funds

We're constitutionally set up to be inactive, following the Warren Buffett idea that you should always judge how you're doing in any given year relative to if you'd done nothing. As long as we've made good decisions and our investment cases are intact, that creates a bias for inactivity.

—Don Noone, VN Capital

One lesson borne of experience is that the best course in investing is often to do nothing. Given the propensity most of us have for tinkering, that's a hard lesson to apply in practice.

Edward Studzinski, Harris Associates

We have a five-year average holding period. Particularly in a volatile market like today's, people are trying to zig and zag ahead of every market turn that they're hoping they can forecast with scientific precision. We like to plant seeds and then watch the trees grow, and our portfolio is often kind of a portrait of inactivity. That's kept us from making sharp and sometimes emotional moves that we eventually come to regret.

—Matthew McLennan, First Eagle Funds

We set an upside target for each holding, which is not the maximum expectation we have, but the level at which we reasonably expect to be able to sell in the future. When we're right, we'll generally hold until the shares reach that upside. The reality is that we can't do the level of due diligence we want on each idea and also turn the portfolio over quickly by constantly trading out good ideas for better ones. So we typically hold companies an average of five years.

—*Steven Romick, First Pacific Advisors*

We believe the most important contributor to the long-term investment performance of the companies we own is earnings growth, not a change in valuation. Because growth is driven by earning high returns on capital and successfully reinvesting cash flow, we tend to be very long-term investors—our average holding period runs about seven years—in order for this virtuous process to bear fruit.

—*Eric Ende, First Pacific Advisors*

To compound returns at a high rate over a long time, it's going to happen because a relatively small number of your stocks go up massively. If we're right on the long-term trends, our bias is to stay with a trade for many years to allow that to happen. We try to avoid getting itchy every time something hits a new high—a stock that goes up a lot over time, by definition, is frequently hitting new highs.

—*John Burbank, Passport Capital*

Given the tax implications of selling, the cost of trading, and the challenge of getting two appraisals right, John Templeton used to have what he called the 100 percent rule, meaning the upside should be at least twice as high before swapping out one position for what you consider a more attractive one. We similarly want to improve our position materially when we trade an undervalued business.

—*Mason Hawkins, Southeastern Asset Management*

It's always been fairly easy for me to stay focused on the long term, but with 30 years' experience reinforcing the importance of that, it's easier to stay patient. In 2008 that patience didn't serve me so well. When the problems started to get attention, conviction that things would be fine in the medium to long term kept me from trying to time the cycle. In the short term, a lot more selling would have been a good idea. Hopefully that was a one-in-50-year event.

—*Robert Robotti, Robotti & Co.*

Buy and hold shouldn't really be part of a value investor's vocabulary. All we know is price and value—if price meets value, whether in three months or three years, there's no justification for just sitting there.

—*Charles de Vaulx, International Value Advisers*

One thing I learned from [Tiger Management's] Julian Robertson is the concept that there are no holds. Every day you're either willing to buy more at the current price or, if you aren't, you should redeploy the capital to something you believe does deserve incremental capital. I sometimes hear, "If my target price is $45, why should we sell at $43?" The answer is simple—I believe we have better uses for that capital than getting the last few percentage points in the move from $43 to $45.

We distribute every day something we call the Sheet of Shame. It shows our ten largest losses, cumulatively from the inception of the position, year-to-date, month-to-date, and yesterday. It's a way of focusing our attention on what's not working. There are only two ways to get something off the Sheet of Shame—which people are eager to do—either eliminate the position or increase the position and be right, earning some of the losses back.

—*Lee Ainslie, Maverick Capital*

We're paid to measure risk and reward. But evaluating risk and reward is a continuous process, not once a year or once a month. So our percentage holdings of names in our portfolio will run up and down based on relative attractiveness.

For example, we may love Stock A as a long-term investment. We buy it at the start of the year at $30 and within less than a year it's up 50 percent. We're just as excited about the three- to five-year prospects today as we were—in fact, probably more so because we've seen that our thesis is on track. But the growth isn't at as reasonable a price now. So in a company like this that we know well, we think it's right by our investors to buy low and sell high as often as possible. It's hard work and we run up trading costs, but we believe over time it dampens volatility and adds return, and that's our job.

—Larrry Robbins, Glenview Capital

We've taken a more active view [since 2008] on adjusting position sizes so they best reflect our level of conviction and return expectations. We're not at all becoming market timers, but we're much less apt today to let a 5 percent position through appreciation become an 8 percent position unless its prospective return has commensurately improved as well. We've also scaled back the maximum position size we're comfortable with to 8 to 9 percent of the portfolio, from 12 to 13 percent or higher before the crisis.

—Michael Winer, Third Avenue Management

You always want to use your capital as efficiently as possible and I think we're fairly good at sizing positions based on the revaluation opportunities present. A lot of value investors may buy at $20, buy more at $15, and then won't purchase another share all the way to $40 or $50. We're not afraid to buy on the way up: If the probability of being right has gone up, the probability-adjusted return can improve even as the share price increases.

—Alan Fournier, Pennant Capital

We generally expect to hold something for a long time in order to realize the value we believe is there. But one thing I learned from [SAC Capital's] Steve Cohen is to be sensitive to when the market over-appreciates something in the short term and to harvest some of your gains. Markets inevitably react to data points that you don't think are truly relevant. Trading around that is a profit opportunity and helps you better manage risk.

—Robert Jaffe, Force Capital Management

When I started in the business, a stock might move 25 cents if there was a sound reason. Today, there's too much information out there and people are misusing it. This creates short-term valuation extremes, which you should often act on. Buy and hold doesn't make as much sense when stocks are hitting price objectives quickly. If we

buy at $10 with a two-year objective of $15 and the stock reaches
$14 within two weeks, we're not doing our job if we don't take
money off the table to buy another stock with a 30 percent discount
right away.

—Robert Olstein, Olstein Capital Management

2008 was really quite profound for me as an investor. It increased
my resolve to hold only companies I deeply believe in because you
never quite know when forces outside of your control set off a tidal
wave across markets that shakes everything to its foundation. During a crisis, the less conviction you have about something, the more
likely you are to handle it poorly and the more likely the company
in question is vulnerable.

I have put forever to rest my longstanding profile of never selling anything ever. I am over that. One outcome of this exercise has
been to more pointedly question the enduring nature of the status
quo and to not hesitate in reducing portfolio holdings when the
uncertainty is too high.

—Thomas Russo, Gardner Russo & Gardner

DEALING WITH ADVERSITY

A key occupational hazard of the value investor's trade is buying into
a beaten-down stock that in relatively short order falls another 20 to
25 percent in price. As long-time value hunter Robert Olstein of Olstein
Capital Management puts it: "When you buy on bad news, it often doesn't
just stop on a dime; there's usually more bad news before things start
to turn. You could probably make 20 percent a year by tapping into my
phone line and shorting my initial buys of every stock. That's how good I
am at timing."

Discerning between timing mistakes and just plain mistakes when
something has gone against you is a top-of-mind issue for most successful
investors. Says Richard Pzena of Pzena Investment Management: "Making
the right decisions at these moments adds more value, in my opinion, than
the initial buy decision."

* * *

We're going to make another decision when we're down 25 percent in a position. Did we just completely blow it? Are we right, but the market is just insane? Or is it somewhere in between?

I believe the biggest way you add value as a value investor is how you behave on those down 25 percent situations. Sometimes you should buy more, sometimes you should get out, and sometimes you should stay put. I've never actually looked, but we probably hold tight 40 percent of the time, and split 50/50 between buying more and getting out.

—*Richard Pzena, Pzena Investment Management*

I'm catching a falling sword in almost every situation I'm in, and I'm trying to figure out if it's falling from the 2nd floor or the 10th floor. But my capital base is big enough and my appetite to stay concentrated strong enough that, if warranted, I can patiently, over the course of three to six months, make the price bottom by buying a little stock every day even as it's going down.

—*Jeffrey Ubben, ValueAct Capital*

When a stock moves sharply after an earnings announcement, the question I want the analyst to answer is whether something in today's earnings report impacted the value of the company in 2015. Are we three years from now going to look back at today's earnings as a seminal moment in our understanding of the business and its competitive dynamics? That can be the case, but more often than not what's perceived as a bad quarter doesn't impact the value of the enterprise. That often means adding to existing positions.

—*Win Murray, Harris Associates*

My threshold for pain is high as long as I believe I'm still right. Historically, we've made a lot more money on the long side when what we thought we were buying cheap went down another 30 percent before finally going up—we always buy more if our thesis hasn't changed.

—*Francois Parenteau, Defiance Capital*

During difficult periods we have always been willing to add risk as the rest of the market is removing it by reducing valuations.

I remember sitting in my office on October 19, 1987, when the market was crashing and getting a call from [Royce & Associates founder] Chuck Royce—who was one of my brokerage clients then—asking me what stocks I liked and why. I walked him quickly through three or four of my best ideas, he asked a few questions that made it obvious he knew the companies at least as well as I did, and then he told me to put in orders to buy 10,000 shares of each, with additional buy orders of 10,000 shares for every 1/8th of a point tick down in the price.

You can only show that kind of resolve with great conviction in your process and your discipline, which increases every time you come through a tough period successfully. It's that process and discipline that is fully under our control—in the end, that's all you should really worry about.

—Whitney George, Royce & Associates

We're a long-term, low-turnover manager, so the office routine doesn't change much [in bad markets]. Outside the office may be a different story, say, with respect to sleep patterns and eating habits. But we always say, "When the going gets tough, the tough do research." One of my biggest jobs is to keep everyone focused. Don't stare at the red numbers on the screen—call companies, call industry contacts to hear what's really going on, dig for new ideas, and just look to take advantage of the volatility.

—Jeffrey Bronchick, Reed, Conner & Birdwell

My mistake in 2009 was that in March—when I should have been buying—I felt things were completely unraveling and started selling my longs and increasing my shorts. I've spent my career trying to think only for myself and in this instance I was so influenced by the external world that I blew it with the type of market call I rarely make. All I wanted to do was take risk off the table, when what I should have done was cancel my Bloomberg subscription and focus on the businesses of the companies we owned. That would have been a far better use of my time.

—Carlo Cannell, Cannell Capital

It's the bias of the information age that people feel isolated when they're not in touch with what's going on. To me it's a good discipline to often say, "I don't really care what goes on in the market today." When you do that you can actually get something useful done. Even something simple like saying you'll only answer e-mails in the morning, at lunch, and at the end of the day sometimes can go a long way toward avoiding unhelpful distractions that tend to arise.

We're very big on what we call battle plans, in which we map out how we'll behave at various price points in the market. John Templeton used to talk often about taking that kind of pre-commitment down to the level of individual securities. Because you've already decided what you should be doing, it allows you to focus your attention in a very useful way when the market is falling to pieces.

—James Montier, GMO

We have periodic devil's-advocate reviews of all our large holdings and a separate analyst is charged with presenting the negative case. It's more than a debate society—the devil's advocate should genuinely believe the negative argument is the right one. We obviously make plenty of mistakes, but that discipline helps us reduce the frequency and severity of them. In investing, that's half the battle.

—Edward Studzinski, Harris Associates

If an individual position decreases by 10 percent from our cost, we conduct a formal review. The focus is on understanding why something has gone down. If the reason is that the sector is down, or pessimism over a short-term trend has increased, we'll typically buy more if we believe the story is still intact. If the reason the stock is down makes our thesis wrong, we'll sell. What happens more than I think people are willing to admit is that we have no real idea why the stock is down, which is a problem. There's no pat answer for those situations, but we're apt to sell when that happens as well.

—Christopher Grisanti, Grisanti, Brown & Partners

A guideline that's helped us control risk is to require a full reassessment of our investment thesis when we've marked down a company's intrinsic value by roughly 15 percent or more. If you have to mark down intrinsic value, you probably made a mistake somewhere. The question is whether what caused the mistake is lasting or temporary, which deserves a fresh look.

—Steve Morrow, NewSouth Capital

We have a rigid rule that if a position is down at least 15 percent from our cost, we force ourselves to either buy more or sell. Human nature in such situations is just to hold, but if our conviction on the idea is intact, we're happy to see it down 15 percent so we can buy more. If that isn't the case, we sell. The down-15 percent positions in a portfolio aren't great, but they're manageable. What we want to avoid are the down-15 percent ones that turn into down-40 percent ones—that's where you really start to blow a hole in your capital that's hard to get out of.

—Joe Wolf, RS Investments

For stocks going against us, we also have three triggers that force a decision: if a stock moves 20 percent or more against us on a trailing 45-day basis, if a long costs us 25 basis points in a month, or if a short costs us 15 basis points in a month. It's almost never a surprise when something gets flagged, but we force ourselves to decide whether this is a great opportunity or whether we've made a mistake and should move on. The majority of the time we end up adding to the position.

—Steve Galbraith, Maverick Capital

We don't have many rules, but when a stock is down materially relative to its peer group we assign another analyst to formally review it and then force ourselves to buy more or get out. Not surprisingly, the analyst who originally recommended the stock is the last person to want to sell it.

—Jeffrey Bronchick, Reed, Conner & Birdwell

We have a formal review process if a stock declines by 20 percent or more from our original point of purchase. The analyst responsible for the idea reviews it fully with the entire team, with everyone focused on identifying what we may have missed. There's no forced action at that point, but if we do decide to average down, we only do so once. Averaging down repeatedly in stocks that are tanking is a great way to destroy a portfolio.

—Brian Barish, Cambiar Investors

We've done research on all of our buy and sell decisions and—based on 20/20 hindsight—isolated how each one adds or detracts from the overall value of the portfolio. We found that we generally did a good job of selling losers and of holding on to winners. Where we didn't do so well was in buying more of things that were falling in price—which is interesting, given how much we as value managers love averaging down. We still have more to learn about this, but I would say we've become even more mindful when looking at whether to buy as something gaps down.

—Mariko Gordon, Daruma Capital Management

You have to be willing to double down when you invest in the types of companies we invest in, where things often get worse well before they get better. I don't want to leave you with the impression, however, that it always works. In the late 1990s I had about a 12 percent portfolio position in Superior National, a big player in California workers' compensation insurance. I increased my position in a rights offering and it got as high as 20 percent of my portfolio. When the workers' comp business in California fell apart, the company turned out to be too leveraged and the shares went from $22 to zero. The lesson wasn't not to be aggressive, but not to be overweighted in anything that's so leveraged that it really has the risk of going to zero.

—Robert Robotti, Robotti & Co.

What's the definition of a long-term hold? A short-term buy that went down.

—James Montier, Société Générale

We're big believers in the notion that losers in this business are the ones who make big mistakes and winners are those who make small mistakes. For that reason we try to be unsentimental about our positions, particularly those going against us. We do not average down after a position gets hit, for example. That's counterintuitive to most value investors, but because there is always a fair chance we'll be wrong, we don't want to compound mistakes. One reason I think indexes beat active managers is that you never see an index averaging down. If we're doing our job, we can always find another idea that gives us the same potential upside or better, and we'd rather go with that.

—James Shircliff, River Road Asset Management

There's an interesting section in *Outliers*, by Malcolm Gladwell, in which he describes how disasters like plane crashes or the Three Mile Island nuclear accident are rarely because of one big mistake. They're more likely to result from a series of small mistakes, any one of which, if avoided, would have kept the disaster from happening. Many investing mistakes we've made have been in companies where a bunch of little things went wrong, which when added together made a big problem. Those types of situations can creep up on you, so I'd say one lesson is to not ignore minor setbacks and to be very aware if they start to pile up.

—Paul Sonkin, Hummingbird Value Fund

We don't interpret meaning in how stocks are priced. People tend to think if a stock falls 30 to 40 percent, it must mean things are worse than they realize. We don't think that way and just stay focused on our estimate of intrinsic value. It can happen that a stock falls 30 percent but we think the business value is down 50 percent, so we sell. More often the stock price falls 30 percent and we think the business value may have fallen only 5 to 10 percent, giving us an opportunity.

—Chris Welch, Diamond Hill Investment Group

With investing, focusing on what's already happened is generally a bad strategy. The decision at any point should be only about looking forward. Just adjusting how you set up your spreadsheets and what you track on reports could help in this regard.

—Dan Ariely, Duke University

If someone has a material piece of information to share about one of our names, I always ask that they first step back and review with me our current shared viewpoint on the stock. That helps us put in context the importance of the new information and to better discuss the extent to which it may alter our conviction and/or target stock price. Someone rushing into my office and blurting out the latest news without putting it into broader perspective increases the possibility we'll make a rash trading judgment.

—*Michael Karsch, Karsch Capital*

I honestly don't feel any of the emotional ups and downs from the market's day-to-day activity. I just don't worry about short-term volatility.

—*Ed Wachenheim, Greenhaven Associates*

We lost some longtime clients during the crisis, one of which delicately referred to me as a "washed-up All-Star" as the market was going down. It's not possible to avoid it eating at you emotionally when the market is going against you. One critical thing I've learned, however, is that whenever I'm the least bit emotional, I don't make decisions. We can all feel the same emotions as the small investor—when you're in that state of mind, don't do a thing.

—*Robert Olstein, Olstein Capital Management*

Sometimes going for a walk or meeting a friend for lunch when the market is down 200 points is a lot better then staring at the screen trying to figure out what to do. You don't have to do anything and most of time you shouldn't. I'm absolutely convinced that regularly clearing your mind helps you make better decisions.

—*Aaron Edelheit, Sabre Value Management*

Humor is an important part of our culture. That's not to say we're cutting up all the time or that we're even that funny, but in a deadly serious business like ours if you can't find humor in what you're doing, it's going to kill you. Having a sense of the absurd eases tension and puts things in perspective when things are going against you. Without that, people burn out or tend in their desperation to roll the dice. That's the last thing we want to do.

—*Robert Kleinschmidt, Tocqueville Asset Management*

When we buy a stock we write down exactly why we own it, which we should be able to lay out in three or four sentences. To the extent those assumptions are no longer valid, we'll sell regardless of how cheap it gets. We're fighting the natural tendency to come up with new reasons to own something, for the simple reason that we've found in our post-mortem work on mistakes that one of the best ways to lose money over time is by owning stocks with changing investment rationales.

—Ragen Stienke, Westwood Management

We tend not to average down. I think this is a common mistake, when you don't realize there's something out there you're missing and you compound the problem. We've instituted a soft stop-loss that is triggered whenever a position causes a 1% loss on the overall portfolio from cost, say a 5% initial position falls 20% from where we bought it. We don't automatically sell, but there's a high bar to keep something in the portfolio, let alone add to it.

At the end of the day, markets are too efficient to totally ignore price action. If we're going to be wrong, we usually know in the first year and can cut our losses. Better to admit it then rather than later.

—Stephen Goddard, The London Company

One thing that helps us maintain perspective through difficult times is that we outline specifically in writing what our investment thesis is and what we expect to happen. If what is happening with the business is in line with our thesis and expectations, that gives us the confidence to stick with something or buy more if the share price tanks.

If subsequent events indicate our original thesis is wrong, we make every attempt to ignore the temptation to keep a stock because it's so cheap or because we can come up with new reasons to own it. That rarely works out well.

—Edward Maran, Thornburg Investment Management

Our bias toward buying and holding has at times made us too quick to rationalize a problem that hits one of our companies as temporary and already priced into the stock. If the problem turns out to be more long term and fundamental, it's likely not fully discounted into the current price at all. We've been blind at times to fundamental changes in a company's business because we think the quick 25 to 30 percent drop in the share price makes the stock too cheap to sell.

One technique that helps me avoid that is to regularly look at what we own and ask as objectively as possible if we would buy the exact same portfolio if we were starting over from scratch with the same amount of money. For positions where the answer is probably no, the likely reason is that the company's situation has fundamentally changed, but I just haven't fully admitted it yet.

—Francois Rochon, Giverny Capital

When something spooks me, I should more often take advantage of the liquidity of the market to get out and finish the work on whatever the new issues are. If you determine the problem is a big one, you can avoid a lot of pain. If you conclude the problem is only temporary, you can usually get back in at a lower price.

—David Eigen, Post Road Capital

I've been at this long enough that I can keep things in perspective. Ben Graham said it well: He said to succeed in the investment business it helps if you're smart and it helps if you work hard, but what's most critical to success is that when you have conviction, you stick with it.

The fact that you go through times when you're out of sync or out of favor, that's good, you should expect that and even welcome it. That's where opportunity comes from. If we'd given up on our conviction in early 2007 [betting against financially vulnerable companies], we would have missed a huge opportunity. That we didn't was a game changer for us.

—Prem Watsa, Fairfax Financial

TAKING A STAND

Shareholder activism has come a long way from its modern rise in popularity in the 1980s. Back then, says one of today's foremost activist investors, ValueAct Capital's Jeffrey Ubben, what passed for activism was little more than "buy shares today and tomorrow throw a hissy fit." While that basic strategy has not gone away, more prevalent is a constructive effort over time to influence company management and boards to make changes meant to increase shareholder value. It's not for everyone—and one can certainly be a successful investor without an activist bent—but many of the best investors in the business see their willingness to push for change when appropriate as a valuable arrow in their investing quiver.

* * *

Most shareholders of undermanaged or poorly managed companies vote with their feet rather than push for changes in management, board composition, or strategy. So, poor management persists because shareholders aren't willing to do anything about it, which we think is an abdication of responsible ownership and fiduciary duty. But even if big shareholders have a willingness to take on a public company, most firms don't have the experience, resources or skill set to do so. We think the fact that we have that ability when others don't is a big opportunity.

The private equity business was built around taking over companies and doing what shareholders should have gotten done. Most private equity firms do not possess secret sauce in terms of management expertise—they're financial engineers. The amazing thing is that the same shareholders who do nothing to effect change at a poorly managed company before a private equity firm comes in to take over line up to pay a stupid multiple for the company when it comes public again.

—Jon Jacobson, Highfields Capital

Michael Price [CEO of Mutual Series from 1988 to 1998] was at the forefront of shareholder activism. His and our attitude became that just selling if you weren't happy wasn't the right conclusion. As the owners of the company, shareholders really deserve full credit for what companies are worth. It's not just our right, it's our *obligation* to do all we can to see that we get that credit. For us, a continuing dialogue with management—public or not—is an important part of what we do.

—Peter Langerman, Mutual Series Funds

What we try to do is buy high-quality businesses at a price that is not reflective of the intrinsic value of the business as it is, and certainly not reflective of what the intrinsic value would be if it were run better. That allows us to capture a double discount. That's a benefit we can have over private equity. They can buy a company and run it better to extract incremental value, but they're typically paying the highest price in a competitive auction, so they don't get that first discount. We don't control, but because we have a track record of making money for other investors, we can often exert enough influence to make an impact.

—William Ackman, Pershing Square Capital Management

We absolutely want to be constructively engaged shareholders. We have 10 to 15 percent of our capital in each of our core companies, so I think it's imperative that we make our views, particularly with respect to capital allocation, clear. For the most part, management appreciates the faith we're placing in their business and in them to get the stock out of the valuation hole it's in. When management is unresponsive, we work to change that.

—Alexander Roepers, Atlantic Investment Management

The basic reason our investment strategy adds value is that board members are classic agents, not principals. The information board members get about what shareholders want comes from the CEO. However well intended, board members mostly lack enough fundamental knowledge about the business to challenge the CEO on the performance of the business or new strategies to create value. Almost always, they don't have enough money on the line to have the sense of urgency we have as owners. It's a blueprint for inertia.

—Jeffrey Ubben, ValueAct Capital

We prefer a much quieter form of activism, but every now and then we need to do more. To get on my soapbox for a minute, I'd argue that the unwillingness of institutional investors to take more of a stand against poor management or corporate governance helped contribute to the 2008 crisis. Silence was not the best response to some of the bad behavior going on, particularly in financials.

—David Winters, Wintergreen Fund

If you think about where the corporate system has fallen down in the U.S., it's when the actual capital has gotten far removed from the enterprise, and the agency relationship between owners and management has gotten so broad and wide. That's when you have disconnects or conflicts of interest. Everything we do tries to shrink the distance between the capital and the enterprise.

Activism to a large extent is trying to truncate risk by eliminating the misallocation of capital, which is less likely when those responsible truly act as if they're spending their own money. When making a decision on a new factory or product launch or hiring plan, people should feel the weight of the capital they are entrusted with. Understandably, given the corporate form, many people running corporations don't operate that way. So when that isn't happening, the ability to improve those decisions through activism is a key way to create shareholder value.

—Michael McConnell, Shamrock Capital Advisors

If our capital base were permanent, we'd probably only do active investments. But it isn't, so the fact that I don't ever want to be forced to sell an active investment in the course of an engagement means we also need to hold passive positions. Historically, around 55% of our portfolio has been in active investments, 15% or so has been in cash, and the balance has been passive.

The 55% of our capital in activist investments has produced more than 90% of our returns. One primary reason we're working hard to increase the amount of permanent capital we have is to devote as much of the portfolio as possible to active positions. Doing that should enable us to earn higher returns over time.

—William Ackman, Pershing Square Capital Management

ATTRACTING ACTIVISTS' ATTENTION

Value investors frequently zero in on situations in which a company by its own devices has veered off course, resulting in lagging performance that is nonetheless perceived as fixable. Nonactivists and activists alike count on the fixes being made, with activists looking in varied ways to shoulder more of the load to insure that happens.

* * *

Every investor wants to find well-managed companies, with defendable market positions, that generate a lot of free cash flow that is reinvested intelligently. The problem is, those companies typically don't have valuations we can accept as value investors.

So we look for businesses that qualify on a few of the ideal characteristics and that we think can improve on the others. In most cases either the management is lousy or the company has had a very bad record in terms of capital allocation. To us, those are the easiest things to fix.

—Jon Jacobson, Highfields Capital

Our interest starts first with the quality of the business. We're not looking for trouble, for quick deals to be made, for fixes, *per se*, or even for board seats. We buy good businesses at good prices, where we're willing to take on the short-term risk—the near-term negative data point—because we think the long-term gain is compelling. If the stock goes up, we look like traditional value investors who made a nice investment.

But probably half the time things don't work out that way. We're 18 months in, with a full position, and the stock is where we bought it or lower. But we've proved out the industry structure, we've proved out our investment thesis, and we really believe in the asset. It's at that point we go to the board and management and say we've been your default buyer, we own 5 to 10 percent of your company, and we'd like to buy more but we won't do so without a board seat. The stock is underperforming, we believe we have a deep understanding of your business, we have a deep knowledge of capital markets, and we want all the information that's available to board members to help craft a strategy that creates value for all shareholders.

We don't pick fights. But when the train goes off the track, you need to do something about it.

—Jeffrey Ubben, ValueAct Capital

Our front-end screening is fairly automated, looking at both performance laggards and where implied expectations are pessimistic. We start with the proposition that the market is right about a company's valuation. If these assets, with this management, with this strategy, in this environment are worth $20 per share, can we identify changes in that composition that would make the market value much higher? More traditional investors might stop there, but we then try to figure out how likely the actions we've identified are to be taken and over what time frame, and, most importantly, how capable we are of helping to make them happen.

—Ralph Whitworth, Relational Investors

In the typical situation that attracts us, we engage with management in order to try to get them to rein in spending on failing growth initiatives, refocus on the good core business, improve cash flow, and put in place a greater level of discipline with respect to return on invested capital.

—Jeffrey Smith, Starboard Value

If I learned anything as a management consultant, it was the importance of identifying where a business has its greatest competitive advantage and then focusing the growth and development of the business on that nexus of advantage. Companies consistently lose sight of that for a variety of reasons, often resulting in what we call "de-worsification." It's a very common issue for us.

People issues are also common. These are very difficult decisions for companies to make, often involving many subjective and emotional variables. When necessary, we try to bring a reasonable and rational approach to difficult decisions that need to be made on both hiring and firing.

As market time horizons continue to shrink, the patience we'll demonstrate to companies that are disappointing us has been similarly telescoped. We're not rude or abusive, but we are expressing our points of view and building coalitions to drive change earlier, more frequently and perhaps more forcefully than we have in the past.

—David Nierenberg, D3 Family Funds

Invariably the companies we zero in on have poor corporate governance, but we're far more interested in how the board makes decisions than in the tick-the-box governance items like whether they have a poison pill or a staggered board. Not enough boards think of themselves as shareholder representatives. That particularly manifests itself in setting compensation plans, which don't focus enough on return on investment and often just reflect what management wants rather than what true shareholder representatives would require. In virtually all of our companies compensation is a central topic of discussion.

—Ralph Whitworth, Relational Investors

Our preference would be to have a constructive conversation with management leading to a positive resolution. I don't think going immediately for the jugular, as some other activists do, is the best way to succeed. If you embarrass people and attack them personally, you're much less likely to have a rational discussion. But we've made it clear that we aren't going to go away.

—Phil Goldstein, Bulldog Investors

Activists need the capital base, experience, and credibility to follow through—by buying the company or going on the board to help fix it—if steps aren't being taken to address their concerns. You need to be more than a yeller and screamer whose biggest asset is that you don't care what anybody thinks about you.

—Jeffrey Ubben, ValueAct Capital

There is growing sentiment that a shareholder perspective in the boardroom is helpful, which was not the case 25 years ago. I'd like to think we've moved past the corporate-raider phase and that most activism today is done professionally with the interests of all shareholders in mind.

Companies have also increasingly realized how unproductive it is to resist shareholder input. When activists show up, management for the most part behaves responsibly and respectfully. That results in healthy, constructive dialogue about how a company should operate. That type of dialogue is absolutely in the best interest of all shareholders.

—Jeffrey Smith, Starboard Value

There's a certain trendiness to activism, driven by the fact that the opportunities for activism aren't always there. In the 1980s you heard a lot about it, but then as valuations changed in the 1990s you didn't hear much about it at all. Now it's popular again, but we've always considered a willingness to be active as just another weapon in our arsenal.

—Barry Rosenstein, JANA Partners

I will say that I have in the past fallen into what I call time traps, where I've spent too much time trying to resolve problem investments. We will pick our battles, but usually we're better off helping our best investments maximize opportunities than trying to perform brain surgery on dogs.

—David Nierenberg, D3 Family Funds

One mistake we made with our investment in Borders Group was taking an active role at the company's request. Given the direction the industry was heading and how hard it was to make anything happen, it wasn't worth the time and energy. Paraphrasing Warren Buffett, when you find yourself in a sinking ship, sometimes the best thing to do is to switch boats rather than keep bailing.

—William Ackman, Pershing Square Capital Management

We prefer to avoid public confrontations with management for three main reasons. First, we're a young enough company that I don't want to run the risk of our entire reputation being tied to a public battle with this or that company. Second, we've greatly benefited as investors from forming partnerships with our portfolio companies. We want to maintain that same access, which requires that when we sit across from management they understand we're a constructive force and not a potential headache. The third thing is just from a legal perspective, being an activist is very time-consuming and expensive.

Activists are, generally speaking, well researched and well informed in their positions and most of the time are fundamentally right. They may have an issue with the free riders benefiting from their work, but the good ones are doing everyone a service.

—Larry Robbins, Glenview Capital

I've got a full quota of righteous indignation and a lot of things turn me off about corporate America, but I've never had the personality for being confrontational. I talk to management at times, both to complain and to offer suggestions, but I'm hesitant to be public or loud about it. If I pushed on an issue and someone called my bluff, I know myself well enough to question whether I'd follow through with a lawsuit or whatever the next step might be.

—Wally Weitz, Weitz Funds

We like to invest with management that gets it and is doing what we think they should. Some investors want to buy cheap stocks where the businesses are run by morons and then force them to do something different. That's not a bad strategy, but that's not how we tend to do things.

—Wayne Cooperman, Cobalt Capital

The fact is, when I feel I have to write a letter and make noise, that almost always means I've made a mistake and the more productive use of my time is to sell and move on.

As a buy-and-hold investor, the perfect outcome is when a company earns high returns on their equity capital for as long as I live. I can hold and have the earnings compound in a tax-efficient way. So, as opposed to agitating for a fight, I'm better off hooking up with people who are great at what they're doing—and are going to keep being great at it for a long time.

—Thomas Gayner, Markel Corp.

CHAPTER 10

Guarding Against Risk

It's become common practice since the financial crisis for nearly all money managers—and those looking to hire them—to place significant emphasis on portfolio risk management. This renewal of focus on risk is far less pronounced in the best value investors, for the simple reason that guarding against the unexpected has always been at the core of how they think about investing. Oaktree Capital Chairman Howard Marks captured the general mindset nicely in this excerpt from one of his many classic investor letters, this one from 2009:

> [I]nvestors shouldn't plan on getting added return without bearing incremental risk. And for doing so, they should demand risk premiums. But at some point in the swing of the pendulum, people usually forget that truth and embrace risk-taking to excess. In short, in bull markets—usually when things have been going well for a while—people tend to say, "Risk is my friend. The more risk I take, the greater my return will be. I'd like more risk, please."
>
> The truth is, risk tolerance is antithetical to successful investing. When investors are unworried and risk-tolerant, they buy stocks at high P/E ratios and private companies at high EBITDA multiples, and they pile into bonds despite narrow yield spreads and into real estate at minimal "cap" rates.
>
> There are few things as risky as the widespread belief that there's no risk, because it's only when investors are suitably risk-averse that prospective returns will incorporate appropriate risk premiums. Hopefully in the future (a) investors will remember to fear risk and demand risk premiums and (b) we'll continue to be alert for times when they don't.

The Baupost Group's Seth Klarman puts it even more succinctly:

Things that have never happened before are bound to occur with some regularity. You must always be prepared for the unexpected, including sudden, sharp downward swings in markets and the economy. Whatever adverse scenario you can contemplate, reality can be far worse.

Guarding against risk is built into every aspect of the best value investors' strategies, from the ideas they pursue, their buy and sell disciplines, how they build positions, how they structure their portfolios, how they manage cash, and how they hedge.

MARGIN OF SAFETY

In Chapter 20 of *The Intelligent Investor*, Benjamin Graham, the patron saint of value investing, introduces the concept of *margin of safety*. Warren Buffett has called this chapter and another in the same book on responding to market fluctuations, "the two most important essays ever written on investing." In its simplest terms, Graham writes that margin of safety comes from "a favorable difference between price on the one hand and indicated or appraised value on the other," adding that "it is available for absorbing the effect of miscalculations or worse-than-average luck."

Echoing but also broadening the concept of margin of safety, most top investors today cite the inherent risk aversion they build into how they identify, analyze, and choose potential investments—and, of course, what they pay for them—as their first and most prominent line of defense against risk.

* * *

Our primary frontier of risk management isn't wide diversification, but the quality of the individual businesses, their balance sheets, and the people who run them. In the financial crisis the businesses we owned held up quite well, even if their stock prices didn't. That type of volatility is risk only if you're looking at a short time frame, which we aren't.

—*Chuck Akre, Akre Capital Management*

People don't believe business quality is a hedge, but if your valuation discipline holds and you get the quality of the business right, you can take a 50-year flood, which is what 2008 was, and live to take advantage of it. We incurred a markdown in 2008, and it was arguably just that. You may have to accept a bit more volatility with our fund than in a long/short fund, but we followed a down 2008 with a very strong 2009 and 2010 and would put our three-year returns up against anybody's. The key is avoiding businesses that get snuffed out at the bottom.

—Jeffrey Ubben, ValueAct Capital

Margin of safety comes from as many places as possible, but primarily from the strength and sustainability of the business model, low valuations relative to book value or cash-flow multiples, and undervalued hard assets or other assets on the balance sheet.

—Jon Jacobson, Highfields Capital

At the heart of value investing is the notion of mean reversion, that by paying a low multiple on a conservative margin you can win with the passage of time as the valuation of the business and the margins normalize. What can break that and cause mean *aversion*, though, are things like fading business models, expeditionary management deploying capital in a dilutive way, and adverse capital-structure contingencies. We make every effort to invest only in the universe of companies where those risks of breakage are as limited as possible.

—Matthew McLennan, First Eagle Funds

The consequence of our investment style is that we end up in good businesses, where the market isn't recognizing how good the business is or the level of cash it generates. Those tend to be fairly low-beta stocks, so even though we have a relatively concentrated portfolio—with between 15 and 20 longs at any given time—we haven't had very high volatility.

—Richard Vogel, Alatus Capital

Investing is often about knowing your strengths and we've learned that we're better at spotting profitable, unglamourous, undervalued companies than we are at identifying traditional turnarounds—by which I mean money-losing companies we expect to get back into the black. As a result, we set a guideline for ourselves that no more than 10 percent of the portfolio will be in companies with negative trailing 12-month earnings.

—John Dorfman, Thunderstorm Capital

I've always told people I have no idea what the market's going to do or when returns will appear in the portfolio. I don't think either of those is predictable. The best we can do today is to focus on companies with balance sheets to weather a credit-constrained world, business models that will be around for years to come, and valuations that are cheap enough to make the wait for recovery worthwhile. That's what we can control—the rest of it takes care of itself.

—Andrew Jones, North Star Partners

Our primary defense against risk, though, is to only buy companies that generate or are about to generate excess free cash flow, after capital expenditures and working capital needs. When problems develop, and they will, free-cash-flow companies don't have to take on short-term strategies that are not in the long-term best interests of the company to survive. They can make strategic acquisitions when others cannot. They can buy back their stock and raise dividends. They also often tend to be the companies that get acquired.

—Robert Olstein, Olstein Capital Management

Given our number of holdings [30 to 40] and our low turnover, we can devote 10 times the amount of time some others can spend on any given position, which means we should know the business better, reducing the possibility that things are going to hit us from left field. That depth of knowledge, combined with the quality of the businesses we want to own, is our primary risk-management tool.

—Eric Ende, First Pacific Advisors

Long periods of prosperity tend to breed overconfidence on the part of investors, which leads to a misassessment of risk. During times of excesses, we concentrate on reducing risk by holding uniquely strong companies.

—Ed Wachenheim, Greenhaven Associates

The most important way we manage risk is to avoid situations where credit risks can overwhelm the story. We'll take the risk that our assumptions about the business turn out to be wrong in fact or in timing, but we want to minimize the risk that value is destroyed or the story doesn't even get a chance to play out because of a balance-sheet crisis. If you put our portfolios against those of other value managers, we're typically in the lowest decile in terms of aggregate debt-equity ratio.

—*Brian Barish, Cambiar Investors*

After learning some hard lessons during the financial crisis, we instituted a rule that any ratio of total assets to shareholders' equity above 2.5 to 1 is an exception, which doesn't automatically mean we won't buy it, but each individual position size will be limited and we won't ever have more than 10 percent of the portfolio in such exceptions at one time. That's nothing more than a recognition that when you're wrong with a leveraged business model, the hit to the stock price can just be too fast and too damaging.

—*Robert Olstein, Olstein Capital Management*

BUILDING A POSITION

One way savvy long-term investors look to mitigate risk is by being in no rush to establish what they consider a full position in a new idea. That the share price can run away from them before they are fully invested is an irritant most are more than willing to accept.

* * *

A full position is 8 to 10 percent of the fund's assets, but we typically work our way there over three or four tranches. At each step we're either gaining more confidence in the valuation and our ability to make a difference or we're not. For example, we generally don't meet with companies until we own a stake, so that's the first step once we've taken a position. As we gauge their response and validate with them and elsewhere how we're looking at valuation, we'll either sell, buy more, or sit on it to gather additional information. Working into positions this way helps manage risk.

—Ralph Whitworth, Relational Investors

We often take R&D positions in stocks [before completely finishing our research]. Action adds a sense of urgency to the work—there are so many things to look at in this business that things can fall through the cracks unless you force yourself to focus. Having capital on the books does that.

When we find out the company's a bad business partner, there are structural industry issues we didn't know about or maybe there's an earnings miss we decide isn't a short-term event—then we'll sell. But if every step of the way you get more excited by what you uncover, those are the companies that become 5 percent, 6 percent, 7 percent positions in the portfolio.

—Ricky Sandler, Eminence Capital

We like to live with smaller investments in a company for three to six months before making a full commitment. It gives us an opportunity to even better understand the company and its business while getting to know management and whether we're all on the same page. Sometimes the stock pops quickly and the valuation gets too high, or we lose some conviction on the attractiveness of the business, or it becomes clear that management and/or the board is not interested in developing a positive relationship. We very infrequently purposefully pick a fight, so we'll just move on. Our goal is that by the time we're ready to commit to taking a 10 percent-plus stake in a company we know the business cold and have bonded with management so that we're really in it together.

—Jeffrey Ubben, ValueAct Capital

Given that we're often buying into the teeth of a storm, it's rare that we feel we have to establish a full position right away. While some stocks may run away from us, we believe we've been hurt less by that than we've benefitted from averaging down as ideas in which we have high conviction first get cheaper, or by adding to positions as our conviction in the business and management grows.

—Peter Keefe, Avenir Corp.

After taking a relatively small position, we'll look to further establish our relationship with the board and management, which
should allow us a deeper understanding of both the organization
and the business. Management will say the business is going to
do this based on how they're managing it, and if that happens,
that's helpful, and if it doesn't, that's also interesting. The analytical process is highly iterative, which we consider a key way to
manage risk.

—Jeffrey Ubben, ValueAct Capital

I've never been so disciplined that I hold off buying until 100 percent of the work is done. A workbench position gets built into a
core position only when we have little or no question about the
business, people and reinvestment opportunities. It takes time to
learn how the business model really behaves and I've also found
that it usually takes a long time to understand when management is
really good. Many of the times I thought I knew right away, I was
dead wrong.

—Chuck Akre, Akre Capital Management

CASH MANAGEMENT

How much cash an equity investor can hold in his or her portfolio is often
limited by the terms of engagement agreed upon with investors. When that's
not the case, opinions still vary widely among top investors on the extent to
which cash is a valuable risk mitigator, or even a strategic asset.

* * *

We don't manage our cash balance in a strategic way. Part of that
is a business decision: people hire us because they believe we know
how to find great unloved companies, not because we're clever going in and out of cash. Part of it is also just realistic. As much as I'd
love to be in cash when the market gets hit, I don't believe I can get
that consistently right over time. And if you make just a couple big
mistakes on timing, it can kill you.

—James Shircliff, River Road Asset Management

By having a high cash balance, one is suggesting that he has some wisdom or knowledge about timing the market for which he or she should be compensated. I have none of that.

—*Carlo Cannell, Cannell Capital*

Many value investors have a very particular view of when things are cheap and when they're expensive and they should hold cash. They portray holding cash as a risk-reduction method. My view is that's just taking on a different risk. You're betting there is going to be regular cyclicality and things are going to get cheap again and you're going to be able to buy them. But if that doesn't happen as you expected, you're screwed. You'll end up like the guys that have been bearish for 20 years and don't have any assets any more.

—*Bill Miller, Legg Mason Funds*

We have opinions on overall risk that impact what we own, but we never have an opinion on the market. I've always found enough companies that meet our standards, so we remain more or less fully invested. I think timing the market is extremely difficult to do profitably. With individual companies, I can pinpoint the relatively few variables I need to get right for a thesis to work. When you start looking at the stock market's direction, there are so many variables that I can't even identify them all, let alone predict or weigh them correctly. My time is more productively spent elsewhere.

—*Ed Wachenheim, Greenhaven Associates*

People we greatly respect think about this differently, but if even in 2007 we could buy a company like Wrigley at 80 cents on the dollar, we think that's a lot more attractive than holding cash. We were getting a substantial free-cash-flow coupon, a strong balance sheet with net cash, and bottom-line earnings growing at double-digit rates. The way we look at things, even at 80 cents on the dollar, we'd expect a rate of return on something like that in the mid-teens annually. And that was available in, across the board, the priciest market I've ever seen.

—*C. T. Fitzpatrick, Vulcan Value Partners*

Our cash balance is purely a residual of whether we're finding enough to invest in.

—Jean-Marie Eveillard, First Eagle Funds

Our willingness to hold cash during fallow periods has enabled us to maintain a strict sell discipline regardless of whether we had anything promising to replace what we sold. This view on cash, combined with a truly long-term investment perspective, has also enabled us to avoid the gun-to-the-head mentality that pressures many investors to own less-than-stellar investments. The world doesn't end when we pass on a borderline investment that later works out; the danger we seek to avoid is the temptation or pressure to make too many borderline investments that later turn out badly.

—Seth Klarman, The Baupost Group

We usually hold less than 20 positions at a time, so no one would ever say we're a place to put all your money, but we behave as if that's what people have done. So we think it's reasonable to have some cash around for emergencies—as Buffett says, why risk what you need for that which you don't need?

We used to think having cash was a byproduct of not having enough to do. But the older I get, the more I see it as a strategic asset. It allows us to take advantage of those great opportunities that come up from time to time. We're just behaving like the companies we like to invest in.

—Bruce Berkowitz, Fairholme Capital

One big reason we like to hold cash is that my inherent nature is to feel something better to buy is always going to come along and I want to have the cash available to buy it. People assume they can always sell something to buy something better, but I don't like potentially selling into a lousy market when the liquidity isn't there.

—Steven Romick, First Pacific Advisors

Ben Graham always made the point that even if you thought you had a portfolio of very cheap stocks, if the market at the time was fully priced, you should have at least 25 percent of your portfolio in something other than equities, such as cash or bonds. To do otherwise would be to delude yourself that your stocks, no matter how cheap they appeared to you, would be magically immune if the whole market was to correct. I've always thought that made a lot of sense.

—Charles de Vaulx, International Value Advisers

If we can't find undervalued stocks we'll let cash accumulate, as we believe cash is a better alternative than owning an overvalued security. I'd argue that having the patience and discipline to save your cash for when the fat pitches come along is probably the most valuable trait an investor can have.

—Eric Cinnamond, Intrepid Capital

Periods of low returns have often historically been accompanied by higher volatility. That scares investors away, but volatility in a low-return world is a blessing for us, because there's more opportunity to buy low and sell high. That's one main reason we have 15 percent of our portfolio in cash, so we can pounce when volatility results in individual stocks being shot down excessively.

—Charles de Vaulx, International Value Advisers

When I was first starting out in the business, you could be more or less fully invested all the time. If there was a downturn in the industrial sector, you could sell the utilities you owned that were doing well to buy the beaten-down industrials. In today's market, everything goes up and down at the same time, so you don't have stocks going up to sell in order to buy the bargains. The best way to take advantage of a big market correction, then, is to have cash. In a normal time, we'll keep around 10 percent cash on hand for liquidity purposes. Given the state of the world today, we're closer to 20 percent.

We'll miss some profits when valuations are running high and we're raising cash. That's just not something we've ever worried about.

—Dennis Delafield, Delafield Fund

MIDAS TOUCH

Holding gold or other precious metals in one's portfolio as a hedge against macroeconomic risks is a common tactic among value investors—one that engenders, however, a good deal of debate.

* * *

Gold is a logical alternative for those worried about governments' ability to manage their finances. If western political leaders adopt practices which result in devalued currencies, large budget deficits and rising inflation, gold to us represents a pretty decent store of value relative to currency alternatives.

—*Robert Kleinschmidt, Tocqueville Asset Management*

After the financial crisis we decided we needed to do a little bit more macro investing, hedging for potential strange outcomes within the system. Having a material stake in gold has been one primary way we've done that.

—*David Einhorn, Greenlight Capital*

There is a survivalist aspect to having such a big stake in tangible assets. As long as governments show such low regard for policies that support the real value of paper financial assets, investing in precious metals is about the only way to guarantee the preservation of your wealth.

—*Eric Sprott, Sprott Asset Management*

We don't look at gold as a commodity, but as a form of insurance against what Peter Bernstein calls extreme outcomes. In most circumstances in which worldwide equity markets would go down—and not just for a week or two—the price of gold would go up, providing a partial offset to the hits we'd take in our equity portfolio.

We don't have a blind commitment to gold. The time may come when we think the insurance premium is too expensive or we'll decide that the insurance is no longer required.

—*Jean-Marie Eveillard, First Eagle Funds*

Gold kind of scares me because very often the people involved with it seem to be slightly insane. My other problem is I don't know how to value it. Unlike an equity that supposedly has cash flow attached to it, or unlike a bond that has a coupon, gold isn't worth anything intrinsically beyond what somebody is willing to pay for it.

I have ended up buying it, however, because I concluded it offered opportunity under two extreme outcomes. If the world went into deflation, then gold would act as a store of value while the financial system disintegrated. On the other side, we know people use gold as a store of value during inflationary times, particularly in a world in which you're seeing competitive currency devaluations.

—*James Montier, GMO*

You could take all the gold that's ever been mined, and it would fill a cube 67 feet in each direction. For what that's worth at current gold prices, you could buy all—not some, all—of the farmland in the United States. Plus, you could buy 10 Exxon Mobils, plus have $1 trillion of walking-around money. Or you could have a big cube of metal. Which would you take? Which is going to produce more value?"

—*Warren Buffett (as quoted in* Fortune)

HEDGING BETS

Beyond more common risk-mitigation methods such as diversification, holding cash, and owning gold, there are an ever-increasing number of strategies—under the broadly defined rubric of hedging—that investors can use to guard against general or specific risks in their portfolios. We focus here primarily on one of the more hotly debated of such strategies, the willingness to short individual stocks and indexes. While some market observers and practitioners consider shorting to be the devil's work, others can't imagine their portfolios—or the market in general, for that matter—functioning well without it.

To Short or Not to Short?

Shorting stocks obviously isn't for everyone and brings with it some unique challenges, not the least of which is unlimited risk of loss on any given position. Both avid proponents and opponents of the practice tend to agree on one thing: it's very difficult to do well.

*   *   *

Without having a commitment to the short side, it's difficult to be offensive when you should be. The highest-return opportunities are available when markets are in free fall, but if you're getting shelled, you may not have the emotional conviction to be aggressively opportunistic, and you may not even be able to do it, because of redemptions. Being able to be offensive when everybody else is defensive, in and of itself, can yield excess returns.

A second element is that as true, committed short sellers, we have to be immensely skeptical, and skepticism is a terrific quality in a value investor. A key reason for our success is that we have a high batting average on the long side. We're better at avoiding mistakes because we're very attuned to those situations where value gets destroyed, or where it isn't really there in the first place, say, because of phony accounting.

—Ricky Sandler, Eminence Capital

Our view is that short selling may not in most years be worth the time and effort you spend on it, but you do it precisely for those years like 2008 when shorting not only offsets losses on your longs, but also produces capital that allows you to average down on the long side. A lot of people in 2007 gave up on short selling because it hadn't been particularly productive for a few years. In retrospect, that should have been an excellent sign something bad was going to happen.

Given all the stylistic differences of value investors, it's easy to forget sometimes what value investing is all about, which I would argue is margin of safety. That margin of safety doesn't just apply to your individual ideas, but also to how your portfolio is put together. The goal should be that in the middle of a storm that puts all the less-seaworthy boats at the bottom of the ocean, your boat, battered as it may be, makes it back to shore. Short selling helps you do that.

—Zeke Ashton, Centaur Capital

Both our shorting and activism have done a good job for us in tempering the downside. No one likes going through a crisis, but our shorts and some activist longs that moved independently of the market in 2008 kept us way ahead of the market and better able to respond to opportunities as they were created. On top of that, I think shorting is intellectually challenging and plays a valuable role in the markets.

—William Ackman, Pershing Square Capital Management

I believe the irrationality in the market generally tends to be more focused on the long side. As a result, I think that overall there are more incorrectly priced short opportunities than long opportunities. I [also] just consider shorting to be more intellectually stimulating. Like a lot of things in the markets and in life, the more intellectual argument is usually the negative one. There's something very satisfying about nailing an overpriced security.

—Robert Jaffe, Force Capital Management

We short because I think it is the most prudent way to manage a portfolio, from a risk perspective, and because I believe the key to successful long-term investing is to avoid losses. We also short because in certain subsections of the market it's easier than buying stocks. There are always classes of companies that are dying. If you really track the mortality rates of companies, you'd conclude that the market does not have the upward bias everyone thinks it does. The market is actually a carefully pruned garden.

—Carlo Cannell, Cannell Capital

We think shorting makes us better analysts. Charlie Munger says you really understand a company when you can articulate the negative scenario better than the person on the other side of the trade. We also think that from a business standpoint, if you've done all the work and conclude the negative scenario is most likely to play out, it makes a lot of sense to be able to short.

—Ric Dillon, Diamond Hill Investment Group

How would you judge an investing strategy with the following fundamental economic characteristics: (1) limited potential returns, but unlimited potential losses; (2) skyrocketing competition; (3) tax inefficiency; (4) aggregate net losses over its history; (5) The elimination of a significant source of income in recent years; (6) risk of asset repossession at creditors' whim? Having spent 15 years of my career doing nothing but short selling—with periods of great prosperity and other periods of fast, painful losses—I can argue with some authority that, as an investment strategy, shorting suffers from each of these characteristics of a bad business.

—Joseph Feshbach, Joe Feshbach Partners

We dabbled in shorting early on, thinking we should take advantage of the bad companies we uncovered as well as the good. In reviewing our shorts after our first year, we found that in each case we would have made money if we'd actually closed out the positions, but we hadn't. We were good at identifying the short ideas, but were terrible at trading them. Our batting average was just so much better with our longs that we decided we shouldn't devote the time to the shorts.

—*James Vanasek, VN Capital*

One general mistake we made in starting our firm was that we told ourselves that we should be hedging against macro concerns when that wasn't really our expertise. Short positions were never going to be a big part of our portfolio, but they took up an inordinate amount of time and added an inordinate amount of stress.

—*James Clarke, Clarke Bennitt LLC*

We do some shorting, but very little. The problem is that shorting requires timing, which isn't my greatest strength. I would guess that for all the shorts we've done over the past 25 years we're at about a $0 profit on them.

—*Robert Olstein, Olstein Capital Management*

Value Destroyers

Whether one shorts stocks or not, the characteristics short sellers look for in their best ideas are illustrative of what long-only investors should typically take great pains to avoid.

*　　*　　*

The first and most lucrative category of short ideas are the booms that go bust. We've had our most success with debt-financed asset bubbles—as opposed to just plain asset bubbles—where there are ticking time bombs in terms of debt needing to be repaid, and where there are people ahead of the shareholders in the bankruptcy or workout process. The debt-financed distinction is important. It kept us from shorting the Internet in the 1990s—that was a valuation bubble more than anything else.

The next category involves technological obsolescence. Economists talk quite rightly about the benefits of "creative destruction," where new technologies and innovations advance mankind and grow GDPs. But such changes also render whole industries obsolete. Disruptive technologies have two sides and always have. You saw it in the 1980s as personal computers wiped out the word-processor and minicomputer markets. What's playing out now is the transformation from an analog to a digital world. While that's created great fortunes like Google's, it's also wiping out whole businesses. Traditional music retailing was one of the first to start going. Then came video rental. Value investors will invest into these types of markets at their peril. Cash flows evaporate faster than you ever dreamed.

We also look for accounting irregularities, which can run the gamut from simple overstatement of earnings, often a gray area, to outright fraud. We're trying to find cases where the economic reality is significantly divorced from the accounting presentation of the business. It's not GE managing earnings—everybody does that. We want to see something way beyond that, where management is going out of its way to mislead. It could be the hiding losses in offshore subsidiaries like Enron. It could be abusing mark-to-market accounting as Baldwin-United and many others did. It could be Boston Chicken, a big winner for us in the 1990s, lending money to franchisees to cover losses and not reserving for the receivables. The biggest abuse in accounting today, often legally, is in acquisition accounting.

The last big one would be consumer fads. This is when investors—typically retail investors—use recent experience to extrapolate *ad infinitum* into the future what is clearly a one-time growth ramp of a product. People are consistently way too optimistic and underestimate just how competitive the U.S. economy is in these types of things: Cabbage Patch Kids in the 1980s, NordicTrack in the early 1990s, George Foreman grills in the early 2000s.

—*James Chanos, Kynikos Associates*

[Blue Ridge Capital's] John Griffin, one of the few investors who is really good at shorting, says you always want time to be on your side with shorts. Taking that to heart, our primary focus on the short side is on identifying secular problems that over the cycle are working against a given company. We try to steer clear of short positions in businesses that have relatively short business cycles, shorts based on valuation, or shorts betting on a bad earnings release.

We often find short ideas when all everyone talks about is how great demand is in an industry, while ignoring the supply side. We've seen that dynamic in some of the component markets for green technology, such as in the light-emitting-diode (LED) space. With the vast expansion of production capacity we can see going on, good luck making money in this business over time.

—Lee Atzil, Pennant Capital

We're looking for companies with weakening moats, often coupled with a resulting deployment of capital into areas in which they have no competitive advantage. Even better is when they're deploying not just excess capital, but leveraging the balance sheet to do so.

—James Crichton, Scout Capital

We don't short on valuation, but rather in situations where we believe a company is violating the law, or has misleading or inaccurate accounting, or has a potential regulatory problem.

—William Ackman, Pershing Square Capital Management

When we're short, we look for deteriorating industry conditions, company-specific fundamentals at risk, and liquidity issues. We will short a good company, even a cheap company, if we think reality will fall short of current expectations. The best way I've learned to short is by making mistakes on the long side—in value traps, for example—and then trying to recognize when others are making the same mistake.

—Larry Robbins, Glenview Capital

We primarily look for material disconnects between our view of economic earnings and the earnings that are reported and people are using to value the stock. It could be accounting related, so we pay careful attention to things like rising accounts receivable relative to total sales, cash from operations that is not keeping pace with net income, and decreasing returns on capital.

We also look for long-term structural declines—kind of the opposite of what we look for on the long side. Wall Street tends not to fundamentally mark stocks down until bad news actually shows up in the numbers. We'll ignore the supposed value today and focus on whether we think the "E" in a P/E is going to be materially less in three to five years.

—*Ricky Sandler, Eminence Capital*

We focus on what we call false hope, where stated company goals are unlikely or unobtainable. We've had success historically with single-product companies, often in the healthcare field. Management tends to be promotional, the companies burn cash because they're growing so fast, and Wall Street tends to love them because they're always raising money. When expectations appear to be that growth will never stop and that the success with one product will be replicated many times over, there's often plenty of room for ultimate disappointment.

—*Robert Alpert, Atlas Capital*

We have a motto, "buy cash flow, short cash burn." If a business is burning cash, they're destroying value quarter after quarter. Two things generally happen. They have to recapitalize on unfavorable terms, which is good for us as short sellers. Or, they can't get financing, which, of course, is nirvana for us as short sellers because the stocks then usually go to zero.

—*Zeke Ashton, Centaur Capital*

When there is a cyclone of wealth transfer into an area, some of the participants in the fledgling industry will be real companies whose products and services will change the world. But there will also be dozens of other companies that are bogus and run by unscrupulous promoters. That's the subset of the market we're attracted to on the short side.

—*Carlo Cannell, Cannell Capital*

I have developed something called the *C score*, which is basically a six-variable method for searching out ideal short candidates that are potentially manipulating earnings. The variables are a growing difference between net income and cash flow from operations, increasing days sales outstanding, growing days sales inventory, growing other current assets to revenues, declining depreciation relative to gross property, plant and equipment and, finally, total asset growth greater than 10 percent.

There's a high probability that companies that score high on those six measures are actually manipulating earnings. By also requiring some measure of high valuation, say a price/sales ratio greater than 2×, we can imagine stock prices for the remaining companies going south quite fast.

—James Montier, Société Générale

It's very hard to short good-business-model, accelerating-growth companies just because you believe they're wildly overvalued. You don't often hear of investors making their fortune by shorting something like Google or Amazon. For value investors in particular, it's better to stick on the short side to broken business models, fads and frauds. There are usually enough of those to go around.

—Glenn Tongue, T2 Partners

We won't short on valuation—say, because Google is trading at 20× next year's cash flow when we think it should only trade at 15×.

—Steven Tananbaum, GoldenTree Asset Management

We're not playing for a multiple reduction, or a reversion to the mean for the industry. My biggest mistakes have generally been because I stayed with shorts just because they were expensive. The multiple game is a dangerous one—valuations can be crazy and stay crazy. We typically want to see something already or soon to be going very wrong. Our best shorts in the past 10 years, in fact, have been more in low-multiple companies, where we believed the earnings were illusionary.

—James Chanos, Kynikos Associates

One thing we like to do on the short side is to wait to see things start to break down before we get involved. Once something starts to crack, there will still likely be plenty of disagreement—reflected in the stock price—on whether or not the business is really broken.

—Alan Fournier, Pennant Capital

I guarantee that in every great blow-up there has been at least one big-name investor involved all the way down. Don't stop your work on the downside because you can't imagine so-and-so owner making a mistake. It happens all the time.

—*James Chanos, Kynikos Associates*

Portfolio Hedging

While many managers who short view the practice first and foremost as a profit center, shorting individual stocks and indexes also can play an important role in offsetting specific risks elsewhere in the portfolio. Some investors articulate well the strategy behind such efforts, but too often the explication is so complex that more questions are raised than answers given.

* * *

To give an example of the type of hedging we do, we invested last year in Arkema, a specialty chemical company that was spun out of France's Total. It had all the classic spin-off dynamics and we saw it as an excellent opportunity to get in at a good price as a low-margin, neglected company was now going to be run by an independent management that could unlock the business value. At the same time, though, we didn't want to be exposed to a cyclical downturn in the chemicals business, so we shorted a basket of European specialty chemical companies that had twice the margins of Arkema and were trading at higher valuations.

—*Jeffrey Tannenbaum, Fir Tree Partners*

We keep our net exposure to the market in a tight band, usually from 0 percent to 25 percent. The basic rationale is that while we're confident in our skill as stock pickers, we're not confident at all in our ability to predict market direction. Another key aspect of our portfolio strategy is to limit exposure to exogenous variables. If we're long a chicken producer we believe is highly undervalued, for example, we'll pair that with a short position in a chicken producer we believe is overvalued because we don't want exposure to the price volatility of chicken, soybean meal or corn, commodities that dramatically impact the unit economics of the business. The more we can hedge against exposures that concern us, the more aggressive we can be in individual long positions based on our view of the fundamentals.

—Tucker Golden, Solas Capital

Our hedging falls into three primary buckets, which vary in emphasis over time. Typically the biggest one is a global market hedge, in which we use things like index options, index futures or credit default swaps to insulate the portfolio, to a defined level, from big market dislocations.

The second bucket is directly related to what we own, in which we'll hedge against a commodity price, a currency, or another industry player in a relative-value trade. In energy, for example, we're usually trying to isolate the relative value between stock prices and commodities futures prices. In those cases, for example, we'll short the oil and gas curve, to guard against the long bet getting washed out if commodity prices fall. Another example would be if we own Ford and believe not only that it's absolutely cheap but also cheap relative to GM or BMW, we may short one of those to hedge against a general auto-industry decline.

The last bucket includes shorts in individual stocks where we're trying to create alpha. It's been increasingly difficult to do this for a lot of technical and competitive reasons, which is why a lot of people have given up on it. We haven't given up, but as a percentage of the hedging we do it's currently the smallest.

—Jon Jacobson, Highfields Capital

Is Shorting Inherently Evil?

We don't share the general enmity sometimes directed toward short sellers, as if betting against stocks was somehow anti-American. Well-functioning markets depend on the transparent flow of information, which can be greatly hindered when critics are attacked not for the quality of their analysis, but simply for being skeptics. "The vilification of critics, be they short-sellers, journalists, or regulators, chills the free flow of ideas and analysis—indeed, chills free speech—by making it so darn expensive," writes Greenlight Capital's David Einhorn in his book, *Fooling Some of the People All of the Time,* written about his experience shorting Allied Capital stock. "If posting an analysis on a website or making a speech gets you an SEC investigation, why bother?"

As in any category of investors, there may be bad actors who should be held accountable for misdeeds proscribed by law or regulation. There may be bad analysis for which the market tends to be a strict disciplinarian. Such safeguards should be fully sufficient to punish wrongdoers, while leaving the free flow of information intact.

*   *   *

I have no problem with taking a negative view on a company, but as it's gotten easier (through the Internet and TV) and more economical (through options markets) to conduct bear raids, there's a much greater risk that short sellers can manipulate the markets and try to bring companies down.

—*Martin Whitman, Third Avenue Management*

From our experience, much long-oriented analysis is simplistic, highly optimistic, and sloppy. Short-sellers, by going against the long-term tide of economic growth and the short-term swells of public opinion and margins calls, are forced to be cracker-jack analysts. Their work product is usually top-notch and needs to be. Short-sellers shouldn't be reviled or banned; most should be celebrated and encouraged. They are the policemen of the financial markets, identifying frauds and cautioning against bubbles. In effect, they protect the unsophisticated from predatory schemes that regulators and enforcement agencies don't seem able to prevent.

—*Seth Klarman, The Baupost Group*

One general benefit of shorting is that it tempers volatility in both directions. Risk is created when markets get overvalued and short sellers help keep that in line. I'd argue that one reason housing got so overvalued is that until very late in the game everyone was on the same side of the trade, which created significant risk in the system. Short sellers also temper volatility on the downside – they're one of the earliest buyers when a stock crashes.

I'd also argue that the shorts who do good fundamental research play an important watchdog role. They have the resources to dig into something that a regulator might miss. Had people listened to Jim Chanos about Enron, or us about MBIA, or David Einhorn about Lehman Brothers, a lot of people's money could have been saved.

—*William Ackman, Pershing Square Capital Management*

It annoys me when management blames short sellers for a variety of ills and then tries to get Congress or the regulators to harass and vilify them. I long for the day when a management team, which has a well-known short seller publicly short its stock, starts its quarterly earnings call with a Q&A session with the short-seller. "We are now going to take all the questions which Jim Chanos, manager of Kynikos Associates, who is short our stock, would like to ask. Mr. Chanos, your line is open. Please proceed." Wouldn't that clear the air?

—*Timothy Mullen, VNBTrust*

Short selling is now a lot more acceptable than it was, but it's still difficult. People question our motives and say things like "What's your vested interest? Aren't you saying that just because you expect the stock to go down?" Well, yeah . . . don't people who are long say positive things because they think a stock's going to go up?

—*James Chanos, Kynikos Associates*

CHAPTER 11

Making the Sale

Despite the obvious importance of doing it well, selling often gets relatively short shrift in the discussion of investment strategy. Investors who speak with great clarity and in great detail about their buying *strategy* often describe their selling *discipline* in three or four bullet points. The language used in explaining how, why, and when they sell a stock can be, for want of a better word, fuzzy.

This attitude toward selling is consistent with research by behavioral-finance expert Terence Odean of the University of California, Berkeley, who has found that investors tend to derive considerably more pleasure from buying than they do from selling. "Buying is optimistic, about what the stock can do for the portfolio going forward," he says. "Selling is generally more pessimistic, about what the stock has already done to the portfolio, which may or may not have been pleasant."

This discomfort around selling is also borne out in research of professional investors' selling practices. As Michael Ervolini, CEO of investment-research firm Cabot Research, puts it:

> *Standard descriptions of the selling discipline typically include: (1) We sell when our thesis for the stock has been realized; (2) We sell when the fundamentals significantly change; and (3) We sell opportunistically when we identify better uses of our capital.*
>
> *These are fine reasons for selling a stock, but they don't particularly suggest strategic thinking. This was borne out in a survey of professional investors that my firm, Cabot Research, conducted in 2008 with the CFA Institute. The results highlighted that most sell decisions are based on judgment, feel, and instinct—less than 15 percent of the respondents said they used a rigorous and calibrated method for identifying sell candidates.*

Even the novice investor can attest that selling carries with it more than its share of emotional baggage. "This stock has been a dog, but I can't sell now because it's got to be about to turn." "This has been a big winner. I love this company, I love this management, how can I sell?" "Wow, up 30 percent in six months. I better get out while the getting is good!"

Novice and professional investor alike are subject to the challenges that complicate the selling process. But the best investors tend to place selling front and center among what they must do well, and are adept in articulating why they sell, their disciplines for deciding when they sell, and the lessons they've learned from painful experience.

WHY TO SELL

In contemplating selling, investors are dealing with the good, the bad, and the ugly in their portfolios. While that can make generalizations difficult, leading investors are typically clear-headed and thoroughly unsentimental about why any given position should be headed for the chopping block.

* * *

We sell for four primary reasons: when the price reaches our appraised value; when the portfolio's risk/return profile can be significantly improved by selling—for example, a business at 80 percent of its worth for an equally attractive one selling at only 40 percent of its value; when the future earnings power is impaired by competitive or other threats to the business; or when we were wrong on management and changing the leadership would be too costly or problematic.

—*Mason Hawkins, Southeastern Asset Management*

Warren Buffett talks about a company's value moving through innovation, imitation and then idiocy phases. We're most comfortable in the early stages when we think we're kind of writing the intellectual property. That's not to say there's not a lot of money to be made in the imitation and even idiocy phases, but it's not our native ground. If we're saying the same thing as the consensus and something is no longer misunderstood, chances are we're selling.

—*Adam Weiss, Scout Capital*

In general, we own a stock because we have a thesis that we don't believe is widely recognized. Once that thesis is widely recognized, there's no reason for us to own the stock. We hope the stock is selling at a certain level at that point, but sometimes it's higher than we expect and sometimes it's lower. But it's not the price that matters, it's whether the thesis is widely known. If it is, we should be selling regardless of the price.

—Ed Wachenheim, Greenhaven Associates

Sometimes we sell when we've been right, sometimes we sell when we've been wrong, and sometimes we sell because there are four more things that became more compelling. There's a common expectation that people who do primary research in the depth we do to arrive at their own fundamental view of what value is over a three- to five-year time horizon should hold the stocks for that long. That can happen, but the reality is it often doesn't work out that way.

When we look at our portfolio and feel we have other, fresher ideas more in the early innings of the market's misunderstanding than the middle innings, we will consistently make that swap.

—Adam Weiss, Scout Capital

We replace portfolio holdings later in their earnings cycle and at the high end of their valuation range with those that have the opposite characteristics. There's not one absolute number against which all ideas are compared. This is the value-added of fundamental research—using our judgment and experience to gauge where companies are in their valuation and earnings cycles.

—Kevin McCreesh, Systematic Financial Management

We are fully aware when valuations are getting stretched, which often coincides with a position getting outsized in the portfolio. In those cases, we will likely take money off the table by managing the position size down.

—Chuck Akre, Akre Capital Management

We pay attention to what I'd call technical exhaustion points, where the trading experience indicates that market enthusiasm is so overdone that there's a high likelihood of a reversal. We also keep on top of our companies, industries, and trends to gauge how well the market is understanding the story. We won't put up big returns holding stocks for which the valuation relative to the ongoing potential indicates the story is well understood.

—John Burbank, Passport Capital

We have for selling what we call the *IBD test*. When our companies start showing up on *Investor's Business Daily*'s hot top-10 lists, that's generally the time for us to get out. When the momentum investor's bible brands one of our companies as a hot growth company, we're usually ready to sell. Sometimes it's early, but we've gotten in early as well.

—Cara Denver, D3 Family Funds

To be successful in any business you have to have a certain competitiveness and a certain paranoia. In our business where they keep score every day and your problems are staring you in the face, you need to be incredibly focused on the problems in the portfolio and constantly assess whether your analysis is right and the consensus is wrong. There's a fine line between having done your homework and having conviction in it and just being stupidly stubborn. The best investors figure out how to walk that line, recognizing their mistakes and moving on when the situation warrants. All of that is very hard—if it were easy, everyone would be good at it.

—Jon Jacobson, Highfields Capital

We try not to have many investing rules, but there is one that has served us well: If we decide we were wrong about something, in terms of why we did it, we exit, period. We never invent new reasons to continue with a position when the original reasons are no longer available.

—David Einhorn, Greenlight Capital

One general principle I learned from [famed hedge fund manager] Michael Steinhardt years ago is that if he had a position, and there was any discrepancy at all factually or fundamentally from the original thesis, he'd close out the position. You could give him 20 good reasons to stay the course and he wouldn't do it. At first I thought he was just being unreasonable and dogmatic, but I realized it was just about probabilities. He might have in his heart of hearts believed that those 20 reasons were persuasive and he should stay the course, but that wasn't how he thought about things. He was thinking "90 percent of the time when something like this happens, I lose money, so I'm going to get out." He wouldn't ever say this might be the 1-in-10 time it's not going to happen.

—Bryan Jacoboski, Abingdon Capital

It's when we're truly negatively surprised that we typically exit a position. If we're surprised, that usually means management is also and that there's something more fundamentally wrong with the business than we thought.

—Steve Galbraith, Maverick Capital

We are required as analysts to present five, six or seven key reasons to own a stock, and if any of those start to erode, that's a warning sign we regularly track that often leads us to sell. For example, we have tended in the past couple of years to overestimate the intrinsic-value growth in media companies. As we scale those estimates back—taking away a primary reason for our owning them—we should be selling.

—Clyde McGregor, Harris Associates

We are prone to the classic value-investor mistake of being stubborn about selling even when the thesis starts to break down. I bought it cheap and now it's even cheaper—I can't sell now! That's complicated by the fact that we're transparent with our investors about what we're doing, and it's hard to admit that what you were arguing last quarter has changed or was just flat out wrong.

We try to apply a couple basic tests to avoid that mistake. One is to be sensitive that when something is taking up an inordinate amount of mental bandwidth, that's almost always a bad sign. We spent way too much time trying to grapple with AIG in 2008, for example, as the bottom was falling out.

Probably the best question we ask ourselves when contemplating selling is, "If we didn't own it, would we be buying it today."

We bought Lockheed Martin [in early 2010] because we liked the hard-to-replicate franchise, strong capital discipline and positive correlation to rising geopolitical tensions. We also thought that defense-spending cuts might be less onerous than expected, especially if the Republicans did well in the next election. When Republicans did do well in the mid-term elections, defense stocks did little because everyone was talking about across-the-board belt-tightening. When North Korea shelled South Korea, Lockheed shares actually went down over the next week. Those were market signals that we listened to, and when we asked if we'd be buying the shares today, the answer was no. Given that we also had many other things to buy, we sold and moved on quickly.

—Daniel Bubis, Tetrem Capital

Buying bargains is the sweet spot of value investors, although how small a discount one might accept can be subject to debate. Selling is more difficult because it involves securities that are closer to fully priced. As with buying, investors need a discipline for selling. First, sell targets, once set, should be regularly adjusted to reflect all currently available information. Second, individual investors must consider tax consequences. Third, whether or not an investor is fully invested may influence the urgency of raising cash from a stockholding as it approaches full valuation. The availability of better bargains might also make one a more eager seller. Finally, value investors should completely exit a security by the time it reaches full value; owning overvalued securities is the realm of speculators.

—Seth Klarman, The Baupost Group

SELLING BY THE NUMBERS

It's by no means a universal approach, but the selling process can be one of the more rote disciplines investors follow: "If X, then we sell." X is, unsurprisingly, usually based on valuation.

* * *

We generally sell at around 90 percent of our estimate of business value and we try to be quite disciplined about it. I've never understood why value investors who are very disciplined on the buy side become momentum investors when they sell, saying they'll wait for the market to tell them when it's the right time to sell.

It seems to me that if you think your portfolio is being hurt by that last move from fair value to overvalued—that that move is greater than what you'd get by going from 60 percent of fair value to 90 percent of fair value in something else—then shouldn't your strategy be to identify names that you've missed that have run up to fair value and buy them for the run to overvalued? Yeah, it's frustrating to sell names and they go up more, but the flip side is you've reinvested that money in something that you feel is more undervalued and should contribute to your returns beyond what you'll get from what you sold early.

—Bill Nygren, Harris Associates

When the stock price gets within our estimated range for intrinsic value, we're sellers. To my mind, capturing a discount to a conservatively estimated intrinsic value is a far easier proposition than betting on the growth of intrinsic value over time. Someone like Warren Buffett, who has an incredible gift for imagining how a company's business and market develops over time, is going to be much better than I am at seeing the potential for growth. There are exceptions, but I usually leave that part of a stock's upside to people like him.

—Jim Roumell, Roumell Asset Management

Psychological issues can come into play, but selling strikes me as fairly straightforward. We'll sell any time we conclude our thesis is flawed or risk factors have emerged that make us doubt the probability of return. In ideas that are working out, if we believe the fair value of a stock that is a 5 percent position and trading at $80 is $100, we start staging out as the position size gets larger and the stock price gets closer to fair value. So we might start selling at $90 and be out by $105. We try not to make it much more complicated than that.

We have a friend who keeps sending us e-mails about all the stocks we sold too soon. But you know what? It's okay to give up the risky profit. We kick ourselves when we turn out to be too conservative by selling at the midpoint of our fair value range. But we can live with that. We specialize in getting the low-risk profits. It's okay with us if other people make money on the high-risk profits.

—Zeke Ashton, Centaur Capital

We try to keep it fairly rigid. When a holding hits some combination of 8x EBITDA, 12x EBIT, or 15x forward earnings, we're going to start selling. Given the types of companies we buy, that means the shares are in the top end of their valuation range and we can't expect enough further upside.

—Alexander Roepers, Atlantic Investment Management

We have an absolute valuation process, with buy and sell prices for every stock in our portfolio. We think in terms of cap rate, a real estate term, which we calculate by dividing our estimate of a company's normalized operating earnings by its enterprise value. We're trying to buy companies at a 15 percent earnings yield and we'll be selling when that yield gets to around 8 percent. At 8 percent you're getting into the rarefied zone where growth and momentum investors are still comfortable, but where those who care about value— including potential buyers of the company—aren't so interested.

—Whitney George, Royce & Associates

When a stock hits 90 percent of our value estimate, we formally review the fundamentals of the position and our estimates. We also may begin trimming, particularly if the position is large or less liquid. At 100 percent of estimated value, we are actively trimming the position. If we still have a position when it gets to 110 percent, we must be out before it gets to 111 percent. This approach gives us flexibility to let our winners run, but only within the boundaries of our valuation discipline.

That's not to say we'll let the whole portfolio sit in fully valued stocks. We keep careful overall track of where our portfolio holdings trade relative to absolute value. The historical range is 65 percent to 82 percent, and right now it's around 76 percent. I'm not doing my job as a portfolio manager if I'm not swapping out stocks trading closer to estimated value with those trading at much bigger discounts.

—James Shircliff, River Road Asset Management

I have a pretty strict rule that if anything changes my perspective on a company so that my earnings estimates fall by more than 15 percent, I sell. You could legitimately argue a stock is even more attractive if its price falls 25 percent and your estimates only go down 15 percent, but that in many ways turns an offensive thesis into a defensive one, a dynamic I try to avoid.

—Jed Nussdorf, Soapstone Capital

Tracking insider selling is sometimes not so helpful, but if you do see an insider aggressively selling when the stock is falling, run. There's only one reason somebody does that, and it's not because they're bullish on the stock's prospects. I couldn't care less if you're paying for a new swimming pool or your kids' tuition—you're selling and think your stock is overvalued, so why should I own it?

—Aaron Edelheit, Sabre Value Management

Our selling discipline reflects our desire to exit investments when they reach fair value, although we do pay a lot of attention to taxes, which are inexplicably overlooked by a lot of long/short funds. The common wisdom seems to be that you shouldn't let taxes cloud your investment judgment, but that's unrealistic to us given the difference between short- and long-term tax rates. We do not like to sell stocks that have worked before owning them for a full year, unless we feel a stock's price exceeds fair value to the extent that the tax benefit of waiting to sell no longer compensates for the risk of a return to fair value, or worse.

—Tucker Golden, Solas Capital

I arrived at a rigid quantitative discipline because otherwise I would have no idea how to sell. It struck me that if you let your emotions dictate when to sell, you risk falling in love with companies that have been doing well and you ride them too long, and then something goes wrong. I guess I have the classic value mentality. It's instinctual for me to want to sell as things go up and I start getting nervous. For me, having something systematic that says ìthis is cheapî or ìthis is fairly valuedî is really, really important.

—Richard Pzena, Pzena Investment Management

GETTING THE TIMING RIGHT

Ask investors to reflect on their mistakes and they frequently cite poor timing—both too early and too late—when it comes to selling. How they come to terms with this timing challenge, and what they do to overcome it, can be highly instructive in understanding their overall investment approach.

* * *

Given our value bias, we tend to buy early and sell early. Often in our best investments the shareholder base changes, from value investors to GARP investors, and we miss out as that full transition takes place and the true believers completely take over. I've come to accept that and consider it kind of inevitable with a value discipline.

—Jon Jacobson, Highfields Capital

As sensible as a buy-and-hold strategy is in a bull market, it can be dangerous in a volatile, downward-trending one. It's a fair criticism that we historically may have held too closely to our aspirational valuation, even after what we considered our proprietary insight had become conventionally held. We're less worried now about the perfect exit and are content with the perfectly good one.

—David Nierenberg, D3 Family Funds

I more often than not sell too soon. To avoid that, I'm trying to better distinguish between cases in which the rise in the share price is still primarily a function of improving business fundamentals and those where multiple expansion has become most important. A rapidly increasing multiple often means too many people are starting to agree with me, which makes me nervous.

—Aaron Edelheit, Sabre Value Management

We've many times sold way too soon. To try to avoid this, we've forced ourselves to look over long periods at where margin and sentiment peaks have been in individual stocks, to really vet how high something might reasonably go.

—Philip Tasho, TAMRO Capital

In cases in which we haven't made a mistake or something better hasn't come along, we've evolved our selling strategy somewhat. We used to have a fairly rigid rule that as soon as something went above the market multiple we'd sell, but we thought we too often were leaving money on the table so we now use trailing stops. That means if something hits the market multiple on the day it's trading at $61, we'll set a stop to sell, say, at $59. If the stock goes up to $63, we'll set the trailing stop at $61, and so on. Hopefully this allows us to better take advantage of people's willingness to overpay for our shares.

—John Dorfman, Thunderstorm Capital

In one stock we sold way too early. Dealing with management was so frustrating that it discombobulated us and we concluded the situation couldn't be fixed. In fact, we should have stepped back and recognized that the attractiveness of the business would outlast management. Within a year of the old CEO leaving, the stock went from the low teens to $40. We had the conversation at $7 about whether to take a much bigger position and pound the table more with management, we just didn't do it.

—Don Noone, VN Capital

When management really makes us angry, we put the file in a drawer for a while and just don't do anything. We try not to sell just because we're angry. If you sell when you're angry, you can imagine everybody else who sells that way reaches the point of exasperation at exactly the same time. That's the kind of thing that creates at least a trading bottom. Better to sit on it for some time, and even if you still hate what the company's doing, you're probably going to get a better chance to get out.

—David Einhorn, Greenlight Capital

We make a clear distinction when selling between compounders and cigar-butt stocks. Once the cigar butts come back, you know to get out because they're just going to go down again. With [something like] Johnson & Johnson, though, you make a judgment call when it hits intrinsic value, based on your confidence in its ability to compound returns and what your alternatives are.

—Christopher Browne, Tweedy, Browne Co.

We will sell when events materially threaten return on capital, the discount rate implicit in the stock gets too low because the valuation has gone up, or if I just have a much better idea. But if a company is doing well and continues to earn an attractive return on capital, I'm in no hurry to sell.

—Murray Stahl, Horizon Asset Management

If we're investing in competitively advantaged businesses run by excellent management, we won't go too wrong even if we hold companies trading above our estimate of intrinsic value from time to time. We've owned Morningstar since its IPO and I can see it one day becoming a $10 billion business. The founder and CEO owns more than half the company and for 25 years has run it at every level to maximize long-term returns. Unless something fundamentally changes in that situation, why would we sell?

—Brian Bares, Bares Capital

Selling for me is rarely about pure valuation. The really good ones are too hard to find—you don't want to part with them lightly. Life experience tells me that if you sell something at $50 and tell yourself you'll get back in if it goes back down to $35, it will go down to $35.01 and the next time you have a serious look it will be at $300. That hurts.

—Chuck Akre, Akre Capital Management

When something approaches our price target, we will reassess it carefully and the decision to sell often has a lot to do with the alternatives we have. We think it's overly bold of us to try to time going in and out of cash, so we're apt to let something we know well run if we don't have something better to buy. Overall, I'd say in my career I've sold too early many more times than I've sold too late.

—Candace Weir, Paradigm Capital

Based on our research, investors who sell winners and hold losers because they expect the losers to outperform the winners in the future are, on average, mistaken.

—Terence Odean, University of California, Berkeley

Once we take ownership of an idea—whether it's related to politics or sports or investing—a lot of changes take place. We probably fall in love with the idea more than we should. We value it for more than it's worth. And quite often, we have trouble letting go of it because we can't stand the idea of its loss. What are you left with then? A rigid and unyielding ideology that can be quite detrimental to clear thought.

—Dan Ariely, Duke University

Some of our biggest mistakes have been in companies on which we initially made a lot of money, but then got so enamored with the business that we didn't realize when it stopped being relatively special. Not only did we not sell when we should have, we bought more as it started to decline. You start to believe advantaged companies should stay that way forever, but the dynamics of markets often work against that and we as investors miss that at our peril.

What's important is to try to constantly reassess investments as if you're looking at them for the first time. That's not always easy, but we find it helps keep us from falling into the trap of assuming key assumptions are intact when they really aren't.

—Paul Tanico, CastleRock Management

Given the importance we often put on management's ability to fix problems, it's inevitable that from time to time we'll fall in love too easily and make excuses for those in charge when the company continues to do poorly. In these cases, my patience works against me and we tend to ride a stock down until I get disgusted and sell it.

—Preston Athey, T. Rowe Price

SALE PROCESS

Given the many potential pitfalls that attend the selling process, savvy investors often implement guidelines or rules meant to limit those pitfalls' frequency and severity. Forewarned is forearmed.

* * *

As our positions have gotten larger, we often find ourselves in situations where we can't trade out positions quickly. There have been cases where we own, say, one million shares and we think we want to sell, but we can only sell 25,000 shares right away. You could say, "Why bother, it's only 25,000 shares?" But our feeling is that's silly—it might only help solve 2.5 percent of the problem, but the problem is now 2.5 percent smaller than it was. We also find that as you begin to exit a position, sometimes the stomach tells you whether you want to keep going, accelerate, or whether it isn't really necessary.

—David Einhorn, Greenlight Capital

When we worked for Boone Pickens, he taught us that the most successful wildcat oilmen were not the ones who hit the most gushers, but the ones who knew when to plug a dry hole. I think we're disciplined about ignoring sunk costs. We mark our investments to market every day and say, "Okay, we bought this at $25 and it's now at $12, what does the upside look like with this new investment at $12?" If it meets our targets, we'll still own it. If it doesn't, we'll get out. People are afraid to admit to clients that something is a bust, but we're pretty good at just taking our lumps and moving on.

—Ralph Whitworth, Relational Investors

We go out of our way with our positions not to look at the original price we paid. All of our summary sheets have intrinsic value and closing price—if you wanted to know the price paid you'd have to go look it up. Anchoring on your cost—I know from experience—can often cause you to want to take some money off the table and you end up selling too early. On the other side, if you're underwater the tendency is to want to get some of it back first before selling. But if it's a mistake, obviously, it's better to deal with it earlier rather than later.

—Bryan Jacoboski, Abingdon Capital

The market encourages all kinds of anchoring. The price at which you bought a stock is very vivid in your mind, but in reality you'd be much better off if immediately after the purchase you forgot the price you paid. We also ascribe importance to 52-week highs and lows, but why that? It would make as much sense to look at the highs and lows over 70 weeks, or 40 weeks.

—Dan Ariely, Duke University

One lesson learned after enduring a few too many round trips is to take more of an internal rate of return (IRR) focus on when to sell—what is the return potential from today, not "I'm holding this until it reaches my target price of $X." We'll still ride things up and down, but it's been less frequent since we starting thinking more in terms of today's IRR. When we no longer believe something can make us 50 percent over the next two years, we start picking our spots to sell.

—Robert Lietzow, Lakeway Capital

We constantly evaluate the key investment-case elements for each of our holdings and prepare an exception report each week that flags any number of issues. These include when there are material changes in the remaining upside to our target price, when earnings estimates are revised downward, when questions have arisen about any existing catalysts, when new risks appear, or when the stock has been significantly underperforming. We usually have a limited number of reasons for owning a stock, so if any of those reasons change, we want to recognize that early and move on.

—Jerry Senser, Institutional Capital LLC

One thing about our process that I believe helps us when it comes to selling is that we lay out specific milestones in writing that we're counting on to support our thesis. We try to be as specific as possible: inventory turns are expected to improve by this much by the end of 2010, or gross margins should increase from 82 percent to 87 percent within two years. Tracking reality against these milestones keeps you from being in denial when something isn't going the right way, and makes cutting it loose easier.

—Mariko Gordon, Daruma Capital Management

There can be emotional aspects to all these investments, so there's a real benefit to having more than one person making big decisions. Our rule is that our investment committee has to be unanimous in order to buy something, but if any one of the three of us wants to sell, we sell it. That way there's never anything in the portfolio that we're not unanimous on.

—*Ralph Whitworth, Relational Investors*

We have three people in charge of the portfolio and we require unanimity on a stock in order to buy. But it's majority rules on selling. The fact is that it's very hard to sell one of your ideas, especially when it's working beautifully. In those cases, it's often been helpful to have the two more rational partners be able to overrule the most enthusiastic one.

—*Christopher Grisanti, Grisanti, Brown & Partners*

We have formed, for lack of a better word, a committee, to which any analyst or portfolio manager can call for more immediate action on a holding than is currently being taken. If the committee by majority vote decides a stock should be sold, that decision, if I'm in the minority, overrides me as chairman and chief investment officer. I agreed to that because no one position should ever be overly disruptive, and because sometimes you need a mechanism to check you when you're digging in your heels. At some point in our careers, because of bull markets, we can start to think we're geniuses. I'm old enough now that I'm well over that.

—*James Shircliff, River Road Asset Management*

Of Sound Mind

CHAPTER 12

Of Sound Mind

Value investors have been eager students of—and active contributors to—
the increasingly popular field of behavioral finance, which draws from
both psychology and economics in an effort to understand the economic
decisions human beings make. These are not the fully rational decisions
that efficient-markets enthusiasts assume, but the messier actual decisions
people make that impact market prices and are driven by a variety of social,
cognitive, and emotional factors. Behavioral finance looks to understand
and explain investors' natural and evolutionarily supported tendencies
toward—to name a few—overconfidence, sticking with the herd, panicking
in the face of trouble, disliking losses more than they like gains, falling in
love with what they own, overweighting more recent information, and crav-
ing the big score.

Of course it's one thing to understand how human nature can conspire against rational investment decision-making, and quite another to
keep it from happening to you. As Warren Buffett puts it: "Investing is not
a game where the 160-IQ guy beats the guy with the 130 IQ. Rationality
is essential when others are making decisions based on short-term greed
or fear. That is when the money is made." In fact, many of the strategies,
processes, and disciplines articulated throughout this book are meant to
help eradicate those irrational and painful "What was I thinking?" types of
mistakes.

Beyond more concrete elements of strategy and tactics, the best investors
often also emphasize the importance of mindset to their ultimate success.
What are common elements of their mindset? They're competitive. They're
contrarian. They balance self-confidence with humility. They're inherently
curious. They're constantly learning. While such traits may be more innate
than learned and more difficult for the outside observer to assess, they're
extremely important in distinguishing the investors who have what it takes
from those who don't.

COMPETITIVE SPIRIT

Over a total of 38 years as a Division I college basketball coach, the late Norm Stewart amassed 728 wins, most of those at his alma mater, the University of Missouri. Known as a tireless recruiter, the first question he would often pose to aspiring high school players was a simple one, "Do you love to play?" All of course said yes, but how they answered was often telling.

Stewart explained that he asked out of a conviction that those who didn't truly love to play would never have the dedication and drive necessary to compete at the highest levels, regardless of how talented they were. This universal insight certainly holds true for investors. If their love of the game isn't evident, it calls into question their ability to play it well.

* * *

What other business is as intellectually stimulating as this? Other than maybe intelligence gathering for national security, I don't know of one. If you like winning, there's a scorecard. If you like game theory and trying to logically deduce what's likely to happen, this is a great application for that and it's very gratifying to be proven correct.

—*Kyle Bass, Hayman Advisors*

I'd use the analogy of a professional baseball player. If you think about what would motivate someone to put so much time and energy into doing something as repetitive as playing baseball, you could probably boil it down to three things. It could be they just like the process of playing the game, because they're good at it and get a lot of personal validation out of it. It could be because they're very competitive and want to be on the winning team and want to succeed in an objectively measured way. Or it could be they're just in it for the money, to become accomplished in the field, and be well compensated for their talent.

For me, I enjoy the process of trying to figure out what's going on in the world and think investing is about as good as it gets in business in terms of intellectual stimulation. Second, I'm very competitive, but in the positive sense of trying to improve and always measuring how well I'm doing that. The third part—making money—is not required, but conveniently and pleasantly is a result of being good at the first two.

John Burbank, Passport Capital

I love the challenge of investing—for a competitive person there's nothing better than when you absolutely nail something that no one else was getting. It's also a great business for people who are intellectually curious. I've followed the battery industry for 20 years, but I learned several new things from my conversation earlier today with the president of Exide. It's a new game every day—why would I do anything else?

—Candace Weir, Paradigm Capital

When I started the business I was motivated by being a real competitor. I love to win, and the idea of being in an industry where you keep score and know where you stand every day was highly appealing to me—and, in the end, seemed inherently fair.

—John Rogers, Ariel Investments

So many things impact the markets, from history, to politics, to popular culture, and those elements change day-to-day. The challenge of working through all that is consistently exciting–and you can see your results on a real-time basis.

—Tom Perkins, Perkins Investment Management

I love learning about businesses and the intellectual challenge of investing. I'm also intensely competitive about generating great returns. I love that you get a scorecard at the end of the day and I love to win. Winning to me is looking back after 30 years and saying, "Wow, look at that track record—these guys did it well and they did it right."

That's not to say I'm particularly fond of those days when you feel like an idiot and your numbers make you look like an idiot. But as a competitive person, I wouldn't have it any other way.

—Ricky Sandler, Eminence Capital

Figuring things out and solving the puzzles is still the most exciting part. It's very fun to think we understand something that it appears most people view differently. Then you get to find out who's right.

—David Einhorn, Greenlight Capital

There's a big difference between loving to win and hating to lose, which has a lot to do with one's approach to risk. Someone who loves to win is willing to take a lot of risks because the euphoria of winning outweighs the bad outcomes. If you hate to lose, though, any bad outcome is not acceptable. To be a great investor, I think you really have to hate to lose.

—Jon Jacobson, Highfields Capital

Investing is a fun game and you want to find the people who are just smitten with it. I wouldn't say for the best ones that it's about the money—it may fall off the back of the truck, but it's not at all why they play the game.

—Joel Greenblatt, Gotham Capital

People who are in a good mood are more inclined to try learning new skills, to see things in a broader context, to think of creative solutions to problems, to work well with other people, and to persist instead of giving up. If you were writing a recipe for how to make more money, those are among the first ingredients you would include.

Jason Zweig, Author, Your Money and Your Brain

I've always considered myself privileged to live the life I do, making a living doing something I enjoy very much.

—Francisco Garcia Parames, Bestinver Asset Management

[My level of competitiveness] was important, yes. I always said that when Tiger Management was going, that our employees would have taken a 15 to 20 percent pay cut if that would have somehow guaranteed us to be number one. That definitely mellows out over time, but I still like winning, which is one reason I've done this same thing for a long time. You can get too much competitiveness, though, and then you're competitive with your subordinates and your superiors and you're kind of a horse's ass.

—Julian Robertson, Tiger Management

I did worry when I shut down my main hedge fund in 2000 that I didn't want my tombstone to say, "He died getting a quote on the yen"—as if I had nothing better to do in the middle of the night than that.

—Julian Robertson, Tiger Management

INDEPENDENT THOUGHT

One of our favorite quotes with clear application to investing is from Spanish/American philosopher George Santayana, who wrote, "Skepticism is the chastity of the intellect, and it is shameful to surrender it too soon or to the first comer." The best investors are without question a skeptical lot, quick to question the status quo or conventional wisdom, and slow to build the conviction necessary to go against either.

* * *

If you subscribe to the thesis—as I do—that the greatest amount of money is made from having great confidence in contrarian positions, I think you'd find the people who are comfortable taking these positions don't tend to fit in with the mainstream.

Going against the grain is clearly not for everyone—and it doesn't tend to help your social life—but to make the really large money in investing, you have to have the guts to make the bets that everyone else is afraid to make.

—Carlo Cannell, Cannell Capital

Figuring out what you should do as an investor isn't that difficult. You can read all Warren Buffett has written or said over the years, for example, and basically emulate that. The hard part is to have the discipline and the patience to execute.

The bottom line is that to be a good investor you need to only buy when it's emotionally the hardest, only sell when it's emotionally the hardest, and do pretty much nothing while waiting for market extremes to offer opportunities to do either. That's all incredibly hard. You often don't know you've been right until months or even years later. Most people need more immediate gratification than value investing typically offers up.

—Steve Leonard, Pacifica Capital

One of the keys to this business is having conviction based on your work that you're right and the rest of the world is wrong. If you don't have that confidence, you'll never buy anything because there's always something that can go wrong. Everyone thought the idea of buying stock in General Growth Properties right before it went bankrupt in the middle of the financial crisis was the stupidest idea they've ever heard of, and plenty of people said so. The stock was at 35 cents a share, down from $63, and we bought 25% of the company. You can't get much more contrarian than that.

—William Ackman, Pershing Square Capital Management

Acknowledge the complexity of the world and resist the impression that you easily understand it. People are too quick to accept conventional wisdom, because it sounds basically true and it tends to be reinforced by both their peers and opinion leaders, many of whom have never looked at whether the facts support the received wisdom. It's a basic fact of life that many things "everybody knows" turn out to be wrong.

How can an investor use that? The uncertainty involved in predicting complex events would argue for some level of diversification and a greater focus on hedging. At the same time, the fact that people tend toward overconfidence and follow conventional wisdom should provide opportunity for those taking contrarian positions against that. The trick, of course, is to have concrete justification for why the crowd is wrong.

—Robert Shiller, Yale University

As value investors, we're quite used to being short on social acceptance at different periods of time. It's always important to keep in mind that our own balance and equanimity should not be based on external perceptions.

—Matthew McLennan, First Eagle Funds

You learn quickly in this business that you're not going to look smart all the time, which inevitably brings criticism. We always remind ourselves of that great Jean-Marie Eveillard quote, "I'd rather lose clients than lose clients' money."

—*David Samra, Artisan Partners*

As it turns out, one of the key lessons of investing is that the best successes are born during times when you're not a winner. I was down 2 percent in 1999 [a year the S&P 500 rose 21 percent] and it was probably my best year. Nothing worked that year, but resisting the temptation to chase ideas I didn't believe in left me positioned for some of my best years thereafter.

It's a long race, not a sprint—if you rely on the market's validation all the time, not only are you going to be very disappointed, you're also going to make a lot of mistakes.

—*Thomas Russo, Gardner Russo & Gardner*

I think our being based in Columbus, Ohio makes it easier for us to be independent thinkers, which is so important to successful investing. When we leave the office, we're not very likely to be influenced by what other investors are talking about because there aren't many out there. I honestly believe that's an advantage—there's no herd mentality because there's no herd.

—*Ric Dillon, Diamond Hill Investments*

One reason our results have been relatively strong is because our mistakes have been in smaller positions and our successes in larger ones. I attribute a lot of that to our partnership: I tend to be a glass-half-full person, while Ed [co-manager Edward Studzinski] behaves more as if the glass is broken and empty. He helps restrain my more aggressive instincts and his natural skepticism has been incredibly valuable.

—*Clyde McGregor, Harris Associates*

We tend to be conservative and deliberate, which often keeps us from buying as much as we should as quickly as we should. Having said that, I think being skeptical and wary about all the things that can go wrong is a good way to avoid making a lot of mistakes.

Anyway, it's my nature to be that way and even if I could change it, I wouldn't really want to.

—*Wayne Cooperman, Cobalt Capital*

An early mentor of mine, T. Edmund Beck, started out during the Depression and used to always say we were in the rejection business—that we're paid to be cynical and that a big part of success in investing is knowing how to say no. He never dwelled on missed opportunities because something else—even the same thing later on—would always come along. I'm a big believer in that approach.

—*Spencer Davidson, General American Investors*

PERPETUAL STUDENT

Unlike basketball, investing is a game at which you should become more proficient with the long passage of time. This can only happen, however, with the mindset of a perpetual student, as conversant in historical precedent as you are in future possibility.

*　*　*

The nice thing about investing is that if you can protect your physical and mental health you should only get better at it over time. Experience improves your ability to recognize patterns and to exercise judgment in difficult situations, of which there have certainly been no shortage in recent years.

—*David Nierenberg, D3 Family Funds*

I enjoy being a perpetual student, and working with good people. I'll probably be here until I go *non compos mentis*. I'll lose my marbles, then they have a right to get rid of me.

—*Martin Whitman, Third Avenue Management*

I generally find the best investors are very open and have almost a child-like curiosity about how everything works. They don't come to the table with preconceived notions. Americans, in fact, are more likely to have this kind of attitude than Europeans or Asians. It's much harder to learn new things when you think you already know everything.

—Oliver Kratz, Deutsche Asset Management

Soon after graduating from college I went through some testing at the Johnson O'Conner Institute and found I have two prominent aptitudes, inductive reasoning and what they call ideaphoria. These don't often go together—one involves a logical progression from specific observations to arriving at broader generalizations, while the other is an unusually high-frequency flow of ideas, many of which are unfocused and non-linear. You don't want much ideaphoria if you're an accountant, but those two aptitudes combined seem to be conducive to investing.

—Carlo Cannell, Cannell Capital

Fortune magazine recently had an interesting article about how successful people work and one of the people they spoke with was Wynton Marsalis, the great jazz trumpeter. He said that if you want to be able to find a groove, you have to practice, practice, practice. You've got to know the scales and you've got to know the basics if you want to improvise.

—Mitchell Julis, Canyon Capital

Things trade at different values from their true worth because human beings look at them in certain ways in certain circumstances. Those ways and circumstances can change, so the tools you use and your thought processes have to evolve. The exact same thing doesn't always work over and over again—the market's too smart for that.

—Lisa Rapuano, Matador Capital Management

One of the things about which we're institutionally most proud is having outperformed the S&P 500 in every rolling 10-year period since 1969. That means we've had to be open to change and not just do exactly what had worked for the previous 10 years, because the best funds in any 10-year period are always the funds optimized to that period—in healthcare, say, or commodities or technology. The biggest risk we worry about is not adapting to the times and participating in change. That's what keeps us on our toes.

—Christopher Davis, Davis Advisors

I'm a golfer, and one of the things I love about it is that you can play the same course 20 days in a row and every day will be different. It just rained, or it's hot, or the wind is blowing from a different direction. You have to adjust all the time for a lot of changing factors, which is also true of investing. People who really love to invest wouldn't have it any other way.

—Robert Leitzow, Lakeway Capital

I've had the good fortune of being around smart investors my whole life, including my father. Because of that, I'm sure things maybe clicked a bit more quickly when I started getting interested in investing. But I'd have to say learning from what works and what doesn't is how you really become a better investor. In the end, the market is the best teacher.

—Wayne Cooperman, Cobalt Capital

You have to have your eyes open all the time and devote yourself, as Charlie Munger says, to lifetime learning. As I like to say, in life as well as in business I'm lucky if I have learned something new every day—and I'm doubly lucky if it didn't cost too much to do so.

—Chuck Akre, Akre Capital Management

Will Rogers once said, "Good judgment comes from experience, and a lot of that comes from bad judgment." I add to my base of experience every day.

—Donald Yacktman, Yacktman Asset Management

One great thing about investing is that, unlike the pitcher who starts to lose his fastball in his mid-30s, my fastball as an investor should keep getting better. I'm one of those guys who says "Thank God it's Monday," because this is as much my hobby as it is how

I make a living. If you don't feel that way, you should probably be doing something else.

—Andrew Pilara, RS Investments

TO ERR IS HUMAN

Critical to the learning process is a rigorous assessment of how and why past mistakes were made. No portfolio manager would admit that he or she makes little effort to learn from mistakes, but we have often found in this regard that words often don't match deeds. Money managers expect executives of the companies whose stocks they own to be open and honest about mistakes, to be quick to correct them, and to be diligent in trying to make sure they don't happen again. Investors should expect nothing less from those to whom they have entrusted their money.

* * *

We have a deliberate process to at least once a year sit down and look at the mistakes we've made. If you do it too often you probably don't achieve much at all because you're constantly looking over things before the mistake is actually clear.

We try to focus more on process errors we can control than just on what went wrong in terms of outcomes. It's also important to make sure you learn the right lessons—it's very easy to learn a specific lesson that isn't very helpful because you won't find yourself in exactly that specific situation again. You want to learn the most general lesson you can from the mistakes you make.

—James Montier, GMO

I'm playing golf in a foursome that includes someone who's a terrible golfer. He's teeing off and takes a big swing and misses, digging up a divot off to the side of the ball and tee. He regroups, takes a deep breath and then does the exact same thing again, digging an even bigger divot in the same place. He looks at his caddy, who walks over and takes the ball and tee and puts it into the divot hole and says, "Try this."

I thought that was hilarious, but it gets to the importance of working hard not to repeat mistakes. We set up our process so that we're formally addressing as many of the answers as possible to the question, "If it turns out two years from now we've made a mistake, why would that be?" It obviously doesn't eliminate all mistakes, but for a concentrated manager, if as a result you make only two material mistakes per year rather than four, that can make a huge difference in your performance.

—Jeffrey Bronchick, Cove Street Capital

We do post-mortems on all of our positions—as well as regular position reviews of what we own—to constantly assess what we got right and what we didn't. That matters because we want to learn from mistakes even if the investment outcome turned out fine because we were lucky. Luck is not a sustainable way to make money as an investor. Avoiding mistakes that you've made before is.

One primary virtue of experience is that you're constantly learning the ways in which things can go wrong. If you internalize that into your process, you're identifying more of what can go wrong and assessing how that changes your investment case. Minimizing the number of times you get blindsided is a very worthy goal.

—Shawn Kravetz, Esplanade Capital

Some investors don't want to dwell on their mistakes, but we closely track over rolling five-year periods how all of our buy/sell decisions are working out. In the same way we don't beat ourselves up for missing something that truly couldn't have been seen in advance, we don't want to take comfort when an investment works out but our analysis was wrong.

—Ric Dillon, Diamond Hill Investments

Mistakes of judgment are the toughest to learn from, because each one is different. They tend to be in companies in which there has been gradual degradation—hard to pick up from the outside—either in the competitive landscape or the culture of the company. Because each case is different, it's hard to draw general lessons and you don't want to learn the wrong one. There were a lot of ways to look at the mistake of buying AT&T when Michael Armstrong took over—successful executive from outside the industry—that would have prevented you from buying IBM when Lou Gerstner came in.

—Christopher Davis, Davis Advisors

I did a simulation of how often a top money manager earning 20 percent per year with a 15 percent standard deviation would lose money over short time periods. A 20 percent return would be about double the market's long-term average return and a 15 percent standard deviation would be lower than historic market volatility. So this is someone who's doing very well.

But on any given day, this hypothetical manager would lose money almost half the time. He'd lose money in 35 percent of the months and in an average of one quarter per year. Once every 10 years he'd have a losing year.

I think it's healthy for investors to remember that even great long-term records are full of plenty of down months and quarters. Remembering that is hard to do sometimes as time horizons in the industry have gotten so short.

—Bryan Jacoboski, Abingdon Capital

My time playing golf taught me some useful lessons as an investor. For one, you make mistakes all the time and you try to learn from them, but it's always about the next shot. It's about properly preparing and then executing to the best of your ability. That's an excellent mindset for an investor to have.

—Pat English, Fiduciary Management, Inc.

I've been doing this for more than 25 years and have learned never to take mistakes lightly. What's most important for us, though, is to stay focused on the discipline of only investing in companies with the characteristics of leaders, laggards, and innovators that we've seen work as investments over a long period of time. That discipline keeps us grounded, and helps us keep mistakes in perspective. Otherwise, you can drive yourself crazy.

—Philip Tasho, TAMRO Capital

Don't be paralyzed by the fear of making a mistake. Understand that the best opportunities usually carry more perceived risks, and distinguish carefully between the risks that matter most and those you can live with. As long as I know the risks I'm taking and the stock prices are compensating me to take those risks, I can live with that.

—Brian Gaines, Springhouse Capital

You want to make mistakes once in a while. If you never make a mistake, you're being too conservative and missing profit opportunities you shouldn't.

—Ed Wachenheim, Greenhaven Associates

BE EVER SO HUMBLE

There's no question confidence in one's abilities is critical to successful investing. To commit one's own and others' hard-earned capital requires conviction, and conviction requires confidence. But as with fine scotch or pepperoni pizza, too much of a good thing can cause problems. It can at times be difficult to see, but quite often even the most accomplished money managers exhibit a level of humility about their craft that, far from a sign of weakness, is often a prerequisite to long-term success.

*   *   *

One can see the investment universe as full of certainties, or one can see it as replete with probabilities. Those who reflect and hesitate make far less in a bull market, but those who never question themselves get obliterated when the bear market comes. In investing, certainty can be a serious problem, because it causes one not to reassess flawed conclusions. Nobody can know all the facts. Instead, one must rely on shreds of evidence, kernels of truth, and what one suspects to be true but cannot prove.

—Seth Klarman, The Baupost Group

You obviously need to develop strong opinions and to have the conviction to stick with them when you believe you're right, even when everybody else may think you're an idiot. But where I've seen ego get in the way is by not always being open to question and to input that could change your mind. If you can't ever admit you're wrong, you're more likely to hang on to your losers and sell your winners, which is not a recipe for success.

—Kyle Bass, Hayman Advisors

It is much harder psychologically to be unsure than to be sure; certainty builds confidence, and confidence reinforces certainty. Yet being overly certain in an uncertain, protean, and ultimately unknowable world is hazardous for investors. To be sure, uncertainty breeds doubt, which can be paralyzing. But uncertainty also motivates diligence, as one pursues the unattainable goal of eliminating all doubt. Unlike premature or false certainty, which induces flawed analysis and failed judgments, a healthy uncertainty drives the quest for justifiable conviction.

—*Seth Klarman, The Baupost Group*

When I worked for New York City, I met an old-time surveyor in my department who had gone broke betting on horses. The first time he had gone to the racetrack he decided to bet on a horse named Surveyor, and the worst possible thing happened—the horse won. This guy figured it was easy money and over the next 20 years he proceeded to lose just about everything he had.

People forget it all the time, but it's important as investors to differentiate between luck and skill. Over short periods of time, you can do the wrong thing and make a lot of money and do the right thing and look like an idiot. We try to stick to what we do well and not get too caught up in what's working at any given moment. In the long run, that sort of discipline will keep you from blowing up. It's a lesson a lot of smarter guys than us have obviously forgotten.

—*Phil Goldstein, Bulldog Investors*

Whatever the environment we try to remain humble, which means maintaining our discipline of buying only great companies with strong balance sheets when they're priced with a wide margin of safety. It's when you're not humble that you end up doing things that will make you humble.

—*François Rochon, Giverny Capital*

Over a long career you learn a certain humility and are quicker to attribute success to luck rather than your own brilliance. I think that makes you a better investor, because you're less apt to make the big mistake and you're probably quicker to capitalize on good fortune when it shines upon you.

—*Spencer Davidson, General American Investors*

We know our investors are going to worry about their portfolios over short time periods, but we explain to them that we won't. We

try to look at short-term market gyrations as nothing more than opportunities to smartly enter or exit a position, subject to valuation
and fundamentals. While I hope that keeps us rational, I wouldn't
say I'm always calm. My style at heart is out of the pages of Andy
Grove's book, *Only the Paranoid Survive*. When our stocks are going down I'm driving everyone nuts to see what we might be missing. When our stocks are going up I'm not any more comfortable.
I'm worried whether they're going up for the right reasons and how
it might all come crashing down. I say we invest paranoid somewhat tongue-in-cheek, because we couldn't take the sizable positions we do if we were truly paranoid. I just worry about it every
step of the way.

—Steven Romick, First Pacific Advisors

I've seen too many businesses—investment firms and others—run
into the ground by impressive people who start to think they're
smarter than everyone else. That's when big mistakes get made.
There are enough ways to screw up in this business without bringing it on yourself because of ego.

—Barry Rosenstein, JANA Partners

Attempting to achieve a superior long-term record by stringing together a run of top-decile years is unlikely to succeed. Rather, striving to do a little better than average every year, and through discipline to have highly superior relative results in bad times, is: (1) less
likely to produce extreme volatility; (2) less likely to produce huge
losses which can't be recouped, and (3) most importantly, more
likely to work.

—Howard Marks, Oaktree Capital

This is the world's best business when you're doing well and somewhat less so when everybody's yelling at you because you're trailing
the market. It's important not to get carried away with yourself
when times are good, and to be able to admit your mistakes and
move on when they're not so good. If you are intellectually honest—
and not afraid to be visibly and sometimes painfully judged by your
peers—investing is not work, it's fun.

—Jeffrey Bronchick, Reed, Conner & Birdwell

The Final Word

Value investors have a long tradition of sharing what they've learned, which we hope to have honored by assembling the insights many of the best money managers in the business have shared with us over the years. We have gone to great lengths to make sure that their words, not ours, have taken the most prominence. Our greatest wish is that you'll find in the wisdom they've imparted insights that will make you a better investor tomorrow, a year from now, and ten years from now. To that end, it's only fitting that we close with the quote we used to lead off our Editors' Letter in the inaugural issue of *Value Investor Insight*, from Warren Buffett's long-time partner—and a brilliant investor in his own right—Charlie Munger:

> *If Warren Buffett had never learned anything new after graduating from Columbia Business School, Berkshire Hathaway would be a pale shadow of its present self. Warren would have gotten rich—what he learned from Ben Graham at Columbia was enough to make anybody rich. But he wouldn't have the kind of enterprise Berkshire is if he hadn't kept learning. I don't know anyone who [became a great investor] with great rapidity. The game is to keep learning . . . if you don't keep learning, other people will pass you by.*

Here's wishing you a lifetime of investing pleasure and prosperity . . . at the front of the pack.

About the Authors

John Heins is the cofounder and President of Value Investor Media, Inc., and Editor-in-Chief of *Value Investor Insight* and *SuperInvestor Insight*. He is responsible for day-to-day operations of Value Investor Media, a media company founded in 2004 to provide investing ideas and insight to sophisticated professional and individual investors.

Previously, Mr. Heins was President and Chief Executive Officer of Gruner + Jahr USA Publishing, Bertelsmann AG's U.S. magazine subsidiary, Senior Vice President and General Manager of America Online's Personal Finance business, and a reporter and staff writer for *Forbes* magazine. He graduated magna cum laude from the University of Pennsylvania's Wharton School with a bachelor's degree in Economics and also holds an MBA from Stanford University's Graduate School of Business.

Whitney Tilson is the cofounder of hedge funds Kase Capital, T2 Partners and Tilson Capital Partners, the Tilson Mutual Funds, Value Investor Media, Inc., and the Value Investing Congress.

Mr. Tilson coauthored the book, *More Mortgage Meltdown: 6 Ways to Profit in These Bad Times*, has written for *Forbes*, the *Financial Times*, *Kiplinger's*, the *Motley Fool*, and *TheStreet.com*, and was one of the authors of *Poor Charlie's Almanack*, the definitive book on Berkshire Hathaway Vice Chairman Charlie Munger. He is a CNBC Contributor, was featured in a 2008 *60 Minutes* segment about the housing crisis that won an Emmy, was one of five investors included in *SmartMoney's* 2006 "Power 30," and was named by *Institutional Investor* in 2007 as one of "20 Rising Stars."

Mr. Tilson was a founding member of Teach for America and the Initiative for a Competitive Inner City, and was a consultant at The Boston Consulting Group. He received an MBA with High Distinction from the Harvard Business School and graduated magna cum laude from Harvard College with a bachelor's degree in Government.

Index